...ity

Collecte...
Jo...

The overall focus of John Astley's Collected Essays is the *sociology of culture*, which - through many agencies, and often pervasively, affects all of our lives in ways that we...

celebrated monograph on The Beatles.

John Astley is currently working on *Herbivores and Carnivores*, a timely investigation into the struggle for cultural values in contemporary society.

By the same author:

Liberation and Domestication (Essays 1)
Professionalism & Practice (Essays 3)

Why Don't We Don't We Do It In The Road?
The Beatles Phenomenon

Culture and Creativity

THE BEATLES AND OTHER ESSAYS

John Astley

The COMPANY *of* WRITERS
2006

First Published in the United Kingdom 2006
by The Company of Writers
www.thecompanyofwriters.com

© 2006 John Astley

John Astley has asserted his right under the Copyright,
Designs and Patents Act 1988.

Paperback
ISBN: 0-9551834-1-3
& ISBN: 978-0-9551834-1-6

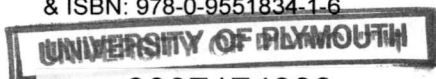

British Library Cataloguing in Publication Data.
A catalogue record for this book is available from the British Library.

Classification: Non-Fiction
Social Sciences/Culture

BIC Codes
J/JB

Bibliographic Data also available:
Nielsen Book Data

Dedication

This book is dedicated to my sons, Liam and Humphrey, who know about music, and are kind enough to share this aspect of cultural creativity with me.

Acknowledgements

I am grateful to Esther Dudley, Stuart Mealing, and Intellect Books Ltd. for permission to reproduce my essay 'Design for Life'

Thank you to Wendy for the typing.

William Morris (1834-96): the British craftsman, designer, writer, typographer, Socialist, and Utopian - is the subject of John Astley's essay "Design for Life."

CONTENTS

Introduction

THIS SECOND VOLUME of my collected essays focuses on 'Culture & Creativity', and offers the reader a diverse range of subjects addressed over many years.

By far the longest essay in this collection is my 1979 attempt to understand and explain 'The Beatles phenomenon'. This was most definitely work in progress, directly related to my place within British cultural studies. As the reader will see there is a good deal of discussion in that essay about my emerging methodology as a Sociologist explicitly concerned with a number of inter-connected issues. These were, and are still, how we might understand the nature and role of culture in our individual and collective lives, the prospect of really understanding everyday life in post-War Britain, and the constant struggle to assert democratic values and practices in society.

I have already reflected on the last of these in the essay 'Herbivores versus Carnivores', which I leave the reader to explore. I should also say that currently I am developing the themes and issues addressed in that essay in to a full-length monograph. Once again, I can assure the reader that this is very much 'work in progress'!

I have included my very brief sketch of Raymond Williams (written as an *aide-memoire* for my students in Oxford) to help address the issue of culture. Within the speculation on, and writing about, culture, we have almost gone full-circle away from discussing 'cultural products' *per se*, and then back again. Williams and his peers wanted to think about culture as more than the highly valued artefacts of social elites. He sought to empower the *ordinary*, the everyday product of human labour, to place value upon the cultural creativity of all people. He demonstrated through his *work,* his everyday labour, that his fellow social beings did indeed contribute to the sum total of intellectual insight, and artefact production in ways that could, should, be meaningful to a much wider audience both individually and collectively. He raised the value attached to the cultural creativity of 'ordinary people', and argued that the very urgency of these labours, set as they invariably are within a context of daily struggles for both survival, and a 'voice' are certainly a resource for hope. I set out some more detailed comments on this toward the end of the 'Herbivores versus Carnivores' essay.

Of course there is a utopian dimension to this kind of approach, and it is certainly there in my own writing. Surely it in no accident that those struggling to break free from the bonds of orthodoxy and servility should envisage a better life in this world: the good society?

My essays here on Morris, Wilde, and Orwell all reflect upon these concerns, these struggles, these hopes. They, like so many other able contributors to this work, were well aware of the urgency and difficulty of 'swimming against the tide.' We should take some pleasure from the progress they made, their valued contribution, indefatigable spirit, and inspiring leadership. It is no less important for us to do the same.

A great deal has been said over recent decades about the tendency of modern societies to create a mass culture, essentially the ways of life of the vast majority of working (class) people determined by the exponential growth of consumer capitalism. Insatiable, philistine, banal, vulgar, acquisitive; 'bread and circuses'. In this approach all power resides with the elites in society who determine cultural values, who own and manage the production and distribution of fashionable products; goods and services, creating and destroying celebrities along the way, part and parcel of the quest for novelty and ever-renewed markets. Choice, of sorts, at a price; namely technical rationality, and standardisation.

However, those who feel that - despite the existence of these tendencies related to the continuing inventiveness and obsessive desire for control of consumer capitalism - there remains a semi-autonomy in our lives. This freedom, such as it is in all its diversity, is essentially our insurance against, and antidote for, cultural dominance, hegemony. The very existence of a 'grass-roots' or grounded cultural creativity, and productivity, is testimony to both the nature of the everyday struggle for power and control that takes place. It also demonstrates loud and clear that the dominant economic, social and political forces in society can be challenged, and triumphed over in all manner of ways.

Some years ago now (see my essay 'Transitions' in *Liberation and Domestication*, 2005) I developed the concept of Ideological Cultural Apparatuses (ICAs) to suggest that the real shapers of dominant values, ideas and attitudes in contemporary Britain are to be found in the organisations related to advertising and the media. My contention was, and is, that the various State 'apparatuses', such as schools, have less and less influence.

So what we see now much more regularly is a desire by researchers and writers to focus attention upon cultural products. There is a steady stream of writing on the culture industries, and in a Williams-ish way a concern about the conditions of production in those industries. There is a tendency in some of this writing to de-politicise the issues; indeed, a valid criticism of some cultural studies is the emergence of an apolitical posture, which seeks to separate scholarship from the everyday consequences of social relationships dominated by inequalities of power.

I certainly do not want to take time here to engage in detailed wrangles about methodologies, and the politics of scholarship, including who is where on the greasy pole of career advancement this year! I am more concerned with the 'snakes and ladders' nature of ordinary people's lives, and what enlightenment, awareness raising, and encouragement can be given via this broader educational labour. There is an element of this in my essays collected together here for the reader to access, speculate upon, and come to their own judgements.

John Astley
Exmouth, Winter 2005

Herbivores versus Carnivores: the struggle for democratic cultural values in post-1945 Britain

2002

In the winter of 1978/9 I sat down to write a long article on 'The Beatles Phenomenon'. I sought in that piece to pose, and answer to my own satisfaction, a series of questions about the nature of popular cultures in post-War Britain, which the rise of The Beatles epitomised.

My main question was why, and how, could a cultural phenomenon like The Beatles happen? My approach was a socio-historical one, identifying significant transformation, for example, and linked to my role as a critical theorist, and a devotee of Raymond Williams. Despite the many failings of that work, I would still stand by a good deal of what was said, and, essentially for my writing thereafter, how I came to explore the broader issues of cultural values. In discussing the cultural antecedents of that pop phenomenon I opened up, and developed in a definite political context, questions about the increasing domination, indeed colonisation, of popular cultures by the commercial nexus. These are processes aided and abetted by those with political power in whose interest it was (and remains) to help create and preside over a largely emasculated and stultified population.

One of the issues I addressed then was the way a revitalised consumerist and liberal looking capitalism could present a feeling of openness while actually maintaining the traditional privileges of the elites. Post-War settlement? Yes. Greater democracy? An emphatic No! I am reminded of those earnest debates in the 1960s about class, parenting, and schooling, seeking to find some State sponsored and acceptable solution to the continued failings of a class-ridden and despotic schooling system. Consider how the 'common-sense' message of Plowden in 1967 about the deprivation, disadvantage, and cultural deficit experienced by working class children required a compensatory educational facelift. As Basil Bernstein pointed out in his 1971 essay 'education cannot compensate for society' the audacity of the already privileged to blame the working class for their failings was quite staggering. Please note that the educational policy arm of the

New Labour State apparatus is referring to social class as a key factor in life chances once again. Is this an appropriate time to re-publish Michael Young's *The Rise of the Meritocracy* (1958)?

The title of this paper comes from the essay 'Festival' by Michael Frayn, the final piece in *Age of Austerity 1945-51* edited by Michael Sissons and Philip French in 1963. (The year of publication just happens to coincide with the breakthrough into international celebrity of The Beatles). Frayn's essay is about the intense struggle between political and cultural values to create The Festival of Britain held in 1951 (to which I went as a seven year old). Frayn used the terms *herbivores* and *carnivores* to identify the two sides battling it out for the very existence of the Festival. He characterises the Herbivores as philanthropic, kindly, whimsical, cosy, optimistic, and middlebrow. The carnivores were 'the other side of the coin', and as Frayn says of them, 'if God had not wished them (the main body of the upper and middle classes) to prey on all smaller and weaker creatures without scruple he would not have made them as they are'. I certainly would not want to subscribe to all of the Herbivore characteristics, because they did in the main see the working class 'as the inert objects of benign administration'. However, I am certainly prepared to start here as part of a debate about what, and whose, values really matter. Many of our contemporary versions of 'the great and the good', along with the 'woolly liberals' much derided by Stalinists like Jack Straw, qualify as herbivores. It is certainly the case that New Labour has risen to power on the back of the forty-year triumph of the Carnivores. New Labour politics is the most recent phase of taking democratic dialogue further and further away from the ordinary people, and the Herbivores alike.

One of my aims here is to argue for a debate, yes, a dialogue certainly, about cultural values, and the lack of opportunity that most of us have to engage with ideas, our own, and other people's. {Habermas' communicative action thesis (1984) is an issue here}. Our lives are dominated by an advanced consumer-oriented global capitalism, which as an entity relies on our choices being manipulated and circumscribed in the interests of big profits and continued economic and cultural domination. (Much as described by Marx in volume three of *Capital*, published by Engels in 1894). This domination is supplemented by a system of quasi represent-ative government that is oppressive because it deals in propaganda, and whose processes are oligarchic and opaque rather than open and transparent as is always claimed in the propaganda. The recent BBC2 series *The Century of the Self* - written by Tim Adams - brought these and other issues out very well, and should remind us of the pioneering work of Vance Packard, who in *The Hidden Persuaders* (1957), for example, drew our attention to 'the packaged soul'.

I want to argue that we are (still) alienated because of the separation from the fruits of our labour and any genuine sense of working for an inter-related personal and social fulfilment. We work for wages, to be choice making consumers, to be permitted to engage with unbounded joy in the status acquisition rush by spending money we do not have. I see no reason to alter much the 'one dimensional man' thesis of Herbert Marcuse in the 1964, namely that 'the technology of advanced industrial societies has enabled them to eliminate conflict by assimilating all those who in earlier forms of social order provided either voices or forces of dissent. Technology does this partly by creating affluence. Freedom from material want, which Marx and Marcuse himself took and take to be the precondition of other freedoms, has been transformed into an agency for producing servitude.' (MacIntyre, 1970). Now, although this 1964 thesis was pessimistic, and over-taken by many subsequent political upheavals apparently demonstrating peoples capacity to throw off their psychological as well as political chains (the collapse of Stalinism being a case in point), I would argue that the servitude remains. Neil Postman, the American Sociologist suggested that we are 'amusing ourselves to death' (1986), and in his essay 'A sad heart at the supermarket' Randall Jarrell argued that half of us is stuffed to death, while the other half is starved to death (1962).

I want to argue that far from escaping the servitude that comes with the apparent freedoms that advanced capitalism provides, we are more and more in debt to these power sources and forces. Look for example at the withering authority of the lifestyle role modelling now part of the daily routine of the mass media.

In the wake of my essay on The Beatles I went on to write about the increasing power of what I called 'Ideological Cultural Apparatuses' (ICAs), the everyday mechanisms by which our commonplace and regularly used ideas, images, and values are recycled for our endless entertainment or titillation. Here we are flattered, have our strings pulled, and generally praise ourselves for being so clever; hedonism and solipsism combined in self-actualisation! We are, of course, constantly on the cusp of consuming some new and essential thing. Another example in this age of information of more knowledge without wisdom!

However, despite all this, I do remain optimistic, and my interest in these cultural processes has been stimulated over many years by the likes of Zygmunt Bauman, who has encouraged me to write and talk about cultural creativity as an antidote to alienation. (1976). This also takes me close to the grounded aesthetics and common culture ideas of Paul Willis (1990). Culture has two senses here: as a functioning analytical concept in understanding social thought; and also as the social reality of cultural actions in everyday life, much in the 'common culture' vein.

There are many social and cultural institutions that can be seen as ICAs, among them the BBC, and other agencies of the mass media of communication. There are the universities and the culture/heritage industries that grow by the day. The latter has the audacity to take what passes for people's real lives (and usually oppressed ones at that), and transform them before our eyes into packages of homogenised history bites, that offer up a simulated version of life in easily digestible form. Even here, in the forms of contemporary domestication, 'we' cannot be allowed to work our minds too hard! It is also worth reminding ourselves that 'history' is written for consumption today, so what values are being promoted - and why?

What is at stake here as well is the power to set agendas. We are not simply talking about the power individuals and organisations have to command obedience, but the way they consistently create the contexts around access and opportunity, about democratic decision-making, or the lack of it. Discourses are shaped; even the idea of having a dialogue around alternatives is marginalised.

For several years at Open University summer school I had the pleasure of giving a regularly updated talk on 'Six Propositions about Culture and Identity'.

These six were:

1. It is to be welcomed that the UK is a more multi-cultural society, but there are continuity as well as change issues here.

2. Human action creates culture, contributing to the personal and social expressions of identity.

3. Culture reflects the diversity and semi-autonomy of 'us'.

4. But, contradictions and conflicts arise. People's aspirations versus forces of control. Struggles occur, often located in particular sites.

5. However, people invariably feel that their needs can only be met by engaging in these struggles.

6. Culture as articulated opposition to exclusion, and these marginal cultures as an antidote to alienation and oppression.

These talks always provoked intense, though overwhelmingly supportive, debates. The dialogue rumbled on afterward for some time, and I always felt that they unleashed a genuine desire among a very diverse group of people to argue and speculate about contemporary society and utopian visions. The very openness of such culturally heterogeneous groups of people brought together in a wonderful educational spirit always seemed to me to be resources of hope.

We have in this country a robust and innovative tradition of studying culture in all respects. This is a radical intellectual tradition, built on the foundations of a radical oppositional political culture that should not be surrendered just because we are constantly swimming against the tide of philistinism and open hostility from those in power.

NOTE:
This is the text of a talk given in Oxford on 19-9-2002 at a conference organised by the Open University's Pavis Centre for Research. The conference was called 'Cultural Returns: assessing the place of culture in social thought.'

REFERENCES:
BAUMAN, Z. *Socialism: The Active Utopia*, 1976
BERNSTEIN, B. Education Cannot Compensate for Society, in
COSIN, B. *et al* (Eds) *School and Society*, 1971
FRAYN, M. Festival, in Sissons & French, 1963
HABERMAS, J. *The Theory of Communicative Action,* 1984
JARRELL, R. *A Sad Heart at the Supermarket,* 1962
MACINTYRE, A. *Marcuse*, 1970
PACKARD, V. *The Hidden Persuaders,* 1957
POSTMAN, N. *Amusing Ourselves to Death,* 1986
SISSONS, M. & French, P. (Eds) *Age of Austerity, 1945-1951*, 1963
WILLIS, P. *Common Culture,* 1990
YOUNG, M. *The R ise of the Meritocracy,* 1958

Raymond Williams: a biographical sketch

1989

Since his death in January 1988, a great deal has been said and written about Raymond Williams' contribution to the intellectual and academic life of Britain. Much of this assessment has pointed to the difficulty of putting Williams into a specific category; was he a sociologist, a dramatist, a novelist, a literary critic and analyst of language, a political activist, a socialist, a Marxist? In fact at one moment or another he was all of these, and more.

Above all else Williams was a *writer* on culture and social life. He can be unequivocally regarded as the leading influence on the development of Cultural Studies in Britain. He was for many years Professor of Drama at Cambridge University.

Despite his influence on many sociologists, and on the 'cultural turn' in Sociology, there is little or no reference to Williams' writing to be found in Sociology texts. He does turn up in books, or chapters, on the mass media, but little else. Some sociologists (including this one) would argue that this says more about the narrowness of Sociology than it does about the lack of relevance in what Williams had to say, and the value of his methodology. This somewhat uneasy relationship between most Sociology and Williams (and Cultural Studies in general) will provide an interesting focus for debates in the next few years as his influence on the analysis of British life comes to be seen as more rather than less significant.

It would not be exaggerating to say that Williams always retained a certain marginality. He was not of mainstream English Literature or Drama or Sociology or conventional Left politics. He was on the critical margins, challenging cultural orthodoxies, in the 'border country', further accentuated by his years in Cambridge. He often commented on his not quite fitting in to this heartland of the English Establishment. Being on the margins, being seen as something of a threat, is an attribute shared by many Sociologists!

Raymond Williams shared with Sociologists (and other social scientists) a concern with devising methods to more fully understand the nature of everyday life and the basis of personal and social action. He was particularly interested in the interrelationship between the social structure of modern Britain; the nature of key social institutions, the persistence of certain roles, the continuity in patterns of power; compared and contrasted with the values and beliefs of the ordinary people.

What forms do our cultural creativity take? What are these social conditions of production? In what ways are these cultures a measure of resistance to domination, exploitation, and inequality? What can we say about the 'sites of struggle' in the day-to-day resistance of the many subjected to the continued undemocratic social control of the few?

In response to these kinds of questions it is not surprising therefore that Williams turned his attention to studies of the mass media, to literacy, and educational issues (especially adult education). He was in the forefront of debates about the commercial influences on the development of our urban and metropolitan lives, but always with an eye for the rural characteristics of the 'border country'. Williams continued to insist that a 'structure of feeling' could be conceptualised in regard to public opinion and the fashionable tendencies to everyday thought and attitudes. This depended much on the real-life material conditions of people's everyday lives *and* the sets of dominant ideologies in society at any given time. To the end of his life Williams insisted that 'culture was ordinary', that what the mass of the people created as interpretations of events, their understandings and cultural creativity was both peculiar to them in their own locality and yet indicative of more universal concerns. It was an optimistic and democratic vision of living culture and its value to the lifeblood of society.

One aspect of Raymond Williams' contribution to our lives was his fiction writing. Indeed his quite deliberate choice of fiction as a vehicle to carry and demonstrate his ideas about self and society tensions were a key to unlocking the door to understanding why we are like we are. He consistently wrote about the importance of the interface between an individual's biography, and a society's history. (And in this respect echoed the work of the American Sociologist C.Wright Mills)

In a very concrete way Williams added to our conceptual vocabulary. His continued interest in the nature (and history) of cultural forms brought him to writing *Keywords* in the 1970s. This has remained one of Williams' most widely known and popular books. (And it is worth commenting on the Penguin paperback versions of Williams' books almost certainly exposing his writing to a wider public.) Keywords are, as he put it himself, the record of an inquiry in to a vocabulary. He was endlessly intrigued by the origins and current usage of words that have continued to play a crucial part in the understandings of our everyday lives. The building blocks of our culture that say so much about the kind of society we live in now compared to both the past, and visions of the future. He was an 'archaeologist' of culture, and an 'architect' of a better, more socially just society.

All of these diverse aspects of Raymond Williams' work, *of his writing,* act as a matrix of analysis and insight, which he bestowed on us. Countless Sociologists, let alone other intellectual workers from other, complementary areas of study, owe a great debt to him. We can repay this debt in part by increasing our understanding of his contribution, and more especially by continuing to engage with our shared values, and using his approaches to influence and shape our work.

A SHORT BIBLIOGRAPHY of WILLIAMS

Drama from Ibsen to Eliot, 1952
Drama in Performance, 1954
Culture and Society, 1958
The Long Revolution, 1961
Communications (Penguin Britain in the Sixties series), 1962
Modern Tragedy, 1966
May Day Manifesto (edited with Stuart Hall and Edward Thompson), 1967
Drama from Ibsen to Brecht, 1968
The English Novel from Dickens to Lawrence, 1970
Orwell (Fontana Modern Masters), 1971
The Country and the City, 1973
Television: Technology and Cultural Form, 1974
Keywords: A Vocabulary of Culture and Society, 1976
Marxism and Literature, 1977
Politics and Letters: Interviews with New Left Review, 1979
Problems with Materialism and Culture: Selected Essays, 1980

Culture, The Sociology of, 1981
Contact: Human Communication and its History, 1981
Towards 2000, 1983
Writing in Society, 1984
Three of Williams' novels formed *The Welsh Trilogy:*
Border Country (1960), *Second Generation* (1964), and *The Fight for Manod* (1979)

The Soul of a Man Under Socialism:
Orwell, Wilde and Morris

1989

In this essay I would like to draw together the interests of three
writers: Orwell, Wilde and Morris in the development of socialism
as a social and economic order and the place of the individual in
that order of things. In the careers of all three men a point was
reached where they could recognise the issues facing both them
and the society in which they lived. The confluence of social
change and personal intellectual development reached a particular
moment in each of them that exposed more than anything else a
concern about the individual and socialism. This should be seen as
a high point in their intellectual development, a mark of their
maturity. They had all arrived at this point through charac-
teristically idiosyncratic development. I am not, therefore, suggesting that these three represent a consensus; they do not. What
does seem important is that all three were engaged in literary
production (and are perhaps best known, or appreciated, for that).
Their writing was ideological, often iconoclastically so. They all
used vital literary devices to persuade; satire, hyperbole, sarcasm.
They were all engaged in speculation about the future political
arrangements of life; and felt it necessary to commit their ideas to
paper.

Orwell and Morris knew much more about socialism and Marx
than did Wilde. However, it is often the case (mercifully) that the
'naïve' interposition can focus upon the nub of an issue, which, in
turn, resonates throughout the discourse on that issue.

Wilde understands the problem, even if he could not put it into
the same theoretical frame as Marx:

> "Society does not consist of individuals, but
> expresses the sum of interrelations, the relations
> within which these individuals stand. As if
> someone were to say: seen from the perspective
> of society, there are no slaves and no citizens:
> both are human beings. Rather, they are that
> outside society. To be a slave, to be a citizen, are
> social characteristics, relations between human

beings A and B. Human being A, as such, is not a
slave. He is a slave in and through society."

(Gundrisse. p.265)

Marx comes to use the concept *social being* to explain the complex
unity of society, history, self and material production.

All three writers believed most earnestly in brotherhood,
fraternity, and viewed socialism as essentially a humanist doctrine
that embraces a fundamental concern with liberty and equality.
There is an acceptance of the need for a planned economy and high
technology industrial development to provide super-abundance.
But, and it is a big but, socialist collectivisation is a means to an
end, and not the end in itself.

Before going on to spend some time on each of these three
writers in detail, it is important to note that Orwell was in a
considerably different position to Wilde and Morris. As Orwell has
pointed out himself:

> "Until the twentieth century, and indeed until the
> nineteen-thirties, all Socialist thought was in some
> sense Utopian. Socialism had nowhere been tested
> in the physical world, and in the mind of almost
> everyone, including its enemies, it was bound up
> with the idea of liberty and equality. Only let
> economic injustice be brought to an end and all
> other forms of tyranny would vanish also. The age
> of human brotherhood would begin, and war,
> crime, disease, poverty, and overwork would be
> things of the past."

*('What is Socialism?' Manchester Evening
News, 31-1-46)*

Orwell had knowledge or 'experience' of the development of
socialist Russia, and was able - along with his contemporaries - to
reflect at great length upon the matter. This is not to say that
experience will of necessity assure greater understanding of any

21

set of ideas or phenomena, but it does certainly provide a further perspective.

To their credit, Wilde and Morris were, like Orwell, very sceptical about the ease with which capitalist culture could be replaced with a state of affairs that in all respects was better.

In his 1948 review of Wilde's essay, 'The Soul of Man under Socialism' (Is it significant that this is the 'year' of '1984'?), Orwell demonstrates just how much in sympathy he is with both Wilde and Morris, at least in the tenor of their ideas and argument. Orwell argues that Wilde is both utopian and anarchic in character. The state will cease to govern and become a distributive mechanism for commodities. Orwell believes that Wilde's future society will be populated by artists, each striving after perfection in the way that seems best to them.

This notion in turn is directly related to Wilde's seminal belief that Man will only be able to realise his personality truly through joy instead of suffering. In this (although Orwell does not draw it out in his review), Wilde is anticipating Eric Gill, one of the foremost members of the English Arts and Crafts movement, who at the turn of the century was to suggest that 'the artist is not a special kind of man, but every man is a special kind of artist'. Gill, like his contemporaries, were in turn the heirs of Morris. Orwell uses this review to express his own misgivings about the possible (and actual) authoritarian tendencies in the socialist movement.

> "Socialism, in the sense of economic colle-
> ctivism, is conquering the earth at a speed that
> would hardly have seemed possible sixty years
> ago" [when Wilde wrote his essay] "and yet
> Utopias, at any rate Wilde's Utopia, is no nearer.
> Where then does the fallacy lie?"

> *(Orwell, CE 4, p. 484)*

Orwell quite rightly underlines the weaknesses of Wilde's argument/analysis, for example, the latter's belief in abundant riches throughout the world, the level and evenness of technological achievement, and so on. However, Orwell comes back to support, and see the value, in Wilde's view:

"Wilde's pamphlet and other kindred writing -
News from Nowhere, for instance - consequently
have their value. They may demand the impossible, and they may - since a Utopia
necessarily reflects the aesthetic ideas of its own
period - sometimes seem 'dated' and ridiculous,
but they do at least look beyond the era of food
queues and party squabbles, and remind the
Socialist movement of its original, half-forgotten
objective of human brotherhood."

(op cit p.485)

Wilde's essay, 'The Soul of Man under Socialism' was first
published in *The Fortnightly Review* in February 1890, and
represents a major contribution to socialist discourse even if, as
was the case, Wilde could not be considered a prominent member
of the 'socialist movement' at that time. Wilde argues from the
outset that the major benefit that would stem from life in a socialist
society would be the true realisation of individualism. It would
allow people to be themselves, and not have to live in the shadow
of other lives. He says that people are surrounded and distracted by
the existence of poverty, ugliness and starvation, and that
understandably enough people with any sensitivity are moved by
such things. But, he suggests, emotions are stirred more quickly
than intelligence. We extend sympathy, a degree of altruism;
which in fact is easier for us to do than engaging in the
fundamental discussions about social change. Wilde believes that
the reformist lurks in even the most enlightened of his
contemporaries. Wilde emphasises that the temporary relief from
destitution and starvation achieved by the generosity of the
reasonably well-off is in fact the worst that could happen, for it
serves to legitimate the existence of conditions taken for granted,
seen as God given, *etc.*

The philanthropist and do-gooder deal with symptoms and no
causes, and are counter-productive agents. This is of course a
strong theme in the plays of Wilde, Shaw and others, in this
period.

> "It is immoral to use private property in order to alleviate the horrible evils that result from the institution of private property."

> (*'The Soul of Man under Socialism, Spring Books, 1963 reprint, p. 915)*

Wilde draws attention to the moral responsibility placed upon the rich to 'do good', and argues that, under socialism, this will cease to exist:

> "The security of society will not depend, as it does now, on the state of the weather."

> *(op cit p.916)*

Socialism, through co-determination, cooperation and *public* wealth creation will provide the material basis for life, for all. But, it will provide more than the *basis* for life, it will create the conditions for a true individualism to develop.

Set against this optimistic sketch, Wilde poses the prospect of an authoritarian socialism; of *Governments* armed with economic power; industrial tyrannies which will not provide the conditions for individuals to prosper. For Wilde, poverty, in the widest sense of deprivation, turns people back into savages, it makes them merely producers of goods and services. These conditions do not make men civilised, literate and philosophical. There are echoes here of Tocqueville's reaction to the factory system, and in Wilde's suspicion of government, the long established opposition to 'Old Corruption'.

One of the most worrying features of everyday life for Wilde is the extent to which the poor and the destitute continue to tolerate their conditions. He does, though, discuss the existence of false consciousness in relation to ideology, hegemony and the process of social reproduction. Wilde does not use these concepts of course. But that is the essence of his argument, and in his terms, for his time, a very sophisticated and far-sighted argument it is.

Like Orwell and Morris, Wilde is an outsider. He does not actually suffer deprivation in any great measure. He comes from a wealthy, well-educated background. He is not one of the masses whose conditions he deplores. And yet he is not accepted among nor admires his own class with any ease or comfort. In this respect, Wilde is again close to Morris and Orwell in his view of what role has to be played by the outsider. They have to be agitators. By example and by deliberate action they have to seek change and encourage others to challenge assumptions and authority in the name of progress.

> "Agitators are a set of interfering, meddling people, who come down to some perfectly contented class of the community and sow the seeds of discontent among them."
>
> *(op cit p.917)*

Wilde cites the abolition of slavery as an example; the abolitionists were 'outsiders' and those in fact least affected by the changes.

Wilde, like Morris and Orwell, realised that he could not become a proletarian; he was stuck with what he was.

Wilde pursues his twin themes of authority and individualism further by arguing that private property will be replaced by public wealth creation and that the new machine age will release men from the unpleasant burdens that they now carry. Government will not encroach upon the lives of people and will have only a minimal role to play:

> "People sometimes inquire what form of government is most suitable for an artist to live under. To this question there is only one answer... no government at all."
>
> *(op cit. p.931)*

Again and again Wilde returns to emphasise that the future socialist society is to be one where the relations between people are ones of equality and freedom. The very fabric of everyday life has been re-humanised so that people draw out the best in others, as in themselves.

> "Man has sought to live intensely, fully, perfectly. When he can do so without exercising restraint on others, or suffering it ever, and his activities are all

pleasurable to him, he will be saner, healthier, more civilised, more himself." *(op cit. p.936)*

The new individualism under socialism will be a new Hellenism. Wilde frequently returns to his belief that property and false needs are the temporary downfall of mankind; that the real riches of the soul cannot be taken from people. Progress is the realisation of Utopias.

William Morris did a great deal during his lifetime. His literary output alone was considerable. In the second half of his life, he devoted his energies to the fight for socialism. Unlike Wilde, Morris did engage the modern socialist movement of the 1880s. He remained, however, an outsider, always arguing for a style of libertarian socialism that was far from the majority view even in his own time. Morris continued to have uppermost in his mind the concerns of the individual and of freedom and creativity. Like Wilde, Morris wanted a socialist society where people could be themselves. He did not want to replace one authoritarian system with another. Morris wrote a good deal on his socialist vision, but the place where his ideas are best represented is in his Utopia, *News from Nowhere*.

News from Nowhere is generally regarded as Morris' most important work. It is certainly his last major composition, written five years before his death in 1896. The work itself is far more than a story of 'utopia'. *News from Nowhere* is essentially a political tract to put across the ideas of a Marxist living in the latter end of the Nineteenth century. The descriptions of London, as the town of the Twenty-first century, are Morris' clear ideas about how human society could and would come about. The creativity of advanced and emancipated Man abounds in an atmosphere of light and joy. Morris created a world in which production was for need and not for profit. The restrictive nature, and inherent anarchy of capitalism, had disappeared, and mankind has been able to pursue the real business of living in a manner that all far-seeing human beings could not fail to agree with. In a word, through socialism human society has at last become *civilised*. One of the failures of *News from Nowhere*, though, is the lack of a clear explanation of the role of science and technology in the development of society. There is no doubt that Morris understood well enough, that far from holding back the progress of the machine, it was vitally necessary to the future of man, that the machine should reach maximum usage. It is, after all, as Morris argues, not for an inanimate object to rule over people; the difference of uses lies in the ownership, and control of the resources. Because Morris did not fully explain this facet of the industrialisation of society, he can be misunderstood. He was certainly not an eccentric old 'feudalist' that hated machines; he hated the class nature of the control of machines.

In *News from Nowhere*, Morris lays great stress on the development of viable relationships between Town and Country. He emphasises the fact that 'town-life', on a massive and squalid scale, came about because of the necessity to house thousands of workers close by the factories. In the future socialist society, when mechanisation and automation has taken over the tedious tasks, man does not have to be huddled together like animals in a zoo.

Despite the enjoyable and very logical descriptions of life and landscape in the Twenty-first century, this is not the most important aspect of the work. By far the most important part of the book, and the most profound in terms of the work of Morris' mind, is the conversation between the 'time traveller' (Morris himself?) and Hammond. The latter is an old sage of the future period, who takes upon himself the neighbourly task of explaining to the guest, the nature of the new society. This dialogue is the vital key to the whole work, and the logical accumulation of Morris' ideas about the order of society. Hammond explains, with tireless patience, how society was transformed from Capitalism to Socialism, initially through a revolution in 1952. The final battle in the revolution, which dispossessed the capitalist class of the 'ill-gotten gains', took place in Trafalgar Square, the scene of many battles in Morris' day. In the dialogue between the men of different centuries, Morris uses the opportunity to draw direct examples, and make comparisons. We should always remember that Morris was not writing for his own amusement, or enter-tainment, or for that matter in an attempt to convert Gladstone and Co. to revolutionary socialism. He was writing to influence those that had even the vaguest notions of change in society; and those that held a clear socialist perspective, and needed the added inspiration of a great piece of prose.

Morris poses the way things are in this world, and remarks upon the changes he sees. Hammond translates this curiosity into an explanation of how society changed, and the real nature of life as it exists in the future epoch. For example, this extract on Education illustrates the point well:

'Said I, "I want an extra word or two about your ideas of education; although I gathered from Dick that you let your children run wild and didn't teach them anything; and in short, that you have so refined your education, that now you have none." "Then you have gathered left handed," quoth he. "But of course I understand your point of view about education, which is that of times past when 'the struggle for life', as men used to phrase it (i.e. the struggle for a slave's rations on the one side, and for a bouncing share of the slaveholders' privilege on the other), pinched 'education' for most people into a niggardly dole of not very accurate information; something to be swallowed by the beginner in the art of living whether he liked it or not, and was hungry for it or not: and which had been chewed and digested over and over again by people who didn't care about it in order to serve it out to other people who didn't care about it. In the nineteenth century, society was so miserably poor, owing to the systematized robbery on which it was founded, that real education was impossible for anybody. The whole theory of their so-called education was that it was necessary to shove a little information into a child, even if it were by means of torture, and accompanied by twaddle which it was well known was of no use, or else would lack information lifelong: the hurry of poverty forbade anything else. All that is past; we are no longer hurried, and the information lies ready to each one's hand when his own inclinations impel him to seek it. In this as in other matters we have become wealthy: we can afford to give ourselves time to grow."'

An important feature of all three writers is their minimalist view of State activity under well developed socialism. They all see the State as representing class and therefore authoritarian interests; bourgeoisie, proletariat or political bureaucracy. It is the contention of these writers that the State will not be required to perform the same functions as it does in their own time. Even for Wilde and Morris, the State was increasingly interventionalist, pushing through more and more legislative control over people's lives. Of course in the Janus-like nature of the modern State, much of this controlling and 'engineering' could be said to be in the interests of the mass of people. However, one of the features of the new order will be that the relations of people will be such, the care, concern, degree of responsibility and so on will be more and more finely evolved; that an 'external' mechanism like the State is not required.

> "…'What kind of government have you? Has republicanism finally triumphed? Or have you come to a mere dictatorship, which some persons in the nineteenth century used to prophesy as the ultimate outcome of democracy? Indeed this last question does not seem so very unreasonable, since you have turned our Parliament House into a dung-market. Or where do you house your present Parliament?'
>
> The old man answered my smile with a hearty laugh, and said, 'Well, well, dung is not the worst kind of corruption; fertility may come of that, whereas mere death came from the other kind, of which those walls once held the great supporters. Now, dear guest, let me tell you that our present parliament would be hard to house in one place, because the whole people is our parliament.' "
>
> *(op cit p.257)*

I have already referred to the advantage Orwell had over Wilde and Morris in that he lived at a time when the socialist experiment was being worked through. Advantage may not be how Orwell saw it, though. One of the most important points to make about Orwell's views is that they were constantly undergoing revision, and yet the feeling of anarchistic, individualistic, outsider rebellion is constantly present. Peter Sedgwick comments upon this in relation to Orwell's remark in the 1946 Preface to the Ukrainian edition of *Animal Farm*, that up to 1930 he, Orwell, did not see himself as a Socialist. Orwell was primarily expressing his disgust with the oppression of the poorer section of the industrial workers. Just as he had expressed his disgust over the treatment of the Burmese or tramps. Sedgwick reminds us that the many disagreements on Orwell's ideological line is largely due to the choice that critics make to see any one time in Orwell's development as that representing the real man. (Peter Sedgwick. 'George Orwell: International Socialist?' *International Socialist*, Issue: June/July 1969)

Two other writers have commented on this aspect of Orwell's descriptive powers coupled with his outsiderish-ness. Raymond Williams has commented on Orwell's observations of the working class, particularly in *The Road to Wigan Pier* which, while being keen and perceptive, fail to be analytical and remain distanced (see R. Williams' *Culture and Society* chapter on Orwell). Dennis Potter made an equally relevant point on Orwell's individualist rebelliou-sness:

> "Orwell's wistful dream floats up out of his weirdly conservative romanticism, his self-induced but inevitably equivocal nostalgia for other (and better) days, his shuddery distaste for most manifestations of modern industrialism, and his angry longing for order, stability and discipline."

> *(D. Potter, 'George Orwell', New Society 1-2-68, p.158)*

By the time Orwell had come to write his review of Wilde's 'The Soul of Man under Socialism', he had moved a considerable way from his polemic in *The Road to Wigan Pier*. His anger is clear in *The Road*...and in a sense it is as much 'trenches' as those he was to experience in Spain. *The Road*...marks a major watershed in Orwell's socialist thought. He moves on from description and polemic, to a reasoned argument for socialism. In this text, though, he is harder, much more iconoclastic about the various strains he denotes in English socialism. In his later years he offers a more mature account.

Again and again in Orwell we find references to the need for the collectivisation of the economy as the first step towards a socialist future. In *Animal Farm*, he uses the struggle of the animals against their exploitation as a metaphor; but he goes beyond the stage of collectivisation to consider at length the revolution betrayed. The betrayers are the intellectuals; arrogant, bureaucratic; in short, not the stuff for democracy and liberty. He raises the nature of the problem in 'The Lion and the Unicorn':

> "Common ownership of the means of production is not in itself a sufficient definition of socialism - centralised ownership has very little meaning unless the mass of the people are living roughly upon an equal level, and have some kind of control over government. 'The State' may come to mean no more than a self-elected political party, and oligarchy and privilege can return, based on power rather than on money."
>
> *(CE, Vol.2, p.80)*

It is not that everyone can be equal. It is not that everyone will be able to do as much for the community. But it will be, from each according to his means, to each according to his needs. However, as these three writers realised, that is arguing for a fundamental turnaround in the affairs of everyday life and living as experienced by most people. People not only have to care about society and about individuals; they have to strive, constantly to shape and refine the social arrangement and organisation of life.

Orwell lived through a period when the CP could call such concerns mere 'bourgeois liberty'; but he and others realised that retaining a central concern with the soul of man under socialism was more than just a prim petit-bourgeois indulgence. Orwell, like Wilde and Morris, found himself cringing at the insensitivity of the 'orthodox communist'.

Wilde, Morris and Orwell had no doubt about the need for the collectivisation of the economy. They 'agreed' that the long-term cultural changes were traumatic. However, the changes were necessary such that the nature of humanity, the quality of life and living could be raised for everyone. They all experienced this aspect of the socialist future in one way or another and wrote about it. Orwell wrote some of his most telling lines in a poem dedicated to an Italian militiaman he encountered in the Spanish Civil War:

> "The Italian soldier shook my hand
> Beside the guard-room table;
> The strong hand and the subtle hand...
>
> Your name and your deeds were forgotten
> Before your bones were dry,
> And the lie that slew you is buried
> Under a deeper lie;
>
> But the thing that I saw in your face
> No power can disinherit:
> No bomb that ever burst
> Shatters the crystal spirit."

(CE Vol.2 p.305/6)

BIBLIOGRAPHY:

MARX, K. *Grundrisse,* Penguin ed., 1973
MORRIS, W. *News from Nowhere,* (1896), 1977 ed.
ORWELL, G. *Collected Essays,* Vols. 2 & 4, Penguin ed.
   The Road to Wigan Pier, Penguin
   Animal Farm, Penguin
   What is Socialism? *Manchester Evening News,* 31-1-46
POTTER, D., 'George Orwell', New *Society* 1-2-68
SEDGWICK, P. 'George Orwell International Socialist?'
International Socialist Issue: June/July 1969
WILDE, O. 'The Soul of Man under Socialism' (1890) in the
Works of Oscar Wilde, Spring Books, 1963
WILLIAMS, R. *Culture and Society,* Penguin, 1963.

Design for Life: The Lasting Contribution of William Morris

2000

Morris entered my life like an aesthetic Trojan Horse; he was there having a significant influence on my development before I fully realised it. But, I have realised it now, in both senses, and it has raised my consciousness about design, about him, about myself, about creativity, and in my creative actions.

It is commonplace to say that Morris means many different things to different people but he does. Anyone with such a diverse range of creative activities is bound to be interpreted in a variety of ways largely dependent on the values and motives of the interpreter. To say that what Morris has become for most people is a social construction is a sociological truism. But we do need to keep reminding ourselves of both the historical and cultural contexts of the interpretations of Morris and his creative output.

> "His largeness of vision is the key to it. Morris was his own emblem of wholeness. He wanted to integrate the city with the country, the present with the past, the public and the personal moralities. Most of all he was concerned with proper human occupation, whether going under the name of work or play. In the late twentieth century throughout the West this is our urgent problem. Technological advance has made ordinary skill and modest pride in work redundant. But redundancy of people brings the threat of disconnection from life."

(Fiona MacCarthy, 1994)

Throughout his adult life, Morris thought and talked about the juxtaposition of useful work and useless toil; how the former was found and lost and needed to be found again and how the latter must be fought against at a personal and a collective level. As you the reader will discover a good deal of what I want to say about

Morris relates to this fundamental issue. For Morris, art and creative work were absolutely crucial facets of the (re)humanisation of people.

Pevsner makes the point that Morris wanted to re-contextualise art and restated Morris in that it 'has no longer any root', and on the question of democratic access to art, 'What business have we with art at all unless all can share it?" According to Pevsner's interpretation, Morris defined art as 'the expression by man of his pleasure in labour' and that 'art' was a 'common culture' or, as Paul Willis would suggest, 'a grounded aesthetic'. Pevsner argues that Morris was very clear that industrial capitalism, the prevailing system/forces/conditions of production would corrupt art, 'Art... will die out of civilization, if the system lasts. That in itself does for me carry with it the condemnation of the whole system.' Pevsner has usually been seen as out of step in suggesting that Morris was looking backwards in his support of handicrafts production. But, to his credit, Pevsner did argue that Morris's 'decorative honesty' was more important in the modern movement than links with the past.

On the question of access, Morris knew the inherent contradiction in the cost of his/The Firm's decorative products. To democratise them, to widen access, would inevitably lead to machine production. Morris was always concerned that mechanisation would open the way for cheap(er) imitations. So the role of the worker-producer is critical. Now, as then, does it matter to the machine operative if they are producing Morris designs? Are they able to transcend their conditions and consequences of production in order to gain pleasure from their work? Is such consciousness any substitute for the work itself? Is there intrinsic and/or extrinsic value in such labour? Because of Pevsner's perception of Morris as a backward-looking designer/producer, he argued that Morris was not a modernist. But as has been pointed out on countless occasions Morris did actually design for machine production, even if he then exercised very tight quality control over all processes from design to finished product. I want to return to these questions of means of production later on.

In this essay I want to consider the value of Morris' creative output, the end-products which are, of course, in the public domain. What I can say here about Morris the private person is limited. I am sure that he experienced many joys, disappointments and frustrations throughout his life; he was a man wedded to his senses, and was, by all accounts, quite emotional at times. So? He certainly had charismatic authority; people of all kinds looked to Morris to give a lead and this he always did, never shirking responsibility.

An example of this that comes to mind is Morris taking on the editorship of *Commonweal* (the newspaper of The Socialist League) from its inception in 1885 to 1890. He also wrote the regular news column in addition to longer articles. This was of course in addition to his design work for The Firm, his lectures, poetry, plays, prose, story writing, and so on.

What I see is that Morris used his personal self, with all the unique characteristics combined with the generalities of his time, class, gender and so on, to create a vast array of visible and lasting achievements and tangible artefacts. Certainly, Morris was a practical man in the sense that he liked to do things (for) himself, he liked to make things rather than engage in endless abstract thinking. And while this is a familiar and over-simplified view of Morris's thinking skills, there is an element to him that reflects R. H. Tawney's famous aphorism: 'Life is a swallow, theory a snail.'

E. P. Thompson, like many interpreters of Morris, emphasised the life-long process that changed and shaped Morris's mind and life. Thompson rightly focused on the romantic-to-revolutionary transformation. In sharing this view I would emphasise the remarkable journey that Morris made from individual artist at the centre of creative activity like Shelley; 'the artist turns into the legislator of the world'. To his lasting credit Morris increasingly realised the inadequacy of the 'romantic artist' conception of the action-taking self and turned his attention more and more to collective actions.

I have said that Morris was a practical man, always designing and making things. It is appropriate to link this aspect of his character to his work as a socialist. 'Morris was not a man given to polite turns of phrase or to rhetoric. All his life it had been his business to make things. Whether tiles, or tapestry, or paper, no detail was too trivial to catch his attention. Now that he had decided that it was necessary to make a revolution, he set about the business in the same manner.' (E. P. Thompson, 1955). Morris came to realise his own praxis: the free, universal, creative and self-creative activity through which a person (or social being) creates and changes his historical human world and himself. Morris came to understand his cultural praxis, his creative practice, in a way that was summed up by Zygmunt Bauman writing about his practice (which as a fellow sociologist, I would share): 'the practical success of sociology so understood can only be measured by the degree to which the opposition between consensus and truth is gradually reduced, and the problem of understanding as an activity distinct from communal life gradually disappears' [my emphasis]. I am also reminded here of Marcuse's claim that the real value of art lies in its capacity to challenge the monopoly of truth! Morris spent most of his adult life doing just that, and - in this brief essay - I want to describe how he did it, and the lasting value of his actions, including the enormous influence he had on the development of 'design' as a practice and education.

Before progressing further perhaps some working definitions of design, linked with reference to education, would be useful.

John Walker, in his book *Design History and the History of Design* quotes Stephen Bayley: 'Design is what occurs when art meets industry, when people begin to make decisions about what mass-produced products should look like.'

Walker emphasises the Ruskinesque view that mass production increasingly separated craft from art and design.

> "It was the gradual introduction of more intensive labour divisions, power-driven machinery, assembly lines, and growing automation which brought about the separation of craft and design, and which prompted the well-known debates about the fate of art and craft in the age of mechanical production and reproduction."
>
> *(John Walker, 1989)*

In many obvious ways, the emergence of Morris & Co. as designers was a contradiction in their aesthetic and socio-moral judgement of the high value of the anonymous medieval craft worker. One way Morris eluded this inherent dichotomy was to be a craft worker himself and not 'just' a designer, retailer and so on. Walter Gropius (of Bauhaus) was moved to observe that 'Ruskin and Morris strove to find a means of reuniting the world of art with the world of work'.

Morris was always aware of whose needs were being met via the process of his designing. Is any designer really engaged with social production for the widest form of need rather than production for profit? Even contemporary examples - like the clockwork radio? However, Ray Watkinson for one has stressed that Morris always sought to develop a relation between function, human life and action taking. Morris, like many of his friends and associations, was very concerned about education. He was only too well aware of the failings of schooling in general and the specific inadequacy of art and technical education.

Colin Ward, one of the 20th century's wisest anarchists, sees Morris as a deschooler, fundamentally opposed to the oppressive and anti-humanist control system called education. Ward makes reference to *News from Nowhere* (Morris's utopian socialist novel published in 1891), in which Morris has characterised a communist Britain without any formal schooling at all but where there is an abundance of life-long learning within the context of 'really useful education'. (And let us not forget that this was a Chartist slogan!) Morris as a Freethinker and secularist comes through strongly here.

I cannot resist quoting Ward, quoting Lethaby (an important figure in the Arts & Crafts movement and first professor of design at the RCA in 1900): 'Those who believe in the condensed ignorance called Higher Education have succeeded with great difficulty in at last creating a dislike for that greatest of blessings, work.' How things change!

Morris had a sound insight into the role of the media and had a few things to say about the growth and role of newspapers in his day:

> "The quality of this joint produce of paper-maker, compositor, and subeditor, confirms my *a priori* reasoning remarkably, for no adventure in this kind of wares has any chance of success if it has more than the merest suspicion of a flavour of literature or thoughtfulness. . .I will not say that the worse periodical is the better the chance it has of success, but that if it intends to succeed it must appeal to the habits that are as much akin

to the reasonable aims of education as is the twiddling of a bit of string by a fidgety person."

(William Morris, 1888)

Morris often commented that the schooling received by the working classes was only good for the creation of discontent and that people are educated to become workmen or the employers of workmen or the hangers-on of the employers!

Not surprisingly, therefore, Morris and his associates focused their energies on the making of socialists via education and agitation.

"The work that lies before us at present is to make socialists, to cover the country with a network of associations. . .(who) have no temptation to waste their time in a thousand follies of party politics."

(William Morris, 1888)

There is a link here with Morris' opposition to the idea of state socialism (one of the reasons why he was often dubbed an anarchist by those in favour of state socialism!). This is because what was important for Morris, educationally, was for people to have a vision of an alternative society to aid their thinking about becoming a socialist on the way to the achievement of a democratic socialist society. Attempts at creating such a society without the existence of people with clearly worked out ideas would be (is) doomed to distortion and exploitation by clever, manipulative rogues masquerading as the friends of democracy. This would eventually lead to failure and the triumph of reactionary forces.

By the late 1870s, Morris was a well-respected expert in design. He served as an examiner for the South Kensington School of Design from the late 70s; and, when the Royal Commission on Technical Education was set up in 1882, Morris was called to give evidence. In fact, he gave 11 printed pages of evidence.

The spur for the Royal Commission was the increasing concern in government (and elsewhere) that the UK's industrial competitors were overtaking them and that the lack of good design and design education was a key factor (along with the usual lack of sound scientific education). It was argued that there needed to be an interrelation between art, design and manufacturing. The question was how could/should a set of art and design education institutions be established to meet this deficit.

One common focus for Morris was the effect of the division of labour on manufactured goods. He attacked the division of labour as both exploitative and short-sighted, as the resulting alienation of workers deprived them of any pleasure in their work or control over it. This process also led to deterioration in the quality of the goods, which was of course a key issue. 'Shoddy is King!' observed Morris.

In his evidence Morris reiterated his view that designers should be familiar with both machine processes and materials in order to get the best from both. He also emphasised the '...commercial importance of originality and beauty. Originality was the linchpin of the Morris business; to a remarkable degree, the identity of the Firm was a reflection of his own personality, thought and aspirations.' (Charles harvey and Jon Press, page 182,1996).

In his evidence Morris also advocated as much practical training in schools of art and design as was possible. Having the opportunity to see a design through all the processes to the finished product was crucial. He also argued that museums should be developed as places where everyone could see a diversity of examples of good practice. Provincial museums, he suggested, should keep a representative range of local products and artefacts. It is always worth remembering that one of the tenets of the Arts and Crafts movement was to use, and be honest with, local materials.

Issues like this have been picked up by recent designers; for example, in 1968 David Pye was moved to say '...economics alone will never justify their (the crafts) continuation. The crafts ought to provide the salt - and the pepper - to make the visible environment more palatable when nearly all of it will have been made by the workmanship of certainty. Let us have nothing to do with the idea that the crafts, regardless of what they make, are in some way superior to the workmanship of certainty, or a means of protest against it. That is paranoia. The crafts ought to be a complement to industry.

However. it has to be said that some people may see Pye's words as a palliative that would be 'the thin end of the wedge'.

Morris' great friend Burne-Jones said of him that: 'All his life, he hated the copying of ancient work as unfair to the old and stupid for the present: only good for inspiration and hope.' According to Elizabeth Wilhide, Morris' great skill 'was his ability to create something entirely new out of his enthusiasm for the past'.

He used his own and others' extensive knowledge of the past, and past art, as a lexicon, to be drawn upon and be inspired by. Over the fireplace in the Red House was the maxim, '*Ars longa, vita brevis*' - or 'Life is short, Art is long!'

Morris' middle-class world was one of decorative confusion. The newly rich and self-conscious property owning middle class was hopelessly uncertain which style to embrace. There was, understandably, a rapidly expanding market place for household goods. It was an eclectic nightmare, dominated by heavy, dark and cluttered interiors. In contrast, Morris sought quality and simplicity. For example, his advocacy of plain white walls, where appropriate, had a profound impact at the time.

He was once moved to comment that, 'I have never been in any rich man's home which would not have looked the better for having a bonfire made outside it of nine-tenths of all it held.'

Morris was quite clear in these matters and wrote and spoke extensively on matters of decorative style. (Those unfamiliar with his advice should go to the original source - and be inspired)[1]:

> "Any decoration is futile if it does not remind you of something beyond itself, craftsmanship involving not only the mastery of technique, but the evocation of the spiritual qualities of breadth, imagination and order."

> *(Elizabeth Wilhide, 1991)*

---

[1] During the writing of this essay I derived great pleasure from re-decorating a room in my 1888 house with Pomegranate (or Fruit) wallpaper (1864) and a wild sage with coriander flat paint on some walls.

Morris is often characterised as someone close to nature. He certainly advocated a careful, reflective study of nature as part of design education. He did this himself and his prose, poetry, lectures and letters are full of descriptive references to nature in general and the countryside in particular. He was a great walker, often to the chagrin of his family and friends! His summers at Kelmscott and in the Cotswolds gave him great pleasure as well as endless sources for his designs. But he did say that drawing and design should be suggestive rather than imitative.

Gustav Holst, the musician, has just popped into my head - another great walker, who went on many rambles with his good friend Ralph Vaughan Williams. They went off collecting folk songs in addition to other countryside artefacts. Holst heard Morris give a lecture in London in 1896 and, after the latter's death in the same year, composed an elegy to Morris (a part of The Cotswold Symphony 1899/1900).

Holst was a young member of the Hammersmith Socialist Society (with his wife-to-be Isobel Harrison). He was involved in the choir and theatricals among other activities. Holst was drawn to the Society in part for its comradeship, which he felt was sadly missing when he moved to London from his hometown of Cheltenham. These feelings in Holst were confirmed much later by Vaughan Williams:

> 'The tawdriness of London, its un-friendliness, the sordidness of both riches and poverty were overwhelming to an enthusiastic and sensitive youth; and to him the ideals of Morris, the insistence on beauty in every detail of human life and work, were a revelation. No wonder, then, that the poetic socialism of the Kelmscott Club became a natural medium of his aspirations; to Morris and his followers 'comradeship' was no pose but an absolute necessity of life.'

Morris was not naïve or sentimental about nature or culture. He knew that the Enlightenment thinkers had seen nature as rigid, as immutable, as controlling, and were dedicated to developing human culture as an expression of freedom and choice. Morris realised that a major problem emerges around the 'need' to control the potentially chaotic development of culture(s); too much freedom would be bad of course! If culture does need organising, even policing, who is to do it? Is this a key contradiction in life for the bourgeois? It is fair to add that Morris was moved to test out the capacity of bourgeois society to make the fraternity aspect of 'liberty, equality and fraternity' actually work, let alone see the other two accomplished. Indeed, a good deal of what Morris wrote in *The Commonweal* (the journal of The Socialist League and edited by Morris) is that if fraternity (or fellowship) is not a living ideology that has transcended the dominant liberal individualist hegemony nothing much is going to change.

> "We are living in an epoch where there is combat between commercialism, or the system of reck-less waste, and communism, or the system of neighbourly common sense."

> *(William Morris, 1895)*

Morris had learnt from Ruskin and other social critics the extent to which the factory system, the historical-inevitable consequence of industrial capitalism, had led to the alienation of human beings, the sense that our own abilities and aspirations as human beings are taken over by other entities.

'Let us grant, first, that the race of man must either labour or perish. Nature does not give us our livelihood gratis; we must win it by toil of some sort or degree.'

This comes from Morris's lecture 'Useful Work versus Useless Toil', and, as mentioned earlier, this sentiment sums up for me so much of his motives. In his outward expression of these values it also became his vocabulary of motives. Morris developed an understanding of cultural and artistic sensibilities and creativity early in his life. He was happy to be the champion of such values and to take action 'against a sea of troubles' that got in the way. However, as he came to realise his values he discovered that the very nature of capitalist society stood in the way. In his first public lecture given on 'The Decorative (or Lesser) Arts' in 1877, he said: 'I do not want art for a few, anymore than education for a few, or freedom for a few.' So he needed to take some action, to do something about it. Morris wanted to democratise art and society because he saw that the former could not be achieved in isolation. In this lecture Morris outlines the highs and lows of craft work. He extols the virtues of design by learnt/traditional skills, experience, and honesty to materials. He also celebrates the collaborative democratic processes of working that are lost to the industrial 'wage slave'. His response is to seek to triumph over this tendency by regaining control of the productive process. 'The artist came out of the handicraftsmen, and left them without hope of elevation, while he himself was left without the help of intelligent, industrious sympathy. Both have suffered, the artist no less than the workman.'

Raymond Williams reiterated this point about Morris and creative labour, that creativity and art versus art and creativity means. . .'Once you say that labour is creative, (it) cannot be confined to the notion of some specialised artistic kind of production.' Or, to paraphrase Eric Gill: 'The artist is not a special kind of person, every person is a special kind of artist!' Morris had understood that the triumph of industrial capitalism had artificially separated out the artist from the workman, the former abstracted to the point of mere style, the latter to increasing degradation as the hand of the machine. One representation of Morris' vision of a society where this dichotomy was healed for the benefit of all is contained in *News from Nowhere*.

Raymond Williams consistently emphasises the meaning of work issues; he is concerned about the way meanings, understandings, were deposited in a culture over time and were therefore fundamental to people's sense of what life and roles entailed (the interplay of the personal and the public aspect of roles). Therefore, if work(ing) were forcibly/undemocratically changed, this central understanding would be shattered and replaced with what?

At this point, I need to briefly revisit the question about the role of culture. I would argue that cultural action can be a proactive realisation of people's desires and hopes, raising issues around a voluntaristic process of change, that in Morris' time, and now, would often be seen as utopian. In the late 19th century, the real context of Morris' practical ideas about change, utopian movements were considered as impractical by Marx and his associates. Marx *et al* conceded that utopian socialists of the turn of the century, like Owen, Saint-Simon, Fourier and Shelly, were understandable because they were not in a position to see the significance of the process of industrial development that would, in a dialectical way, inevitably create the conditions for the rise of a class-conscious proletariat and the revolutionary transformation of society. The weakness of contemporary utopianism for Marx was the insistence by such socialists that voluntaristic action by individuals played any part in the process of change. One of the reasons why Morris has often been seen as an anarchist (like Proudhon, say) and not a socialist is precisely because of the former's deep suspicion of any form of hierarchical politics as an inevitable manifestation of a stratified social order, elitist cultures, and so on. But Morris, quite rightly in my view, held to his utopian vision throughout his life because utopianism criticises the present, postulates a desired alternative which requires effort-labour, by hand and by brain, to bring it into being, and which is certainly not inevitable given the capacity of the forces of the status quo to resist reformulations of the future. This is a constant theme in Morris, as with other utopians, embracing ideas about 'the earthly paradise', 'arcadia' and so on.

I am reminded of my introduction to a paper I gave at the Morris centenary conference in 1996, on 'The Soul of Man under Socialism'. This is the title of an essay by Wilde and my paper sought to discuss the links between Wilde, Orwell and Morris [*refer this present collection*], and their profound influence on my sense of self and my creative *raison d'etre*.

> "It has long been my conviction that cultural creativity can be an antidote to alienation. The expending of human labour, by hand and by brain, is central to our sense of self and the development of identity. We quite literally recreate ourselves through this creative action, we choose the road of dialogue, questions are raised, contradictions are sharpened and brought into focus, and conservative/oppressive forces confronted in the quest for transformation.

> "I say *can* be an antidote because there is plenty of evidence that a considerable amount of cultural production in the name of enlightenment

is anything but enlightening or liberating. George Steiner has once again recently questioned our collective (and private 'bolt hole'?) assumptions with his observation that artistic excellence has less and less to do with progress and decency. He argued that great musical performances, art exhibitions, drama festivals, architecture and so on have not only co-existed with political madness, they have adorned and celebrated it. So, yes, cultural creativity can be/are resources for hope, but *á la* Raymond Williams we need to look carefully at both the vocabulary of motives behind this private and public action and the prevailing conditions of production...Morris, Wilde and Orwell...are linked through their belief in the value of cultural creativity as an antidote to alienation, and their visions of the future, including the 'education of desire'. They were all only too well aware of Mannheim's distinction between the ideologies, or fictions that run our lives so much, and the utopias or wish dreams that we have."

(John Astley, 2005)

This does of course raise key issues about the organisation of practice to which I must return later but for now let me cite Lethaby: 'Designing is not the abstract power exercised by a genius. It is simply the arranging how work shall be done!' How different from my contemporary world of media - adverts - commercially dominated 'art'! To quote T. J. Clarke, chronicler of Modernism '. . .art, in our culture, find itself more and more at the limits, on the verge of emptiness and silence.'

Morris came to understand the politics of culture well before he gave that 1877 lecture but, in the last 20 years of his life in particular, he interwove, like one of his designs, the development of his art and his politics. Morris referred to himself 'as a Modern' and this has not been lost on others then, and since.

"Politics, I should say, is the form par excellence of the contingency that makes modernism what it is. This is why those who wish modernism had never happened (and not a few who think they are firmly on its side) resist to the death the idea that art, at many of its highest moments in the nineteenth and twentieth centuries, took the stuff of politics as its material and did not transmute it. I think of... Morris."

(T.J. Clark, 1999)

Clarke also draws Morris into his account of the role of the 'exhorting classes' and suggest that a good deal of this middle class rhetoric has to do with guilt. There is also here the issue of 'the civilizing process' *á la* Norbert Elias, the 20th century social theorist, and Morris was only too well aware of these pressures. Morris spoke on the contradictions of being a wealthy man and argued that it would have been futile for him to be philanthropic with a carefully managed portion of his money. Instead, he devoted his later adult life and wealth to the socialist movement and the quest to transform society. It is a familiar view that the interrelation between thought and ideal are central to modernism and this was certainly true of Morris.

A regular theme in debates about modern life has been to do with material culture, the objects that are produced (and the processes of producing them) in relation to our needs and wants/desires. Designers/manufacturers and so on depend for their livelihoods on our endless desire to consume goods/objects, which add to the stock of material culture. The value we place upon such goods is largely relative to the particular contexts of our immediate needs and our cultural contexts: who we are, our group membership, our values, and so on. But it is also related to dominant ideologies, those pervasive sets of ideas that in an aggressive, or more relaxed and subtle way, persuade us of the appropriateness of (conspicuous) consumption, the quest for objects of desire, reaching fetish proportions much of the time. Marcuse, in his book *One Dimensional Man* reflected, like Morris, on the stultifying nature of a commercial nexus. So to both para-phrase and take liberties with Le Corbusier on his definition of design, 'ideas made visible' is pretty open!

One of the key issues for Morris, as for us in the 20th century, was the extent to which the specifics of art and design have overlapped. Indeed what 'we' have done is to take art and turn it into material culture with increasing enthusiasm. Walter Benjamin's ideas on 'the work of art in the age of mechanical reproduction' are relevant here, and have focused attention on the popularising of art objects. There are many examples of designer objects taking on the aura of art: look at expensive adverts say (entering into debates about aesthetics, of course, any Dada-ists out there?). It is more commonly the opposite that is true, *i.e.* more and more art has been transformed into material culture. More of us have gained access to these 'art objects' via manufacturing and therefore the nature of these objects has changed because of a wider range of meanings. This 'democratising process' does not prevent art from remaining non-reproducible and valuable in this traditional way but it does and has greatly increased the overlaps between the motivations of designers and artists and also affected the meanings placed upon these objects by us as consumers, alongside whatever aesthetic posture we may strike.

Morris was engaged with thinking about how to transform the conditions of production in the 'decorative arts' to raise quality and increase access. He predated Benjamin (and others) in this concern.

> "One of the foremost tasks of art has always been the creation of a demand which could be fully satisfied only later. The history of every art form shows critical epochs in which a certain art form aspires to effects which could be fully obtained only with a changed technical standard, that is to say, in a new art form."

> *(Walter Benjamin, 1973)*

Fiona MacCarthy quotes Morris on his constant drive for perfection, the quest that drove him on: 'I mean that I can never be contented with getting anything short of the best, and that I should always go on trying to improve our goods in all ways, and should consider anything that was only tolerable as a ladder to mount up to the next stage - that is, in fact, my life.'

When Morris says, 'Have nothing in your houses that you do not know to be useful - or believe to be beautiful,' he means it! (Unlike, say, this author's contemporary environment dominated by the norm of commercial and monetary interest masquerading as aesthetic criteria and judgement.) He is not being cautious or holding back from asserting his beliefs; he is a proselytiser for the development and deployment of the resources for hope.

I need now to turn my attention more specifically to 'The Firm'. I have already said something of Morris's character and his goals in life, his values and approaches to art and design. The establishment of 'The Firm' in 1861 enabled Morris and his friends to put their values into practice and, for example, to engage in the collaborative working model that they espoused.

> "Having among their number men of varied qualifications, they will be able to undertake any species of decoration, mural or otherwise, from pictures, properly so-called, down to the consideration of the smallest work susceptible of art beauty."
>
> (*From a Firm publicity circular of 1861*)

Good technique and mastery of material was fundamental to Morris: 'As he believed that you could not design anything without understanding intimately how it was to be made, he taught himself one process after another.'

When embracing a medium, technique or material new to him, he would spend time researching traditional products to learn how it was done. Hence his many visits to museums and the like. He moved painstakingly through weaving to embroidery to carpet-making and to dyeing; even, in this last instance, spending weeks mastering the making of the dyes themselves. If what he wanted did not exist he would make it himself or work with others to do so. A famous example of this was his creation of a whole new set of typefaces for the Kelmscott Press. This sound basis in technique served Morris well and he went on to teach many other people, including family and friends.

So having established 'The Firm', Morris and his associates went to work. The ambition of Morris and his colleagues to set new standards in the decorative arts drew added strength from their realisation of how well placed they were to carry out Ruskin's injunction to create the market rather than merely supply it; making products "educational instruments that would be more influential for all kinds of good than many lecturers on art, or many treatise writers on morality."

It is quite clear that Morris only 'went back' in time to go 'forward' in design and production, and to overcome the inadequacy of contemporary products. He was prepared to invest time and effort into getting the basic principles sorted out before he took any project forward.

> "Mere originality was not enough, as Morris himself stated 'however original a man may be, he cannot afford to disregard the works of art that have been produced in times past when design was flourishing.' Thus his textile designs, what at first were naturalistic and free flowing, underwent a radical change in 1876 as a result of his discovery of medieval woven textiles at the South Kensington Museum..."

(Charles Harvey and Jon Press, 1991)

'The Firm' became very successful and Morris was particularly identified with these achievements. Their collective output was considerable and Morris was constantly creating. For example in the decade from 1875 Morris made 21 designs for wallpaper, 32 for printed fabrics, 23 for woven fabrics, together with 24 machine-made carpets; plus tapestries, embroideries and all his other activities! (For those interested in more detail, Harvey and Press's book is extensive on the development of 'The Firm', in addition to providing a valuable overview of Morris' life.)

Once 'The Firm' was well established Morris also 'returned' to his poetry, languages and translating. It is worth remembering that Morris was such a renowned poet that when Tennyson died he was offered, and declined, the poet laureateship. Throughout the growth years of 'The Firm' Morris stood by his principles and reiterated these key themes for a wider audience via his many lectures on art and design. This, for example, from his lecture 'The Aim of Art' in 1887:

> "Therefore the Aim of Art is to increase the happiness of men, by giving them beauty and interest of incident to amuse their leisure, and prevent them wearying even in rest, and by giving them hope and bodily pleasure in their work; or shortly, to make man's work happy and his rest fruitful. Consequently genuine art is an unmixed blessing to the race of man."

> *(Quoted in Harvey and Press, 1991)*

And clearly one of the reasons why Morris championed the decorative or 'lesser arts' was because far more ordinary working people were engaged in producing fabrics, pottery, glassware, furniture, clothing, metalwork and so on than in *fine* or *professional* art of any kind.

In this respect Morris was constantly restating the golden rule of ethics, namely, do unto others, as you would want done to you! A clear aspect of Morris' design for life was to consider, speculate about and work out what was needed to transform peoples' lives via a revolutionising of society, of social relations. His critique of conventional politics also embraces the inadequacy of labourism in the UK: the trade union consciousness of limited demands of more pay and better conditions within capitalism.

As I have mentioned before, Morris' fullest account of the processes contained in this transformation to a communist society is in *News from Nowhere*, which should be read by anyone who even vaguely suspects that all is not well and that something else might be imagined and worked for. As I have already indicated, Morris wrote and spoke about socialism a good deal, and it is worth briefly quoting him on this specific issue:

> "...What I mean by Socialism is a condition of society in which there should neither be rich nor poor, neither master nor master's man, neither idle nor overworked, neither brain-sick workers, nor heart-sick hand workers, in a word, in which

all men would be living in equality of condition, and would manage their affairs unwastefully, and with the full consciousness that harm to one would mean harm to all - the realisation at last of the word COMMONWEALTH."

(Quoted in A.L. Morton, 1984)

When I take stock of Morris' influence, it is, inevitably, essentially, with Morris the complete man; the all-rounder, the holistic social being; where certain key values and principles formed the structure for his life and work. I have also felt like this throughout my adult life. As a professional sociologist I occupy this role full-time; I do not take on this self only at certain prescribed times during the day. My co-existence as an educator is the same: I am always at it, seeking opportunities to develop awareness and understanding among my fellow beings, trying to raise consciousness and create opportunities for learning to take place. This may sound horribly 'right-on' and pompous, but it has real intrinsic value for me; these creative, inter-active, collaborative and essentially social actions are life. There can be virtue in practice.

We gaze upon the artefacts and the processes; we contemplate the scheme and shape of things to come, our life and loves, our work in progress.

We engage texture and colour (once a Fauvist always a . . .); we would rather spend an evening in the deep red resonance of Dionysus than in the thin atmosphere of Apollo's company! We are prepared to stand by a commitment to authenticity, try to be honest to materials and methods, in preference to the endlessly shifting surface life of simulation.

There is pleasure to be derived from this focus on the value of human labour that should lead to the good, the virtuous society.

Morris has been dead for over one hundred years, but his legacy lives on; anyone who takes life seriously, who is concerned with the opportunity for creativity and happiness for all, has a great example to follow. Morris' values, principles and approach to work in general and to a life as artist/designer and educator in particular, still stand as a model for us all. We should take up his invitation to focus on the issues that confront us today.

Morris has certainly repaid my investment of time and effort into his vision, his design for life. This essay is about what I have taken from him and why I value it. I also hope to demonstrate how I seek to repay my debt to him, in the full knowledge that without some commitment to reciprocity in human relations we really are lost, or to give Morris the last word, 'Fellowship is life'.

BIBLIOGRAPHY:

ASTLEY, John: '*The Soul of Man Under Socialism: Orwell, Wilde and Morris* (centenary conference paper), 1996 [included in Collected Essays 2 - *Culture and Creativity*, 2006].

BAUMAN, Zygmunt: *Hermeneutics and Social Science*, Hutchinson, 1978.

BENJAMIN, Walter: *The Work of Art in the Age of Mechanical Reproduction in Illuminations* (p.239), (Ed. Hannah Arendt), Fontana, 1973

CLARKE, T. J.: *Farewell to an Idea. Episodes from a History of Modernism* (p.407), Yale Univ. Press, 1999

Ibid. p.21.

HARVEY, Charles & Press, Jon: *Art, Enterprise and Ethics: The Life and Works of William Morris* (p.182), Frank Cass, 1996

HARVEY, Charles & Press, Jon: *William Morris. Design and Enterprise in Victorian Britain* (p.41), Manchester Univ. Press. 1991

Ibid. p.95.

Ibid. p.111

Ibid. p.228.

HEYWOOD, Andrew: In the *Journal of the William Morris Society*. Vol xi no.4 Spring, 1996 (p.43/4).

MACCARTHY, Fiona: *A History of British Design 1830-1970* (p.24), George Allen & Unwin, 1979

MACCARTHY, Fiona. *William Morris: A Life for Our Time*, (p.vii.), Faber & Faber, 1994

MARCUSE, Herbert: *One Dimensional Man*, Sphere, 1968.

MORRIS, William. The Commonweal (30-6-1888, p.5), quoted in The *Journal of the William Morris Society* vol xi, No 1 Autumn 1994.

Ibid. p.5

MORRIS, William: *Hopes and Fear for Art, Five Lectures*, 1921 edtn. (first pub. 1882), Longmans, Green & Co.

MORRIS, William: Lecture, 1895 (p.113), quoted by Thompson in ICA Exhibition publication, 1984

MORRIS, William: in ICA Exhibition publication, 1984.

MORRIS, William: *Useful Work versus Useless Toil*, 1884, in MORTON, A. L.: *Political Writings of William Morris,* Lawrence and Wishart, 1984.

MORRIS, William, quoted in Briggs: *William Morris: Selected Writings and Designs* (p.89), Penguin, 1962

MORTON, A. L.: *Political Writings of William Morris,* Lawrence and Wishart, 1984.

PEVSNER, Nikolaus: *Pioneers of Modern Design* (p.22), Penguin, 1960

Ibid. p.23.

PYE, David, in Harris, Jennifer: *William Morris Revisited: Questioning the Legacy* (p.48), exhibition publication, Whitworth Gallery, 1996

SHANKLAND, Graeme, quoted in Briggs: *William Morris: Selected Writings and Designs* (p.176), Penguin, 1962

THOMPSON, Edward P: *William Morris: Romantic to Revolutionary*, Lawrence & Wishart, 1955

WARD, Colin: Morris as Anarchist Educator, in *William Morris Today,* ICA Exhibition publication (p.128), 1984

WALKER, John A: *Design History and the History of Design,* Pluto (p.27/8), 1989

Ibid. p.38/9.

WATKINSON, Ray: *William Morris as Designer* (p.7), Studio Vista, 1967

WILHIDE, Elizabeth: *William Morris, Décor and Design* (p.38), Pavilion, 1991

Ibid. p.43.

Ibid. p.64.

WILLIAMS, Raymond: *Culture*, Fontana 1981.

WILLIS, Paul: *Common Culture*, Open Univ. Press, 1990.

William Morris: a biographical sketch of a political life

2005

William Morris did not need to get into politics to make his name, to become famous. By the time he did engage with The Democratic Federation in 1883 (the year of Marx's death) he was already very well known as a poet, designer, successful business man (having set up 'The Firm' in 1861), architectural activist and so on, and so on. It was his values, principles, and deep-rooted sense of social injustice that drove him across the 'river of fire' in to active political life - a 'crossing a border' experience taken out of 'necessity and desire'.

In his 1950s' book on Morris, subtitled 'Romantic to Revolutionary', Edward Thompson argued that this transformation was characteristic of Morris' practical and wholehearted solutions to the problems he faced. When there was no viable or acceptable alternative he engaged in 'making a revolution'.

However, this romantic and revolutionary duality to Morris was to re-appear regularly in his ideas, for example around the tricky issue of 'the soul of man under socialism'. Oscar Wilde was to focus very specifically on this problematic in his essay of 1890, but it was never far from Morris' considerations, particularly in the looming bureaucratisation of socialist and labour politics.

One key aspect of this discussion is the acceptance by the leadership of the labour movement that a mass (culture) society actually existed, and that this burgeoning mass needed to be controlled, and - eventually - administered into welfare capitalism. When he eventually came to set up The Socialist League in 1884 he and his associates explicitly distanced themselves from 'State Socialism, by whatever name…'

Morris stuck closely to the view that there are really no masses, only ways of seeing people as masses. Morris' inherent romantic temperament, well established by, and in his aesthetic values, checked any possible tendency towards a socialist corporatism. One contributory manifestation of these values was in his outlook on using 'the past' (as an archive and resources of images, ideas, and practice) to inform his contemporary take on the nature and consequences of industrial capitalism, and what his responses to it should and could be.

Thompson for one has defended Morris' utopianism, putting in to a context of a distancing from the vulgar Marxism of scientific socialism. Michelle Weinroth in her 1996 book, *Reclaiming William Morris*, argues much the same, commending Morris' 'rhetoric of dissent' as a crucial aspect of his place in the pantheon of utopian writers.

Morris' insistence on the opportunity for all to engage in 'useful work rather than useless toil' was at the heart of his growing awareness of the limitations of bourgeois ideals. His reading of Ruskin was vital in this respect, and that set of ideas was well summed up by Herbert Marcuse when he argued that 'the real value of art lies in its capacity to challenge the monopoly of truth'. This form of approach to 'art' took Morris beyond Ruskin into a political domain, which required the former to substantially reassess his ideas on future life.

Unlike many of his labourist associates Morris came to the Marx-influenced Democratic (later Social Democratic) Federation from an anarchistic, romantic/humanist, and practical perspective. Quite simply he believed that everyone should have the opportunity to be happy, be creative, and share in the immense personal and collective value of a beauty enriched life. Morris always acknowledged his privileged background, and indeed in later years spent most of his inheritance on funding his ambitious schemes - such as The Firm. By the time of mature adulthood he came to understand the nature of political barriers that stood in the way of all people sharing in the life experiences that meant so much to him. He came to understand that the only way out of this impasse was to 'make a revolution' in the everyday lives of people, to liberate all people; freedom for all is freedom for each!

The seeds of late-Nineteenth and Twentieth century adult (and workers) education lie in these ideas. The motivation for self-help, freedom of thought, and socialist aspirations became increasingly powerful in successive generations. A distinctive characteristic of Morris' ideas is in the juxtaposition of social structure, culture, and biography.

These very ideas have underpinned the (socialist led) adult education movement and, of course, were later to become 'officialised' in the curriculum developments called Cultural Studies.

Morris was confronted by, and challenged by, an accumulation of practical tasks, just like learning to make dyes, or embroider, or create a design that suggested the complexity of natural forms.

The intellectual side of socialism for Morris was often problematic. He acknowledged that he found Marx's writings difficult, if interesting. Morris did not seek out membership of Marx's coterie, but perceptively asserted that 'Marx is on our side!'

The Democratic Federation's call to 'Agitate, Educate, and Organise' was tailor-made for Morris the practical man, intuitive adult educator, and proselytiser.

Fiona MacCarthy subtitled her 1994 biography of Morris, *A Life for Our Time*, and this theme has been reiterated many times since by people reflecting upon, for example, Morris' ecological and environmentalist concerns. As mentioned above his constant drawing upon the natural world is a key facet of his creative action. He argued that art, craft, and design should suggest nature, not seek to imitate it. His sensibilities concerning his environment are regularly addressed in his juxtaposition of town and country, the urban and the rural, the industrial and the agrarian. Raymond Williams was to develop these concerns in his 1973 book *The Country and the City*.

Williams was to write of a 'structure of feeling' in our attempts to understand everyday life and culture, and took these sentiments into his fiction, particularly that on the Wales/England Border Country. Morris did of course do the same, not just through his early and voluminous poetry, but through his 1890 novel *News from Nowhere* (a joke about utopia, of course), where even the Thames Valley weather had been transformed into a balmy paradise following the socialist revolution of the 1950s, and several years of communism. Morris (and Williams) were talking about knowable communities, and seeking to emphasise how a genuine socialist democracy would enhance, and reproduce organically, the co-operative and collective nature of local community life, rather than try to control and domesticate it in the way most Labour politics has sought to do. Morris' relationship with 'the past' was similar to Williams' concept of the 'knowable community' in the sense of always having it with you (as a resource for hope and so on) even when 'crossing a border' into some different, even hostile domain. Morris' clearly had an understanding of the complex issues related to cultural continuity, and change, that constitutes both 'the past', and contemporary, everyday life.

In his 1958 book *Culture and Society* Williams commends Morris' political analysis skills, and argues that the latter is fine political writer. Williams also refers to Morris' self imposed restricted use of the words *civilization*, by which he meant the consequences of industrial capitalism and the machine age, and *culture*, by which he meant the bogus 'cultured' life-style of the bourgeoisie.

Orwell is another writer concerned with 'the soul of man under socialism' in a world of false meanings and double-speak. This issue was developed in his novel *Nineteen Eighty-Four* where the struggle of 'the last man in Europe', Winston Smith, is conceptualised by, among other abominations the process of obliterating the countryside. A further reason why Morris was, and is, seen as a talismanic political figure is in the portrayal of him as a 'whole man'; not off-centre, alienated, and anomic in the conventional contemporary view of our lives. A large part of Morris' appeal today is in his assertion that creative practice is virtuous, which regularly returns him to consider the social conditions of production, craftwork, and the role of mechanisation. Morris was not anti-machine but he did question the motives for technological change, and who had control over those processes. In this respect Morris' focus on the interplay between social structure, culture and biography raises questions about the value of human labour.

Socialists in the post-1945 years have returned again and again to the central notion that socialism has the vision and potential to create, through praxis, the 'new person'.

For example, note the resurgence of interest in the 1951 Festival of Britain, which briefly flourished in that summer of hope and inquiry, despite the outright opposition of Churchill and his band of misanthropic and anti-democratic conservatives.

This struggle for democratic cultural values continues, and to paraphrase Eric Gill, and other Arts and Crafts movement luminaries, 'The artist is not a special kind of person, every person is a special kind of artist!'

In the struggle to help achieve an informed and educated people, Morris understood the limitations of the capitalist press, and in his usual way, set about redressing this imbalance by establishing *The Commonweal*, the journal of The Socialist League, in February 1885. This was a popular newspaper in most senses, and attracted among others the collaboration of Eleanor Marx and Edward Aveling. Morris would have been a critical observer of our contemporary drift away from the highly contentious role of the 'ideological *state* apparatuses' of British social democracy (for example, for Louis Althusser, in the 1960/70s, mass state education) to the virtually unrestrained 'ideological *cultural* apparatuses' of contemporary life. What, one wonders, would Morris have made of an advertising-saturated media locked into meritocratic fantasy and consumer fetishism?

Morris commented on the severe limitations inherent in newspaper growth of his own day; this is a contemporary equivalent of what we now refer to as 'dumbing down!' He argued that journalism must appeal to habits that are akin to the reasonable aims of education, and not what he saw around him, like 'the twiddling of a piece of string by a fidgety person'! Morris, and later, Williams, would further comment on the 'disappearance of the word', let alone the concept of *education*, from our political language (more recently, this is discernible in the State's reconfiguration of adult and community education).

Morris' concerns with an educating media have echoes in the idea of 'the civilizing process' discussed by Norbert Elias and others in recent decades. The now constant attacks on the idea and scope of public sector broadcasting would have angered Morris, and he would certainly have been in the Bernard Crick type alliances linking any hope of a democratic citizenship with protection of an independent BBC.

Between 1883, when Morris formally engaged with socialist politics, and his death in 1896, he criss-crossed the country giving numerous talks, linking together, and inter-weaving,his ideas and concerns. However, despite all such strenuous travelling and talking his political epicentre remained Hammersmith in west London. The local branch of The Socialist League became a crucial base, and lasting inspiration for so many, from the open-minded and inquisitive, to the dedicated activist. It was in this milieu that the young Gustav Holst encountered Morris, and drew inspiration for his developing musical life. Holst was of course to write 'Elegy: in Memoriam William Morris' (part of his Cotswolds Symphony) in 1899-1900 to record his debt to a great man. Holst was to stay close to Hammersmith all his life, and in the 1930s wrote his piece 'Hammersmith' for the BBC.

So, in conclusion, why choose to write about Morris now, one hundred and nine years after his untimely death? One key reason must surely be the desperate need we have for some outstanding political leadership on the Left. Now more than ever we need some people of vision, passion, and selfless, unswerving commitment to fundamental social change in contemporary Britain. This is not to say that there are no good people engaged in the struggle for democratic socialist values, of course there are, and frustrated though many may be, they fight on as best they can. Many people continue to 'swim against the stream' of a political life dominated by the Tories of all parties, a pusillanimous, and self-seeking Parliamentary Labour Party, and an Establishment firmly in place. The many honest people who recognize only too well the desperate state of our political life today need to be galvanised into action. We can be optimistic about the new anti-global capitalism movements among the young. Green politics and the like all demonstrate a growing awareness among people of the myriad ways in which the rich and powerful hold sway over our everyday lives in an increasingly impoverished world.

However, it remains the case that we need people of Morris' charisma, to take the struggle to a higher level, and re-unite the 'foot soldiers' of that struggle for the benefit of all.

Let me finish by recalling what Robert Blatchford wrote on Morris' death: 'I cannot help thinking that it does not matter what goes into the *Clarion* this week because William Morris is dead. . . he was our best man, and he is dead. How can we think of the movement today but as a thing struck motionless?'

Fortunately, the struggle was not left motionless for long, and now we must look to Morris and others for inspiration to take up the banners once more.

"Why Don't We Do It In The Road?"

The Beatles Phenomenon

John Astley, Oxford
1979

Reissued with a new Preface, 1989

CONTENTS

PREFACE
[1989]

This essay was written in 1979. I began the writing during a Christmas vacation, must have been 1978, and finished the research and writing during the year. Elements of text need updating, in view of the passage of time, and some of the material I would now question, quibble with, over and so on. I hope that I have moved on since 1979, having learnt something from the development of cultural studies and myself. However, I have rejected revision, on more than one occasion - well before now - and have gone instead for a re-launch. If it is good enough for the pop world, who am I to deny such a proposition? The core of the narrative remains relevant, since I was (and am) intent on dealing with that phenomenon, as it existed, not with the biographies of the four individuals after they went their separate ways. If anything, some of my views on the *context* - *eg*. 'post-War Britain' and 'Youth' - have changed (expanded, really) rather than what I have had to say about The Beatles.

I would, though, like to make a few points in this Preface by way of reconfirmation of the need for the project in the first place. I would also add, with all due modesty, that the central themes have held up well with the passage of time.

My main aim in 1978/79 was to write about The Beatles as a cultural project and product alongside the much more important and interesting questions about the formation of the project and product. In this respect, my intellectual debt to Raymond Williams is clear to see. I was always primarily concerned to unravel, for my own satisfaction, the reasons that lay behind the emergence of The Beatles; how could a cultural phenomenon like that/them actually happen?

It is clear, even from these remarks, that I have looked at The Beatles as a cultural phenomenon and not focused my attention on 'you know who' as individuals, *etc*. This is not to say that there is nothing about them in the text, there certainly is and it is important in at least two ways. Firstly, I have always been concerned with the interface between the history of society, social structure, social roles and the history of any one person bound up in all that collective stuff. Secondly, it is necessary to be reminded of the fact that it is real persons that do the social interacting in everyday life and not simply, or abstractly, their cultural forms or stylistic representations. It may well be that the form the interaction takes is shaped, influenced or determined by certain cultural forms at any time. Indeed a great deal of what I wrote ten years ago is precisely about this. Much of what I have written about youth or youth cultures has embraced a concern about the role of music in real people's lives and the crucially related questions about identity formation, life apprenticeship(s), the self and social accountability.

Another key theme in the text that I would stand by is the changing nature of post-War Britain. In the text, I made an attempt to describe and explain changes in production and work, and the shifts away from a society whose sentiments were clustered around producing and *working* to a society increasingly influenced by *consuming*. New technologies, new welfarists' deals, new sets of expectations and aspirations had begun to reorientate people, turn their heads, well before 1962-3. However, the confluence of so many changed and changing aspects of life in Britain, as discussed in this study of a cultural phenomenon was one of the issues I was fumbling towards. The new technologies: records, hi-fi, guitars, TV, and so on, crowded in on us. The questionable new and liberating forms of non-work - leisure - coinciding with the peculiar situation of the young at that time, linked in vitally with the promotion, deification, of pleasure, helped to create a climate where the movement of an essentially working-class set of social and musical phenomena were taken up (and hijacked) by the middle class. Post-War affluence met plurality and diversity in the popular music or 'pop' gold rush. One important feature of the pleasure business was the careful, or even careless, maintenance of good old cultural forms of domestication, romance, love (sex) and marriage. Who said love and profit could not walk out together?

I still believe in the city, the street, as a focus. The whole question of city sounds has continued to interest me. I am still convinced that the white urban blues of the young industrial classes is the essence of Rock 'n' Roll. Okay, the downbeat reflections on life in the blues have been supplemented with an upbeat form in soul and, crucially, an indigenous young black culture has been added since the 1960s.

The question of a cultural tradition remains important. The past (real and myth) is constantly plundered to good and bad effect and

I am more and more aware of the fact that not only does art continue to emulate life, but also that life most certainly imitates art!

Indeed, one of the crucial questions posed here is, "what actually constitutes the past?" Our pasts have been subject to constant rewriting, parody and pastiche. Even if it were possible 'at some time in the past' to say what the past was, can we really be so sure any longer? Pop continues to be one key dimension to Britain's burgeoning heritage industry.

As society and our lives change, are transformed by all manner of agency, popular cultures (if we can still use that generic term with any certainty) continue to be the site of struggles for and about power. The contradictions of everyday life that contributed to the creation of and reflection upon a cultural phenomenon like The Beatles are still with us.

This small corner of cultural analysis may still prove relevant and helpful to anyone trying to make sense of the last forty years or so.

INTRODUCTION

So much has already been said and written about The Beatles (and the 1960s in general) that yet another book about 'The Fab Four' might seem unnecessary. I hope to disprove that idea with this offering. Essentially the text has been written out of my own dissatisfaction with what has gone before. A good deal of biography has appeared over the last ten to fourteen years. Many books have been written on the place of youth, youth cultures, rock and pop music, *etc.* in the same period of production. I have deliberately refrained from calling them history; of either the epoch or The Beatles or both. It seems to me that these various texts - from authorised biography or 'cultural capsule', to 'let's tell it how it really was' pieces - invariably lack any sense of history, as process of change, as analysis of phenomenon with a view of how certain social relations are created, maintained and destroyed. Most of the work on The Beatles to date has a static, pseudo-objective 'snap-shot' feel about it.

One of the focuses of this book is to argue for a feeling of the *images* of post-War British society in Rock and Roll music. What needs to be brought out here is that rock and roll cannot be looked at as a 'thing in itself'. Nor can we look at post-War British society without considering the enormous influence of rock and roll on people's lives, values, attitudes and behaviour. However, we cannot merely locate our interest in the individual sphere of activity and consciousness. An ontology is useful, of course, but I hope to relate some ideas of collective responses as well, particularly as an aspect of social change and cultural devel-elopment. What is needed is to look *through* rock and roll to gain a set of images; an impression of what post-War British society of the 1950s and 1960s was really like. However, these images cannot be static ones. They cannot merely be nostalgic cameos, guaranteed to cast feelings of rapidly advancing senility into the most ardent 'Peter Pan' of Rock and Roll. Anecdote is not enough. The raconteur is invaluable in any attempt to create a view of relations and practices 'as they were', but we need to place our foundations of understanding and analysis on firm ground, rather than the shifting sand. Any retrospective view is tied up in a multitude of *collapsed events*, but these events are not in a linear plane of social development. As reflective, choice-making humans we produce history as part of our daily grind. The later, selective, process of editing and juxtaposition is seductively easy. As Goldman suggests, we need to keep in front of us a notion of changes, critical to any history.

> "Man is defined by his possibilities, by his tendency to enter into community with other men and to establish an equilibrium with nature. Authentic community and universal truth expresses these possibilities, over an extremely long historical period."

> (*The Human Sciences & Philosophy* p.118/119)

If we can come to comprehend the phenomenon of the 1950s and 1960s, we might be able to understand how and why a phenomenon like The Beatles came to be, dwell, change and pass away, only to be 'reborn' time and time again in people's lives and consciousness. Our project must be two-way. We need to look through a perspective of Rock and Roll to understand a good deal of what was happening. We also need to create this understanding of post-War society so as to formulate ideas about The Beatles and their contemporaries.

"Why Don't We Do It In the Road?" becomes not just a statement from The Beatles, but an expectant cry in the air of the future and *events* to come. . .the creation of history. Greil Marcus makes a point in *The Rolling Stone Illustrated History of Rock and Roll* that:

> "The release of the 'Sgt. Pepper' album in 1967 was an event to savour. Almost immediately, 'Sgt. Pepper' was certified as proof that The Beatles music, or at least this album, was art. But what mattered was the conscious creation of event, the way in which the summing-up-the-spirit-of-the-times style of the music (which for the best part has not survived its time) was perfectly congruent with the organising-the-spirit-of-the-times manner in which the album

was released and received, which is to say that 'Sgt. Pepper', as the most brilliantly orchestrated manipulation of a cultural audience in pop history, was nothing less than a small pop explosion in and of itself. The music was not great art; in its intensification of the ability to respond, was."

(p.176)

Marcus is arguing with others that The Beatles and their products, *e.g.* 'Pepper', was a massive unifying/synthesising factor of youth in the western world - a further aspect of the dialectic, the historical process, was reached here in this event - "Why Don't We Do It In The Road?" McCartney screamed, or the youth screamed or shouted or asked. The possibilities were amazing, but contradictory. "Why Don't We Do It In The Road?" epitomised the understatement, contradiction, irony and paradox of The Beatles as characteristic and symbolic of western/British youth in the 1950s/1960s.

"Why Don't We..?" is saying at least two major things: Firstly, *'Let's do it'* - e.g., make music, a name for ourselves, entertain, liberate ourselves - for ourselves; let's not rely on the distanced showbiz glam of Tin Pan Alley and the USA. Secondly, let's get out there in the world and mark out a bit of ground for ourselves. Let's show 'Them', but 'Us' as well, that we can do our own thing. We can have and express opinions, that our values may well express change and an ingenious recalcitrance, but what's wrong with that? Let's strike a posture, be distinctive, draw on tradition, but be innovative; experience and experiment brought like converging streams into a myriad whirlpool with unknown depths, hidden dangers, but the prospect of adventure and perhaps social change. ". . .No one will be watching us" . . .is the supreme contradiction, posing, as it does, the 'tongue in cheek' juxtaposition with "Why don't we do it. . ?" Our lives are commonplace and typical, and yet they are not. For some of us, like The Beatles, we become corporative, and the sum becomes greater and somewhat different than the individual parts. But in the most humble sector of our civilisation, young people find and found themselves encouraged to adopt the conventional wisdoms of the epoch. Youth are greatly affected by dominant ideology that seeks to inculcate an acceptance of the circumscription of their minds and behaviour. Who could forget Paul Johnson's moral fusillade in 1964?

> "Those who flock round The Beatles, who scream themselves into hysteria, whose vacant faces flicker over the screen, are the least fortunate of their generation, the dull, the idle, the failures: their existence, in such large numbers. . .is a fearful indictment of our education system, which in 10 years of schooling can scarcely raise them to literacy... the core of the teenage group - the boys and girls who will be the real leaders and creators of society tomorrow - never go near a pop concert. They are, to put it simply, too busy. They are educating themselves. They are in the process of inheriting the culture which, despite Beatlism or any other mass-produced mental opiate, will continue to shape our civilisation."
>
> *(New Statesman. 28.2.64)*

I do not intend to write about **The Beatles** *per se* in awed tones. I am not advocating another version of idol worship. We have seen enough ritualised sacrifices made at that particular altar. The Beatles as four Liverpool lads, were pretty commonplace. They all stood an even chance of a reasonable future; none of them stood a reasonable chance of an exceptional future.

With hindsight, can we say, argue, that The Beatles had genius? If we are not prepared to place that collective supremacy on *their* shoulders, are we prepared to go as far as saying that Lennon and McCartney had/have genius? If we turn to the dictionary for guidance/criteria we find the following:

> "Natural ability, special mental endowments; exalted intellectual power, instructive and extraordinary, imaginative, creative or inventive capacity."

Certainly we might argue some or most of these factors, but there again so did plenty of other indigenous musicians of the era.

So where do we start? What factors shall we look at that have contributed to The Beatles phenomenon? May and Phillips, in their introduction on 'The Merseysound' (in *British Beat*, 1974) put forward a very prevalent view of The Beatles phenomenon in particular and pop in general, they say, for example:

> "The Beatles' story has something today of the unreality of a dream and it is hard enough, even for those who lived through it, to remember just how great an influence John, Paul, George and Ringo exerted on the world in the period from 1963 to 1968. Those who never witnessed the scenes of Beatlemania of 1963 to 1964, or who never felt the whole of society changing as a result of The Beatles and the lifestyle they represented, can never be expected to believe how powerful were the forces at work."
>
> *(p.6)*

I would like to make two points here.

Firstly, it seems somewhat naive to suggest that The Beatles, dynamic force as they were, were a major agent of social change in post-War society. Can it be argued that Rock and/or Pop really changed social life so dramatically? They were certainly *part of* most decisive social and cultural changes, but a great deal of what was/is arguably 'society' did not change overmuch. The major forces within and making up society did not radically alter, Beatles or not. In many ways it could be argued that *even* 'The Beatles' became absorbed into existing social structures, economic and social relations of Britain in the 1960s. Their overt commercial and social exploitation, as a 'Band', might be a case in point.

Secondly, I would want to argue that May and Phillips, in their enthusiasm to tell it 'as it was', only add to the mystification of Rock Culture and The Beatles phenomenon. They implicitly suggest that 'the phenomenon' defies analysis; can this be so? I hope it is not conclusively the case that such a cultural phenomenon as The Beatles cannot be more fully comprehended, always accepting, of course, that the matter is a complex one. It is not good enough to substitute 'folk' history, masquerading as value-free description, for a rigorous analysis of the phenomenon in its historical and cultural context. It is demystification that we need, despite the fact that it may be speculative.

The success of a study, of the 1960s say, must be judged by the interrelation between a descriptive explanation of the phenomenon (the events) and personal involvement on the one hand, while on the other hand, attempting an analysis of the epoch. Too many 'studies' and/or accounts of The Beatles have been attempting one or the other approach - the key task is, surely, to significantly *relate* and *interrelate* the two.

Here then, personal experience (biography and autobiography) can be seen in a wider theoretical framework.

In this way, the notion of 'images' of The Beatles era can be realised. How are we to see *the period* and *the phenomenon* through perspectives on society, social life, values, *etc.* in general. Or, to take a leaf from Hoggart's book *The Uses of Literacy*, I want to attempt:

> " . . .close attention to the phenomenal detail and representative concreteness of working-class life and culture"

and

> ". . .broad intuitive grasp of cultural movements and tendencies."

I shall attempt to locate The Beatles phenomenon in the framework of a cultural explanation of the post-War period in Britain in general and Liverpool in particular. I will not attempt to deny their special quality, their particular 'magic'. But I will not go on as if they were a set of 'genies' in their smoke-coloured bottles waiting to be invoked to entertain and please us. The Beatles phenomenon has to be located in real-life, post-War Liverpool; not the least of which concerns was being able to escape from it, as Bert in 'John, Paul, George, Ringo and Bert' by Willy Russell reflects:

> ". . .Up until now there have only been two ways of getting out of Liverpool, being a professional

footballer or going to sea; now we've got being a
Rock and Roll star; we should be grateful!"

The task ahead is not an easy one and is beset with numerous
methodological problems. I have already suggested that this is not
a 'sociology of The Beatles', although it does contain a good deal
of sociological analysis. But the way ahead does have its dangers,
as suggested, for example, by Stanley Cohen:

> "There is a delicate tightrope to be walked when
> writing about, say, pop culture. Intuition and
> concrete detail without theoretical sensitivity
> degenerates into colour supplement trend spotting,
> yet more theory piled upon theory, a Talmudic
> reading of sacred texts. . .interspersed with grat-
> uitous references to the concrete, becomes sterile
> and, above all, inaccessible."
>
> *(THES. 30-4-76)*

Or, to put it another way, in the words of the old Zulu proverb:

> "A dog with a bone in its mouth cannot bark!"

In describing events, in attempting to place them into some sort of
coherence, I shall need to avoid the trap of a scientism and
positivism that only allows me to stick to verifiable fact. I will
need to ask for a little 'willing suspension of disbelief' now and
again to relate what I know and what I feel was taking place.
Chances will have to be taken, as Robert Desnos suggests in his
poem (to paraphrase): "This Pelican of Jonathan's laid a white egg,
and out of it came a Pelican, astonishingly like the first, and this
second Pelican, laid in its turn. . .This sort of thing can go on. . .if
you don't make an omelette."

As a participant in, and observer of, the several events of the
1960s and The Beatles phenomenon, I cannot claim to be impartial
or have a value-free approach. Nor can I claim that as the
particular observing subject to a series of objects (such
phenomenal events as I may have encountered, experienced and
relate) I am at all happy about my problematic relationship.

Andreski (in *Social Sciences as Sorcery*) pointed to such a difficulty:

> "Most of the intellectual difficulties besetting the study of society. . . stem from the disparity in size, longevity and power between the object and the investigator."

Most present enquirers into cultural forms in general, and rock and pop cultures in particular, are familiar with the difficulties I have outlined. We can draw on the work also of the 'cultural pessimists': Eliot, Leavis, The Frankfurt School, for example, who have argued (and their words go on echoing still) that, "capitalist culture, like capitalism itself, is in a crisis" - the 'final death-throes' in fact.

These various writers, from 'right and left' of the political spectrum, have argued that the bourgeoisie is incapable of creating a culture that is alive and vital and progressive. Only a gloomy 'life denying' civilisation is possible. These theorists arrived at this point of view by plucking the idea and existence of 'culture' and its development from its economic social and historical parameters. They have raised 'culture' to an abstract level, 'culture as a whole'. Little attention is then paid to the realities of the economic situation, and so political consequences within (the relations of) capitalist society are taken for granted. The bourgeoisie has failed, the working classes are bought off and pathetic, revolutionary force has gone out of productive and social relations alike. One of the worst consequences of this pessimistic view of 'mass culture' is a notion that sees the mass as uncritical 'pawns' in a declining cultural spiral. I want to reject this view, not for the least because it fails to see the inherent contradictions of repression and enlightenment, or conservative and progressive forces within, as central features of the same sets of relations, productive or consumptive or otherwise. One of the continually fascinating and optimistic aspects of the cultures of a capitalist society is the lack of homogeneity and the very paradoxes and ironies that pervade everyday life. This is not to turn a 'blind eye' to the exploitive and alienating characteristics of such cultures, but to draw out the fact that despite the repressions and stultification, human beings do and will achieve a degree of autonomy in their cultural relations that breaks out of cultural 'straitjackets' time and time again.

> " . . . 'Music, music, foul as a day in spring, as ugly as a flower, as hateful as a butterfly's wing!' snarled the Head Blue Meanie to Max, his assistant.
>
> 'Yes, your Blueness,' cringed Max.
>
> The Head Blue Meanie turned navy blue with rage: 'What was that?' he screamed. 'Say that word again and I'll beat you pink and purple and back to blue again! Meanies never take 'yes' for an answer, it's far too positive. Watch what you're saying, Max, my boy. Start saying yes and you might start thinking positively and the next thing you know you're in the grave danger of being happy.'
>
> 'Yes, I mean No, Your Blueness,' said Max, shaking his head as if he were nodding it, and nodding with a gesture suspiciously like a shake.
>
> 'Are the missiles and troops ready, Max?'
>
> 'No,' nodded Max.
>
> 'Good, launch the attack,' rapped the Head Blue Meanie.
>
> 'No, your Blueness,' agreed Max - and that was how the invasion of Pepperland was started."
>
> *(Quoted from the Yellow Submarine screenplay*
> *by Lee Minoff)*

We must recognise the contradictions of our society in order to understand the nature of cultural phenomenon. Our particular perspectives will all focus upon particular concerns and issues, but we need to be cautious and sceptical throughout.

> "A perspective is a way of seeing things, but, as Kenneth Burke has pointed out (in *Permanence cnd Change*, 1965), the symbol, in this case language, is by definition selective, arbitrary, concealing, disguising and dissembling, as well as broad and inclusive, conventionalised, re-vealing, guising and assembling. . .a way of seeing is also a way of not seeing."

> *(From the introduction of Youth and Sociology ed. by P. Manning and M. Truzzi - 1972)*

Any history of The Beatles and their 'careers', with an explanation of the phenomenon, is - like rock culture and life in general - full of challenges and escapes. We need to perceive these to begin to estimate what took place and why. "But the fool on the hill sees the sun going down, And the eyes in his head see the world spinning round." (From the 'The Fool on the Hill', Lennon & *McCartney - 'Magical Mystery Tour', 1967).*

I have already tip-toed around the periphery of the *mystery* of The Beatles phenomenon. Beyond mystery again is the role of 'magic' in transforming these four Liverpool layabouts into the uncrowned cultural leaders of western youth. Wilfred Mellers, in his entertaining book *Twilight of the Gods* (1972), quotes Collingwood (1937) on magic:

> "Magical activity is a kind of dynamo supplying the mechanism of practical life with the em-tional current that drives it. Hence magic is a necessity for every sort and condition of man."

In Mellers' mind, this is linked up with at least one aspect of The Beatles' function, *i.e.*, as dreamweavers (this comes out nowhere more clearly than the *Magical Mystery Tour* where all sanity is reduced to the ridiculous and *vice versa*). It is also tied clearly to the other fundamental aspect of life in parts: air, fire, water and earth - form the basic physical parameter of that life. Mellers suggests that the fact that these elements are to be found in The Beatles' temperaments: Paul/Air, John/Fire, George/Water, Ringo/Earth, only confirms their ability as creators, and thus as Gods, perhaps?

I will not attempt to argue that The Beatles were somehow endowed with 'genius' or 'mystical powers'. I simply do not know about such things. I might as well just leave the question open.

However, I do want to suggest the fundamental significance of The Beatles in the era of the 1960s. 'The Beatles phenomenon' was truly amazing, and no matter how we might be able to be less than circumspect with hindsight, we can only make educated guesses as to why it was *then* and why *the* phenomenon, albeit derived from them, was so far reaching in its consequences.

I am not going to say that The Beatles transformed the world as such. I am *not* about to argue that The Beatles were the leaders of a generation. Nor do I want to suggest that The Beatles were unique in all respects. What I will pursue here is the idea that they reflected, characterised, influenced and even epitomised an era.

Manning and Truzzi, in their book on *Youth and Sociology*, discuss the ideas of Robert Lifton, particularly what Lifton calls 'protean man' - in this context, *varied and variable youth.*

> "Instead of focusing on the changes in social structure (which he clearly takes into account), Lifton attends to consequences of an apparent lack of deep commitment to adult values and rules. In addition to citing the importance of drastic and destructive change, Lifton concerns himself with the symbols which people use to order their social relations. He finds modern man *symbolically* dislocated, seemingly torn out of the context of the social institutions on which he depends. Self and institutional order no longer mesh from the point of view of actor, but seem to float without clear connection . . .
>
> Powerlessness comes not only from a failure to see the self as capable of being controlled, but also from seeing his experience in the context of rapid change caused by other sources."
>
> *(p.384)*

This point by Lifton, drawn out by Manning and Truzzi, is clearly valuable in terms of the consciousness of people (even praxis) and the way in which people 'acquire' and use a perspective or 'world-view'. This then has something to do with their epistemological position in the world and their relation to symbolic aspects of living everyday lives which inevitably comes upon questions of cultural phenomenon.

My feeling is that The Beatles phenomenon is, to an un-determined degree, in disjuncture with The Beatles. Of course I do not mean that they are not umbilically linked, but that the *Beatles phenomenon*, the incredible impact of which is difficult to overestimate, is not the same as The Beatles and even less so John Lennon, Paul McCartney, George Harrison and Ringo Starr.

We make, of necessity, a cultural, consciousness, 'jump' from viewing The Beatles to viewing the 'Beatles phenomenon'. We have adequate testimony, for example from 'The Beatles' themselves that they came to lose sight of what The Beatles had become. They also came to despise many aspects of The Beatles' corporate image, created and manipulated during the process of the making of the 'Beatles phenomenon', the cultural legacy of which has tended to outlive the doubts and fears voiced at the time.

> "You see, we believed The Beatles' myth, too. I don't know whether the others still believe it. We were four guys . . . I met Paul and said, 'You want to join me band?' Then George joined and then Ringo joined. We were just a band that made it very, very, big that's all. Our best work was never recorded. . . because we were performers."

> *(John Lennon, 'Rolling Stone' Interview, 7-1-71)*

> "I've never really done anything to create what has happened. It creates itself. I'm here because it happened. But I didn't do anything to make it happen apart from saying, 'Yes'."

> *(Ringo Starr - quoted in 'The Beatles Illustrated Lyrics'- Vol.I)*

As ever, the final word seems to belong to Lennon, when he sings (to paraphrase): "I don't believe in Kings/I don't believe in Elvis/I don't believe in Beatles". (from Lennon/Plastic Ono Band' album produced by John, Yoko and Phil Spector, 1970).

This is all very anecdotal and ambiguous to a degree that many will find unacceptable as an objective insight into the 'Beatles phenomenon'. However, it seems clear to me that we need to work on at least those two levels of an objective (but obviously not value-free) analysis of the post-War era that paved the way and created the conditions out of which The Beatles phenomenon could come, on the one hand, while on the other hand offering an assessment of the generation of culture - the music, the 'life-style', the euphoria, the artefact, the consciousness, the history, the legacy. A degree of abstraction here is not an esoteric enclave. If we accept that 'music' has a double origin, intellectual and emotional, we can agree with Martin Cooper, the critic, when he says that music is an ambiguous language, the meaning of which will be dependent on the context. Not necessarily the context of the time of production itself of course, for the individual (*e.g.* I have 16-year-old students 'into' The Beatles at the moment), but certainly in terms of a historical context of time of which this or that cultural phenomenon is an aspect. Can we go down the road of the phenomenologist?

> ". . .any significance assigned to music must be ultimately and *necessarily* located in the commonly agreed meanings of the group or society in which the particular music is created."

> *(Quoted from 'Media, Social Process and Music'*
> *from 'Whose Music? - a Sociology of Musical*
> *Languages', John Shepherd et al 1977, p.7)*

This suggestion is correct, of course, but it says everything and yet nothing very concrete. Music is universal. But music is culturally specific, as there is not a universal ear or a universal context. The Beatles and their music found an audience in a vast range of cultures. However, The Beatles phenomenon is essentially culturally specific in that it was the confluence of events in post-

War British society that created, that could create, *that* phenomenor. Let me take Shepherd's notions a step further then.

> ". . .Implicit in the central assumption of this book is the view that the meaning of music is somehow located in its function as a social symbol. It is the word 'meaning', which creates the greatest problem in this context. For most people a symbol has meaning because it refers to something outside itself. Pictures have meaning because they refer to something in physical reality, and words have meaning because they refer to concepts and ideas. But to suggest that a piece of music has meaning because of extra-musical references is, at the least, highly contentious. The logical alternative has thus been to look for the meaning of music within the structure of individual pieces. . ."
>
> *(p.7)*

I would agree with Shepherd *et al* that it is necessary to look further than 'the structure of individual pieces' for an analysis of meaning. For example, once The Beatles had 'made it' in the mid-1960s, several critics, who perhaps leapt in where angels feared to tread, waxed long on the messages/meaning carried by individual pieces. Now you see it, now you don't! So, what are we approaching here? An attempt, perhaps, needs to be made to synthesise such phenomenological insights within a historical materialist context?

> "An approach to the understanding of the social construction of reality may best be made through a consideration of the role played in that process by symbols. A symbol may be thought of as any occurrence in the world, whether or not produced by man, which carries a *generally* agreed meaning for the members of a particular group or society.
>
> Societies can only arrive and continue to exist through communication, that is, the creation

and exchange of symbols. Symbols are not self-contained phenomena. . .the meanings of symbols and sets of symbols are originally derived from *specific* and *real* situations. . . Once a symbol or set of symbols have been created in response to a new situation these symbols, in retrospect, colour that situation. When people look back on a series of events they do so by means of and *through* the symbols created to define it."

(op. cit. p.9)

Let me then be more specific and anecdotal in relation to this viewpoint of Shepherd's. 1968 was the 'watershed', perhaps, in the post-War period of popular culture. It was in 1968 that production of LP records first equalled the production of 45s (49 million, give or take a few). People began, in fact, to talk of *albums* and not merely 'long players'. I can remember buying 'Pepper', 'Wheels of Fire' (the Cream), and the Moody Blues 'Days of Future Passed' at this time, and being very conscious of the change from the five or six tracks- a-side of material compiled from 45 songs or releases. Since then, production of LPs has outstretched that of 45s.

It is significant that 1967/9 marks the period when several strains of Rock and Roll music begin to come together which demand a different concept of recording. That juncture of 1967-68 is, after all, the 'moment' of 'Sgt. Pepper' - the 'concept' and 'complete work of art' album in one. It is also the period of massive output from 'the underground' and 'progressive' bands in the USA and the UK (with all the attendant record labels, investment levels from the majors, *etc.*). It was also the time when bands (like the Cream, say) produced 'live' albums with recorded tracks that took up most of, or a whole side of, the album.

As for The Beatles, Lennon regarded the post-1963 live performances as boring repetition. Instead, he was always keen to concentrate on the studio. As The Beatles' liaison with A & R men like George Martin developed, Lennon saw his own, and The Beatles, *musical* development in the context of the studio. So the studio became a platform, not merely to record an already conceived, tried and trusted piece, but to experiment, to probe, and to take the great leap in the dark. In 1968, The Beatles launched Apple:

> ". . .to open the way to artistic fulfilment for writers, musicians, singers and painters who have hitherto been unable to find acceptance in the commercial world."
>
> *(Apple Corp. press release c. 1968).*

How contradicting and ironic was to become their situation, especially that of Lennon, perhaps. How often he seems to have looked back from some other moment in time, to that juncture, and sorely regretted, been confused by, what seemed a really good idea at the time.

Time and time again we return to the contradictions of the era and 'The Beatles phenomenon' in this particular instance. In attempting to construct an understanding of such cultural events we weave our way through issues of social being, of reality, that only give further weight to Lukacs claim that:

> ". . .Even in everyday life, phenomena often conceal the essence of their own being, instead of illuminating it."
>
> *(From 'The Ontology of Social Being - on Marx',*
> *p.15)*

It is hardly surprising that an observer, like myself, or the reader of this piece, should find as much, if not more, difficulty in understanding the events of the time than did say, Lennon or the other 'Beatles' at the time (in the 1960s) or since. Certainly we might impute some difficulties for the 'actors' themselves in that they could not perhaps form a view or perspective that took account of their own historical place within it. After all, the essence of irony is that the 'actors', the protagonists if you like, do not fully comprehend their situation. The way to gain control over an historical problem is to create a perspective of it, which may be difficult for those caught up in the very nitty-gritty of events themselves. Analysis from any historical standpoint might be a good deal easier. Marx, for example, did attempt to stress this in *Capital*:

> ". . .all science would be superfluous if the outward appearance and the essence of things directly coincided."

('Capital', vol. 3, Moscow, 1962, p.797)

Let me suggest one further anecdotal example of the contradictory situation for 'The Beatles'. One of the least significant books written about 'The Beatles' is Dilello's *The Longest Cocktail Party*. However, one of the interesting aspects of Dilello's book (he was the Apple Corporation 'house hippy') is the notion carried in the title, *viz.* the (longest) cocktail party. This suggests, indeed reflects fairly accurately, a degree of *gentrification* of The Beatles in the late 1960s.

There is an assumption here that at some stage in their corporate development as The Beatles/a marketable commodity *etc.,* they adopted certain values, postures, modes of behaviour *etc.,* that aligned them socially with 'respectable' elements of society. Now, if we go along with this notion, what problems does it pose? Was it due to their maturation, settling down? Was it due to their new-found wealth, status and prestige? Did the kudos that they achieved on a worldwide basis turn them towards a way of life lifestyle that was fundamentally unfamiliar to them? Can we see this as an aspect of their social being, the ontology of Lennon, say, which is yet a further aspect of underlying contradiction for them? Alan Williams, in his account of things, *The Man Who Gave The Beatles Away* (Williams and Marshall, 1975), emphasises his shock at the change taken place in The Beatles on re-contacting them again in the late 1960s.

> "Recently, I had a meeting with Ringo and George at the Apple headquarters. I walked in, carrying a carrier-bag full of my tipple, a dozen bottles of special strong beer. George and Ringo were surrounded by a dozen very expensive and high-powered international lawyers. . .
> . . .When I staggered out of Apple, feeling little pain, George was telling one of the staff:

'We should have recorded this chat with Alan
Williams tonight. It's ages since anyone dared to
talk to us like that, I think it did us a lot of good.
Two years ago we would no doubt have had him
thrown out.'

I've always called a spade a spade. More so
than ever these days . .."

(p.232 & 235)

I hope to be able to show in the following few pages that The
Beatles phenomenon was/is of major significance in post-War
British cultural life. But I also want to argue that the analytical/
philosophical approach that I have used to create this study can be
used as a method elsewhere. It is a 'way of seeing' cultural
phenomenon that seems relevant to me, though I am conscious that
the approach is somewhat inexact. I would like to feel that looking
'yet again' at 'The Beatles' can be excused for the reasons I have
already outlined, and through the ideas and notions I will develop
in the next chapters.

Again, let me emphasise that I am not suggesting that 'The
Beatles' were the 'greatest ever' rock and rollers or cultural
ambassadors of youth, or whatever. I do want to suggest, though,
that they had a *certain* greatness. This is an aspect of The Beatles
phenomenon that was able not merely to characterise and
epitomise their own condition in relation to youth in general, but to
suggest momentous possibilities for the future - individual and
collective futures. They offered something outside of themselves;
often unselfconsciously; they offered a vision of the epoch to
come.

Before embarking on my enterprise any further, I should add a
few words about overall content. I see it as follows: my study will
be concerned with a sociological understanding of the complexity
of such a cultural phenomenon in post-War Britain. The study
contains four main areas, not that these can in any way be
autonomous.

Firstly, I am concerned to discuss present understandings of
mass/popular culture, an aspect of which has been the
development of rock and roll and pop music in the 1950s and
1960s. What led to the emergence of particular forms of popular
culture in this period? What were the antecedents? What are

meanings and the significance of such events in British society? What can a study of popular culture in this period tell us about the nature of society and the social changes that have taken place, set against the persistent patterns of social attitudes and behaviour? Can a study of popular culture in any way be a 'barometer' of life in a capitalist-industrial society like Britain? What can we say of the future?

Secondly, I want to see these issues in relation to conceptions of 'youth cultures' in society. I want to elaborate some established views of the creation, nature, and role of divergent attitudes by and towards youth in society.

These two themes will essentially require an analysis of the economic and social situation of Britain since the war and the relation that may well exist with the development of certain cultures, world-views, *etc.*

I will want to concentrate particularly on the post-War reconstruction of Merseyside, attempting to put together an analysis of life in such an industrial and urban situation.

Thirdly, out of this analysis will grow a discussion of 'The Beatles'. I will not dwell overmuch on biography (*e.g,.* Hunter Davies), or pop journalism (*e.g.,* Braun, Melly, Palmer or Cohn), or musicology (*e.g,,* Mellers) or symbolism (*e.g.,* Aldridge), and instead attempt to synthesize the many diverse and critical themes bound up with a cultural analysis of The Beatles. I would hope for something of a holistic approach to have emerged in this context.

The moment of The Beatles and the 'Mersey Sound' needs some degree of assessment, while attempting to avoid the 'snapshot' anecdotal approach, or the cliché and the sensational. I want to assess and evaluate The Beatles emergence and 'career' both up to and beyond their 1964 watershed. An attempt will be made to analyse the phenomenon in the wider context of their time. How is it that this could have come about and developed in the form that it did? What must British society and cultural relations be like that such cultural 'events' as The Beatles phenomenon can take place?

Lastly, the whole work will be bound up in an ongoing discussion about methodology. I shall attempt to discuss the theoretical issues associated with the study of such a cultural phenomenon and to tease out methodological problems inherent in such a study. I have attempted to clarify my own assumptions and prejudices in the light of past and existing ideologies of cultural analysis.

I trust that the study will break some new ground and be stimulating enough to encourage others to join with me in a discussion towards greater understanding.

> "Thought is a constantly living endeavour in which progress is real without ever being linear and in which it can never be said to have come to an end and be finally complete."

> *(Lucien Goldman - 'The Hidden God')*

Society and Culture

IT SEEMS INEVITABLE that any discussion about Rock and Roll is going to be couched under a general rubric of popular or pop culture. I say inevitable, because of a number of reasons.

Firstly, the development of a musical form like Rock and Roll is undoubtedly an aspect of the culture. This development is not a linear or evolutionary one; it is haphazard, dialectical, full of contradiction and paradox. I am not going to attempt to answer all the appropriate questions. Opening this particular 'Pandora's Box' is not merely problematical; it is just not possible to arrive at such a paradigm on a culture.

Secondly, Rock and Roll has been seen to do with the working class in the main. It has been seen as a mass working class phenomenon, hence the notion of 'popular' i.e. something of a 'folk' idiom; for example, as expressed by Jan Wenner, editor of *Rolling Stone* in 1968:

> ". . . one easily forgets it today, but rock and roll was a phenomenon of the lower classes. It was dirty, raunchy, unrefined, too physical and tasteless."
>
> *(Issue No.20, 26.10.68, p.15)*

This theme has been replayed many times; successfully I felt, in *Rock Dreams,* that kaleidoscope of pictures and words put together by Guy Peellaert and Nick Cohn and published in 1974. Ranging from Joe Turner through early Presley, the authors catch the recalcitrance, posturing and downright affront of the good taste that made them such great performers. "Joe Turner at forty-two pounds. . . can drink both bourbon and beer/Can tear down walls with his bare hands/Can chew pig iron and spit it out as razor blades/Can kill a man with a smile," *etc.* Then came Elvis - another 'phenomenon'. Not so surprising then that decent Americans everywhere were dismayed and disgusted, threatened and frightened by 'the Pelvis'. Not surprising that the early TV coverage of Presley concentrated on shots from the waist up. An extract catches the mood well:

> "Good Hard Rock. Barbarians at the gates; into the breach created by Haley and Presley, there

surged battalions of converts, wild men with uncombed hair, fluorescent suits and voices like power drills, who jumped on pianos or did the splits, grovelled on their knees, shook their hips or battered themselves into states of bug-eyed trance. Last-ditch desperadoes, emerging from the swamps and backwoods to blow up everything that Tin Pan Alley had held most sacred decorum, good taste, and true romance. They sweated, roared and swaggered to the limit; tore the temple down, and razed it to the ground."

(Peellaert and Cohn)

As will be obvious to any observer, there are echoes here of the punk scene of the mid- to late-1970s. There are also echoes of the pre-Epstein Beatles in their Liverpool and Hamburg days. Lennon was well known in the Ripperbaum for his cursing and trick of spraying previously consumed lager at his audience. Rock and Roll is, by definition, to do with sex. We have experienced how numerous, originally explicitly sexual songs, were 'cleaned up' before being re-recorded (usually by a white cover artist) and released on the mass record-buying public. Anyone involved personally in Rock and Roll in Britain in the late 1950s and early 1960s could not fail to have noticed the sexual connotation of music, lyric and attendant dance. I can well remember the particular antics of my Art School's band lead singer (Tony Hole, where are you?) adding a particular embellishment to The Beatles' line: "I'll get you in the end!" Rock and Roll music has been an incitement to 'dance'. As Bernard Shaw once said, "Dancing is the vertical expression of a horizontal desire". All manner of extra-mural activities can, did, and do lead from the Rocking and Rolling.

Rock and Roll has been essentially idiosyncratic, and yet always collective[1]. It - Rock and Roll - has reached great heights and amazing depths. It has exemplified the best and the worst in

---

[1] In an earlier era, Eric Gill (he of the Arts and Crafts movement) suggested that: "The artist is not a special kind of man, for every man is a special kind of artist."

people - and social life. Inevitably then, as suggested by Charlie Gillett, there are many contradictions:

> "[The new] Rock and Roll offered either an aggressive answer to harsh experience or a blissful escape from it."

(C. Gillett, 'The Sound of the City', p.326).

We cannot assume, though, that aggressive answers or blissful escapes are always segregated: one of the first 'wisdoms' of Rock and Roll is that not all that seems to be the case is 'necessarily so!' All that is really going on is that this Rock and Roll stuff is part of the post-War era of the western world in general, and the USA and the UK, in particular. It is part of, a contribution to, and dependent on and derived from, the cultures to be found in those societies. However, the sources of relationships are problematic - to say the least. Many scholars, pundits, critics and observers, have had their misgivings about the relationships and their consequences:

> "Mass culture threatens not merely to 'cretinise' our taste, but to brutalize our senses, while paving the way to totalitarianism." (B. Rosenberg - quoted in *Towards Sociology of Mass Communications.*

(D. McQuail, 1969, p.25).

Now of course not everyone has been as apocalyptic in mood as Rosenberg, but we can testify to many similar assumptions and sentiments on this side of the Atlantic.

Generally speaking, there have been two strands of argument on mass culture. I would recommend the reader to two sources here: Raymond Williams' *The Long Revolution* (Pelican edition, 1965) and Alan Swingewood's *The Myth of Mass Culture* (MacMillan, 1977). On the one hand, the conservative critics of the right and left of the political spectrum (for example, Leavis, Eliot, Horkheimer) have suggested that mass culture represents the failure of the bourgeoisie to maintain their high art cultural promise. There has been a failure by the bourgeoisie to live up to the ideals of the nineteenth century belief in themselves and the *world* they produced - objectively and subjectively.

A technological epoch in the 20th century has given a mass crassness to culture: brutalised, devalued, and imparted, if you like, an essence of *monosodium glutamate* to art and culture. Clearly size, sheer numbers of people participating in 'Art', is an aspect of this argument, along with a belief that the individualistic core to 'art' (individualism serving a central focus of concern for the bourgeoisie) has been circumvented by an attempt to the mass production of art to be consumed within a mass market. It seems to me that 'electronic art' (*i.e.*, Rock and Roll music) is clearly an example of this mass opiate. The barbarians are at the gates. For Attila the Hun, read Chuck Berry, Jimi Hendrix, and John Lennon.

On the other hand, we have the social democratic/pluralist faith in the evolutionary progress of a democratisation in society in general and culture/art along the way. In its way, this notion is related to the belief that social relations have been made increasingly more tolerable for the working class through the extension of basic rights and responsibilities. It is like the idea that the extension of citizenship to the great mass of the people (voting and representative government, extension of trade unionism, greater state intervention, *etc.*) has facilitated a greater share in the good things of life in general. After all is said and done, I am sat here watching the Electric Light Orchestra (ELO) on BBC2, having just read, in a mass circulation newspaper, how much money the Arts Council is going to spend on my behalf. What a lovely set of contradictions there!

Turning to an analysis of The Beatles phenomenon in this context, Joan Peyser, in her article 'The Beatles and The Beatless' ,touched on an issue of great contemporary concern:

> "Are we entering an era in which musical high art, as we have known it, is coming to an end? The medieval poet-musician, who passed on his art through an oral tradition, has a contemporary analogue in the Rock and Roll performer. He is a central, contributing member of a society that is moving steadily away from notation and inexorably toward the preservation of the musical object on record and tape. No notational

system is capable of reproducing the complex texture of a Beatle record or the sophisticated manipulations the sound engineer immobilises on it. What is preserved in the music is the performance itself; the record is the message. Marshall McLuhan's thesis that the visually oriented and literate society of Western man is being replaced by an acoustically oriented, electronic society received its firmest confirmation in the most logical field. The compositional tradition, associated with notation that has prevailed since the beginning of the Renaissance is being replaced by an overwhelmingly oral tradition, in both art and rock music. Art music, for the moment, has excluded all but the most cerebral, specialised listeners. Rock is all embracing, having absorbed elements of blues, folk, jazz and the serious avant-garde.'

(Essay in 'The Age of Rock' edited by Jonathan Eisen, Vintage Books, 1969).

A point can be made here about the relation of the mass culture thesis to the kind of democratisation of culture suggested by Peyser and McLuhan. Certainly, the electronic media, including TV of course, are distinctively aspects of the last four decades or so. However, we need to be careful not to assume that the technological innovation of electronic media, in the modern era, have been essentially liberating. It is true that the development of such forms of communication have taken place at the same historical moment as political reform in the western world and that the centralised and instantaneous nature of these electronic media has meant messages potentially reaching a mass audience, but we should avoid a simple connection. The printed word, demanding a reading audience, has also now reached a much bigger audience than ever before. The mere fact that Joan Peyser *writes* about The Beatles and Rock and Roll, which in turn requires *reading* by the individual, reflects the contradictions inherent in the relation between the literate and oral dimensions of contemporary culture.

Along the way, most assumptions about mass culture have included a strong sense of the possible 'diversions' that can now 'use up' the mass of the people's non-work time. Vicarious and gratuitous pursuits, ephemeral by their very nature, heap themselves upon one another in an endless orgy of consumption. "If they didn't want it this way, we wouldn't give it to them" is the Producer's anthem.

I do not find either of these world views acceptable. In fundamental terms, I dismiss them because of their underlying conservatism, their overriding conception of the working class as a homogenous mass, unto whom things can be done willy-nilly; often, perhaps, in the name of progress.

Robert Lynd touched on this debacle in his treatise 'Knowledge for What?' (in 1938):

> "Our contemporary world is losing its confidence in the inevitability of progress. Men's ways of ordering their common lives have broken down so disastrously as to make hope precarious. So headlong and pervasive is change today, that to scholars, historical parallels are decreasingly relevant as present guides, because so many of the variables in the situation have altered radically. The scholar-scientist is in acute danger of being caught in the words of one of Auden's poems, 'Lecturing on navigation while the ship is going down'."

I was strikingly reminded of this when ardently watching The Queen's 1978 Christmas speech. She (Her Majesty) chose as her theme, the continued (continual) faith in the path of progress. She drew on radio broadcasts by George V and George VI to illustrate this shared concern with the gradual evolution of society into a viable and well integrated plutocracy. What marks these contributions is a touching faith in the ability of capitalist society and relations to create an equitable situation in the future.

The *Daily Telegraph* used to run an advert that stated: 'Times change, values don't'. The message is ambiguous (beyond their play on the title of the rival *The Times*); *The Daily Telegraph* reflects, represents, and indeed reproduces the notion that, despite all the changes taking place in the world, the underlying values of bourgeois society have a permanence and meaning that is not affected by those changes. Clearly, this is nonsense. One of the most characteristic aspects of life in post-1945 Britain is the degree to which values have changed; especially those of post-War youth. Amid the changing 'life-styles' of the last three decades, it is possible to discern a continuing *discontinuity* in the development of social life and relations under capitalism. The contradictions do not, perhaps, appear so sharp as they did in the inter-war years of overt social and political divisiveness, but I would argue that the underlying contradictions of everyday life have been reinforced by changing values, changing aspirations, and events. There is a constant mocking-point to the idea of post-War progress in society, daily supported by evidence of rising standards of living and expectation, daily undermined by evidence of a deepening alienation. Raymond Aron in *Progress and Disillusion* (1968) reflected this concern:

> "[Man] . . . 'created' himself in the course of the centuries as he discovered more and more effective means of production. *But* in creating himself, he also *lost* himself; alienation is the historical adventure of humanity divided into antagonistic classes. With the advent of the capitalist regime, the adventure reaches its final phase; gradually the evolution of the means of production and the accumulation of capital will eliminate the distinctions, which forced the many to make sacrifices for the comfort and well-being of the few responsible for the progress of culture. Never has humanity been so estranged from itself as in the capitalist regime. Never has it been so close to putting an end, once and for all, to alienation, to the divorce of men from the social order in which they live."

This underlying, everyday, contradiction is never more evident than in the 'progress' and 'adventure' of popular music and Rock and Roll in the last twenty years or so. It is the contradiction that allows RCA executives to make policy decisions to invest X million dollars into 'Revolutionary' music in the late 1960s. The corporation provides a greater audience with the opportunity to hear alternative views of social reality, while making vast profits (while at the same time manufacturing electrical equipment used by the USAF engaged in the destruction of Vietnam). The 'Rock music' industry does, understandably, reflect such contradictions of post-War relations. The concern over production and control is vital here. Mazaros in his 'The Necessity of Social Control' paper (Isaac Deutscher lecture, 1971) touched on this:

> "In the course of human development, the function of social control had been alienated from the social body and transferred into capital which, thus, acquired the power of grouping people in a hierarchical structural-functional pattern, in accordance with the criterion of a greater or lesser share in the control over production and distribution. Ironically though, the objective trend inherent in the development of capital in all spheres, from the mechanical fragmentation of the labour process to the creation of automated systems, from local accumulation of capital to its concentration in the form of an ever-expanding and self-saturating world system from a partial and local to a comprehensive international division of labour, from limited consumption to an artificially stimulated and manipulated mass-consumption, in the service of an ever accelerating cycle of reproduction of commodity-society from 'full-time' confined to a privileged few to the mass production of social dynamite, in the form of 'leisure' on a universal scale, carries with it a result diametrically opposed to the interest of capital. For in this process of expansion and concentration, the power of control invested in capital is being *de facto* retransferred to the body as a whole, even if in a necessarily irrational

> way, thanks to the inherent irrationality of capital
> itself."

This, in Mazaros' opinion, raises the whole question of the internal contradictions of the relationship between capital and labour. Capital *reified* and alienated from the social processes of production can only 'control'. The increased power of the working class (proletariat in final terms) is to take control of and over what they already *produce*. 'Workers Control' has come to be a slogan in the past decades, but it represents a major shift in consciousness, in that control is seen to be taken away from the capitalist class. This also raises the question of syndicalist attitudes in the demand for workers control. In this sense of increasing demands for control, is it any wonder that the capitalist class get so upset about strikes, sit-ins, workers' cooperatives and union power, *etc.*, that 'hold the nation to ransom' and attempt to infringe on Capital's right to control, manipulate, and exploit.

It is noticeable that social democrats spend a lot of time talking about workers participation (based on the German codetermination model). In essence, this turns out to be like the employee directors in British Steel, an ear without much of a voice and no teeth at all.

I would like to return to these concerns later, but for now, I feel moved to attempt to relate these problems of the evaluation, assessment and prognosis of mass or popular culture to wider issues concerning youth and socialisation.

On a sunny Sunday afternoon way back in September 1978, I sat on the grass at Shepherd's Bush Green and listened to a young black reggae band. It was part of a carnival organised by the Anti-Nazi League. There were a good few hundred people there; sitting, standing, listening like me. As it happened, I was on my own, but of course not alone. I felt that I shared so much of the culture that was a living tradition and contemporary process around me, especially the public dimension of the music and the politics. If democracy and popular culture mean anything, they mean this. In this moment, like the drowning man, I could see many aspects of my socialisation spread out before me. So to say: "There are places I remember . . .In my life I've loved them all." ('In My Life', Lennon and McCartney, 1965)

At this juncture, I would like to explore some themes of socialisation, which greatly concern and worry me. How do we move between the individual and collective worlds with the degree of familiarity that we do? What sets - or creates - frameworks for our social practices; the dimensions of our everyday lives? But especially, I want to touch on the question of youth in our society. 'Youth': a category, term and concept at one and the same time open to biological and social position. I want to attempt an analysis, in part, of just how 'youth' in society find themselves in the situations that they do and what the consequences of these situations and realisations may be. Along the way, I hope to elaborate on the question of mass or popular culture and the place of Rock and Roll within that culture.

One of the central contradictions of our industrial and urban life is a lurking nostalgia for a rural 'golden age'. From the Romantic revolt of the early nineteenth century to today there is a constant, if minority, tendency to look back to a time, form of social organisation and place free from the strictures, frustrations and ugliness of the industrial and urban situation. It is, of course, difficult to pin down. It is a parallel aspect of our developing and changing cultures that almost defies coherent, rational, objective analysis, and yet the persistence of this anti-urban 'man' feeling is testimony to its strength and significance. Despite attempts to organise such existence and feeling and movement of discontent into collectives, *viz.* 'The Romantics', the ecology and anti-pollution campaigns, the anarcho-syndicalist 'drop-out' contra-cultures, the 'Hippies' *etc.*, the tendency is essentially individualist and existential in its most dominant and vocal forms.

Now it seems to me that a good deal of the revolt against the industrial-urban environment is wasted energy. The corollary of such discontent and revolt has usually been to seek some rural alternative, often idealised, if not mythological (*e.g.*, William Morris and the activities of the Pre-Raphaelite Brotherhood in 1840-50 period). It seems that, rather than face up to the issue of the structural unsuitability of the industrial/urban environment, dissidents look elsewhere for a solution. Perhaps the lack of certain structural, social and political changes in the industrial-urban environment is in part due to the reluctance of articulate, mainly middle class voices, to do something about the situation they so despise? (It is worth adding here there the 'disliked' environment would include the repressive-engineering role of State bureau-cracies, national and local, planning blight, politicians' antics, the arbitrariness of economic pressure groups, *etc.*). Power is grossly unevenly distributed in the industrial/urban environment, but so then is it throughout society. Retreat to a rural enclave or haven will not solve the essential contradictions or power relations, although it may appear to alleviate the immediate tensions of the individuals concerned.

Clearly consciousness plays an important part in the definitions of the situation. Reference points or 'signposts' are crucial. The middle class-ish antagonism to the twin evils of industrialism and urbanism have often resulted from an awareness of the structures and strictures imposed by the very organisation of social life through industrialisation. This phenomenon is not now peculiar to societies with capitalist/free enterprise economies, even if that is where the origins and predominant tendencies lie. There is a mass of sociological evidence in this field, with specifically the contribution of Ferdinand Tonnie's *Community and Association* in the 1870s, to the publications of the Community Development Project Collective (*The Costs of Industrial Change,* and *Gilding the Ghetto*) in the 1970s. It is necessary to add that revolutionary tendencies among the middle class and intelligentsia have often recognised the long-term inadequacies of ideas a return to some rural bliss of lost innocence.

What of the great mass of people, the working class, under such circumstances? The alienation that is suggested exists among the mass of industrial-urban populations, creates its own process of double-bind in the cultures. Most working class people do not have the opportunity or consciousness to 'opt out'. It is worth comm-enting that a great many people will not exhibit a consciousness for 'opting out'. Class or community consciousness is not always a viable alternative to personal understandings of the inter-personal relations of a culture.

The dominance of work roles in society does not afford most people much scope. Work is centralised and the worker has to move to the work with few exceptions. What has been the response to this? In most cases, it would seem fair to argue that the mass of people feel they have to suffer their lot. Alternatives do not present themselves in any viable form, even if they do exist. It is no use wishing that things could be different; the persistent pattern of economic and social relations more or less dictates the pattern of living and working. Most people accept the situations they inherit. These acceptances of the situation are passed on from generation to generation as cultural, even subcultural, norms. You make the best of what there is. The dominant ideologies within our cultures reassert at every step; family, neighbourhood, school, work, *etc.*, that *this* is the way things are and should/can only be. Dip into the matrix of social relations at any point and the persistence of notions of permanence of structures or chances is there to be found. The dominance of such influences is reified of course, and often presented as 'the fickle finger of fate'.

> "Why do we have this sense of similarity - what is it about situations or episodes which allows them, however temporarily, to take on a phenomenal unity?"
>
> *(S. Cohen and L. Taylor, 'Escape Attempts', 1976, p.50.)*

Who writes the scripts? What has occurred has predominantly been reaction and action *within* the context of the industrial/urban environment. What responses are feasible, what alternative modes of living, surviving, that there are, are formulated and worked out within the said environment. This has predominantly occurred in two ways. On the one hand, the demand for reform; an attempt to democratise and thereby have some external control over the environment. This can possibly make the organisation of everyday life more responsive to the needs and desires of the population. On the other hand, it is possible to recognise the emergence of alternative modes of living, within the industrial-urban environment, to those of the dominant culture. Adaptation to given circumstances, to mainly externally enforced and legitimated structures, is a means of making the harsh, uncomfortable and uncompromising, more acceptable and valuable. Collective responses to environmental pressures can often alleviate some of the worst characteristics of social life, even if these developments are limited to only partial relief. The meanings which people place upon certain aspects of their lives may not point towards the eventual elimination of alienating structures. Such meanings, though, may provide a reality that gives some 'breathing space' to make sense out of the nonsensical. But, of course:

> "The mental management of routines, however existentially consoling, leaves the world unchanged and unchallenged. Our daily life retains its behavioural shape for all our mental juggling."

> *(Cohen & Taylor op. cit. p.46)*

The young are perhaps the social grouping in the industrial/urban environment that most bear the brunt of the contradictions thrown up by that environment. They are developing within a 'ready-made' world that is very reluctant to adapt to their needs and desires. They are clearly, explicitly and implicitly, expected to conform to the mores, persistent cultural patterns, whatever they may be.

> "Growing up is essentially an apprenticeship to work. Accounts of family life are filled with material details of working life, your parents, the jobs you did, both in the home and outside, while at school, your first experiences as a wage-earner. Even recreation may be purposefully related to the disciplines of work...For a minority, especially those living in the older industrial areas, the traditional apprenticeships may still hold, along with the economic institution itself. For the rest, and especially those living in the inner city, the accounts of childhood and youth are increasingly dominated by the themes of free time, rather than labour time. For some, every sector of experience may come to be measured against how much or little purchase it affords on that kind of autonomy."

> *(P. Cohen and D. Robins, 'Knuckle Sandwich',*
> *p.7)*

Innovation by the young, in an attempt to reconcile themselves with the environment, to make it more habitable and responsive, may not always be met with enthusiasm and understanding. The family, neighbourhood, school, agencies of law and order, the media, the workplace, *etc.*, are crucial agencies within, and that constitute, the environment, for the young (see also *Learning to Labour*, Paul Willis, 1978).

In most cases, these agencies, for better or for worse, consciously or otherwise, are set on a path to circumscribe the behaviour and often, thereby, attitudes of the young. The persistence of such agencies of socialisation helps to explain the continuance of patterns of cultural and social behaviour. It also helps to explain the resistance that these agencies meet within their everyday dealings with the young. The consciousness of the young, especially the working classes in the industrial-urban environment, invariably means that responses to their situation take place 'within' that environmental context and not at some abstracted distance.

> "What we would argue, in general terms, is that the young inherit a cultural orientation from their parents towards a 'problematic' common to the class as a whole, which is likely to weigh, shape and signify the meanings they then attach to different areas of their social life."
>
> *(J. Clarke, et al in 'Resistance through Rituals',*
> *1975, p.29)*

Whether all responses and resistances are consciously worked out or not is another matter, but in any case, the 'stage' of and for action, the 'battleground' in some respects, is essentially there in the industrial/urban environment. Murdock and McCron (in Youth and Class; the career of a confusion' in *Working Class Youth Culture*, 1976) point towards a class analysis of youth and implicitly at the heart of sociology itself. They suggest that the work situation shows the clearest demonstration among youth and emphasises, not only the individual situation, but the *class* situation, *i.e.*, it is one thing to show that *an individual* is degraded, bored and alienated by work, it is something else to show that a *class* finds itself in such a situation with little or no power to change the relations that permeate everyday life. Here, Murdock and McCron point to the difficulties of subcultural analysis, in inducting back to class, as a significant factor, rather than starting out from a position where *class relations* form the most fundmental axis of social life.

It is not surprising, then, that we find these themes, issues, discussed in relation to mass or popular culture.

I would not want to argue that there is a rigid deterministic relationship between social and economic factors and aspects of mass or popular culture, but the influences of the interrelations and interaction are clear. The relations are complex ones, but that does not mean shying away from an attempt to be analytical.

The social significance of popular culture is clear in that we both react to phenomena and act out, produce, create, phenomena in society. The way in which we give meaning to our lives and those of others is central to our place in a complex matrix/network of economic, social and political relations.

The manner in which we find our 'way about' life requires us to use 'signposts'. Some of these signposts we produce and create ourselves, some are part of significant others' social constructions and we look to them for guidance and direction. The dialectic between experience and experiment lies at the heart of popular culture. The fact that we are individuals with our own consciousness, understanding, awareness and world views, does not preclude us from being part of commonly held, collectively generated consciousness as well. Indeed, our own 'signposts' may lead us to believe in and rely on, collectivist as well as, or instead of, individualistic notions.

> "There is no 'subcultural solution' to working class youth unemployment, educational disadvantage, compulsory miseducation, dead end jobs, the routinisation and specialisation of labour, low pay and the loss of skills. Subcultural strategies cannot match, meet or answer the structuring dimensions emerging in this period for the class as a whole."

(J. Clarke, op. cit. p.47)

Reference to the emergence of 'Rock and Roll' would seem germane to this discussion.

Charlie Gillett in the introduction to *The Sound of the City* positions himself within the frame of reference suggested above:

> ". . .The city's sounds are brutal and oppressive, imposing themselves on anyone who comes into its streets. Many of its residents, committed by their jobs to live in the city, measure their freedom by the frequency and accessibility of departures from it. But during the mid-fifties, in virtually every urban civilization in the world, adolescents staked out their freedom *in* [my emphasis] the cities . . ."

He goes on to outline, hint at, a possible reason for the antagonism which often exists between the dominant culture and dominant ideologies and those innovations and excursions into city 'survival kits' taken up by the young:

> "Rock and Roll' was perhaps the first form of popular culture to celebrate, without reservation, characteristics of city life that had been among the most criticised. In Rock and Roll, the strident, repetitive sounds of city life were, in effect, reproduced as melody and rhythm."

Gillett goes on to say, later in his book, that perhaps 'pop' music had either been a blissful escape from, or an aggressive answer to, the harsh industrial/urban life. There is much talk these days of the culturally deprived. The term is ambiguous to say the least. What it has usually come to mean, certainly in 'cliché sociology', is that the way of life of some sections of the working class is inadequate and, by definition, deficient of essential moral codes and cultural norms. Through 'no fault of their own' many people find themselves part of a seamless web of circumstances that disqualifies them from taking their rightful place among the citizenry.

I see deprivation in the industrial/urban environment in its literal context, *i.e.,* some people *are* deprived of some resources, opportunities, hope, *etc.*, by *other* people. I also recognise a tendency whereby certain people, perhaps collectively organised for that 'purpose', involved in this depriving, belong to social classes. What exactly is being *held back* - or inadequately distributed among the population - could vary enormously. Perhaps it is the right to a decent job, or house, or entertainments, or schooling? Fundamentally, I see the industrial-urban deprivation issue as a sometimes conscious, sometimes unconscious process, whereby some people, groups, classes, institutions, do actually deprive others of essential resources, both material and intellectual, thus limiting options and choices.

It seems to me, therefore, that popular culture, for example, and forms of expression through music (like Rock and Roll) can be seen as a response to such deprivation. Not that it is a passive outcome of a one-way process linked to the social pathology of some people, but as a means whereby people, especially the young, can exert some frames of reference and influence of their own.

Again, I would want to emphasise the persistence of spontaneity in this process. It seems clear that the *creation* of alternative ways of seeing and doing, in this context, are often not analytical, clearly through responses by people. Sometimes it is *deliberate*, of course, where threads are seized upon here and there and developed, perhaps as a direct response and/or challenge to externally voiced cultural and moral norms. "Putting on the agony, putting on the style," as Lonnie Donnegan sang in the 1950s, was as relevant then, as much of the self-conscious posturing since. It may also be that what starts out as an *alternative* posture, played out within the existing overall structures, ends up as oppositional or *vice versa*.

This same point has been argued many times over and from diverse methodological perspectives. For example, in *Everyday Life in the Modern World* (1968), Lefebvre argues:

> "Thus everyday life, the social territory and place of controlled consumption, of terror-enforced passivity, is established and pro-grammed, as a social territory it is easily identified, and under analysis, it reveals its latent irrationality beneath an apparent rationality,

> incoherence beneath an ideology of coherence
> and subsystems of disconnected territories linked
> together only by speech."

The expression of certain attitudes and behaviour reflect, as suggested above, certain forms of culture from which we, and others, can draw certain meanings and understandings of the situation. The views that are expressed by people in society, their outlook, beliefs, *etc.* are traditionally termed *world views.* These world views rest very largely on our knowledge of our situation in the world of values, attitudes and behaviour. How we receive our *knowledge* of social arrangements within society is open to some discussion by social scientists. Some believe that we are socialised into a pretty strict view of things, and that in brief, external constraints and dominant structures will largely determine the outcome. Others argue that our view of the world, of everyday social life, comes about via our interaction with others within the context of ongoing social structures. Values, beliefs and attitudes, which in turn transform themselves into behaviour, are the products of such social interrelationships. World views in this sense are created as much by the active involvement of individuals within social relations, as by any externalforces, shaping and constraining roles, *etc.* These highly complex discussions take place on at least two planes. Personal epistemological issues, concerned with how and why individuals come by their own views of knowledge and, in the wider context, what has come to be known as the 'sociology of knowledge'.

This latter area concerns the overtly *social* context of our understandings and consciousness, our knowledge of ourselves, others, the world. Lucien Goldman, in *The Social and Physical Sciences* lays out one view of the issue:

> ". . .the sociology of knowledge may study world
> views on two different planes, that the *real*
> consciousness of the group, as researchers such
> as Weber, have studied them, for example, or
> that of their *coherent,* exceptional expression in
> great works of philosophy and art, or even in the
> lives of certain exceptional individuals (the latter
> plane corresponds more or less to the maximum

of potential consciousness). The two planes complement and mutually support each other. Though it may not seem so at first, it must be said that, the second plane is often easier to study than the first, precisely because world views are expressed there with more clarity and more preciseness, whereas a study of the development of a new world view in a *real* consciousness of a group offers a much more difficult task, on account of the multiple forms of transition and the enormous complexity of entanglements and mutual influences which constitute social life."

(p.130).

I believe that what Goldman is arguing here is crucial to an understanding of popular culture. Much of popular culture, *e.g.* Rock and Roll is the product of creative activity and output. If we listen to the creations of The Beatles, for example, we may associate ourselves with the view that is expressed there. Either in the lyric (direct) or in the music (indirect and much more subjective) we may identify a paradigmatic world view that we can agree with, or reject, *etc.* It is then, in a sense, a ready-made product for us to consume, or not, as we wish. We can though, hope to identify a view. In the *unexpressed* world of social activity we will have to draw our own inferences from uncollated sources. The *facts* of social life are much less conveniently organised for us. Human *facts* never speak for themselves but yield their meanings only when the questions put to them are inspired by a philosophical theory of the whole.

In term of organising and understanding such facts as the world-views of ourselves and others, we will express notions about consciousness, awareness. Goldman sees here the significance of class as a collectivity that imposes itself as *class consciousness*. He addresses himself to the complexity of social enquiry:

". . .In sociology, knowledge is found on the double plane of the knowing subject and object studied, for even external actions are the actions of conscious beings who more or less freely choose and judge their mode of conduct. The physicist has to take into account only two levels of knowledge, the ideal norm, the applicability of the conception to things and the actual learning of his time, the value of which depends upon its distance from the former. Now, if the physicist must take into consideration only these two levels of knowledge, the historian and especially the sociologist, must take into account at least one intermediary factor between them, the maximum of potential consciousness of the classes which constitute the society under analysis."

(p.118).

If we take the case of Rock and Roll as cultural phenomenon, as input, incursion into our lives, our consciousness, we can perhaps see the significance of what Goldman is saying in relation to what Hoggart has to say on the same subject. Hoggart, in his *The Uses of Literacy*, looks at phenomenon in society, as an aspect of culture, *as* culture and the nature of society and the relationships that make-up society. For that, read: the phenomenon that relate to our understanding of *interaction* in social life. This is the meat of *The Uses of Literacy*, and was taken up in Hoggart's inaugural lecture at Birmingham (CCCS) in 1963.

"I wonder how well we would be able, imaginatively, to apprehend, let alone articulate the complexity of, for example, personal relations, if it were not for literature *working as literature*, densely recreating. I do not mean that we all need to have read the best books, but what has the fact that they have been read and that their insights and something of their fullness have, by the subtle and ramified processes of mediation, passes into the general consciousness, what has that contributed to the richness and flexibility of our understanding of our own experience?

. . . Literature then, has to do with 'knowledge', with meanings. It is not primarily analytic or

> discursive, or it would be something else,
> something valuable perhaps (say, philosophy),
> but not *art*. Only here in art is life embodied,
> recreated, in all its dimensions, so that a
> particular moral choice is bound up with this
> time and that place, with that other person and
> those habits."

Perhaps what can be argued for one aspect of cultural phenomenon, literature, could be argued for Rock and Roll? The difficulty in actually being definite about socialisation is an important consideration to me. It is often easier to be secure in hindsight, but that raises knotty problems of history at all stages of analysis. Greil Marcus, for example, senses this difficulty in his book on aspects of American Rock 'n' Roll.

> "A good part of the impact of Rock 'n' Roll had
> to do with its anachronistic essence, the way it
> seemed to come out of nowhere - the big surprise
> that trivialized the events that governed daily
> life. Rock 'n' Roll gave the kids who had seen
> no alternative but to submit to those events a
> little room to move. Any musicologist, neatly
> tracing the development of the music, can tell us
> that Rock 'n' Roll did not come out of nowhere.
> But it sounded like it did."

(G. Marcus, 'Mystery Train', p.18).

Liverpool in post-War Britain

AT THIS POINT, I would like to outline some pertinent concerns about the development of post-War British politics, and the economic changes that have taken place. I feel it is necessary to sketch, in a general way, the characteristic aspects of post-War British society to facilitate a greater awareness of influential factors in the creation of everyday culture.

If you look at photographs of people in the late 1940s, they look like people in the 1930s. If you look at photographs of many places in the late 1940s they have been directly, visually, affected by the war. Now, clearly, the people *were* affected by the war. Their lives were often traumatically transformed by events. It was inevitable that a massive degree of economic and social reconstruction had to take place after the War. Towns, houses, factories, railways, schools, *etc.*, had to be replaced - economic and social life had to be regenerated. However, it is also evident that reconstruction of society was to take place in political and social life also. Numerous contemporary sources point to the great shock wave that was felt at the landslide victory of the Labour Party at the polls in 1945. The Atlee government embarked upon perilous seas of national reconstruction with that mixture of egalitarian zeal and reluctant collectivism so typical of British social democracy. The degree of contradiction within the government and parliamentary Labour Party was only equalled by the level of contradictions in post-War British culture. Where was Britain to go? What role was the nation, which had held sway over the biggest of all empires, to play in the post-War league of nations? What measures should, could, would be enacted to transform British society from a self-consciously socially divisive one, into a society with a greater degree of equity and social justice?

Gradually, *via* a whole series of piecemeal measures and events, British social life began to take on a different look, a distinctively post-War look. I recall going to the Festival of Britain in 1951, and can still sense the feelings of awe. I recently saw a contemporary film of the separate-worldness of that moment. As it was, the 1951 Festival (like the 1851 before it) concentrated its activities in London, hardly reflecting a cultural cross-section of British life. The post-War Labour politicians had organised their ideas around a planned intervention into everyday economic and social life. Their overall package of reforms - from the establishment of a Welfare State to the nationalisation of public utilities like coal, to the incorporation of the Bank of England into the Treasury's fiscal role, marked their determination to preserve the fundamental basis of a capitalist economy and social relations, while shifting more power to the citizenry and creating the guidelines for increased upward social mobility for the working class as a whole. As I will elaborate below, this increased degree or level of State intervention into everyday life marked both a fundamental necessity for the rational and efficient management of capitalist society and a continuing trap of applying 'first aid' to a progressively contradictory social order. The post-War economic revival, generated by multi-national investments, expanding consumer markets and growing public expenditure, created a level of prosperity that had some significant affects on post-War culture. A great deal of discussion took place in the late-1950s and early-1960s about affluence, embourgeoisement, and consensus. The 1945-51 Labour government laid an important basis for a pretty inevitable process given the prevailing circumstances. The extent of political stability, fragile in retrospect, enabled an era of Conservative rule to last for thirteen years of "You've never had it so good" election budgets, inflationary fiscal policy, and the institutionalisation of the leadership of labour. As has been suggested elsewhere, the degree of economic mismanagement was colossal, even by Tory standards. The years 1952-55 were fortuitous in that the world market for industrial products greatly increased, world commodity prices were down, and the terms of trade benefited British capitalists ("Full employment without inflation", as it was argued by *The Economist* in 1954). In 1954, Butler, as Chancellor of the Exchequer, had predicted that Britain would double her standard of living in 25 years. Between 1955 and 1959 that forecast seemed feasible. On the crest of the boom, MacMillan was to argue, in 1959: "Life is better under the Conservatives."

However, as has been suggested by, for example, Bogdanor and Skidelsky (in *The Age of Affluence* - 1971), the 1950s - as an opportunity for British capitalists to take stock, reinvest, retool, *etc.* - was not grasped. It seems that concerns of short-term greed replaced the more successful 19th century policy of long-term greed. Galbraith agreed in *The Affluent Society* (1958) that the USA (and by default UK) "a developed society which had, in large part, solved the problem of production and could concentrate its energies on other things." Like, for example, the 'problem' of consumption. Galbraith, in the USA, reflected the real tendency inherent in post-War British economic management to pursue post-Keynesian policies of budgetary control, fine-tuning and the like. The leading politicians of the 1940s/1950s came to embrace the policies, even if they did not understand the theories or comprehend the context. The likes of Galbraith assumed that the 'problem of production' was solved because of an increasing equity between boss and worker. This clearly was a mirage. The working class in Britain (as elsewhere to an extent) did improve their position relative to the share of profit taken by the owners of industry. Because of the high demands placed on production, many sections of workers were able to bargain themselves into, often considerable, short-term gains in their pay and conditions. This inevitably reduced the percentage of the return to capital kept by the owners of capital. The workers, in a piecemeal way, took a greater slice of the cake. The 1950s was a period of relatively full employment based on high levels of production and output. Regional unemployment was an endemic problem, not adequately dealt with by successive governments. For example, when unemployment was at a steady 1% in the south of England, the figure was 2½-3% in the north. The young, healthy and skilled tended to flow out of the underdeveloped parts of Britain (including, of course, Merseyside). Capital also moved to the already successful, prosperous section of the society, and away from the very areas that most needed the investment. Despite the rosy picture painted by politicians in general, the economic growth rate in the 1950s was poor. UK levels of growth in output were below that of the USA and continental Europe for the whole period from 1951 to 1964. However, the situation was somewhat masked by a reduction in defence expenditure and improvements in the terms of trade for Britain. (It is ironic to think that the activities of CND might have contributed to a reduction in defence expenditure, which, in turn, helped to improve, in the short-term, the position of the political systems that created the context of nuclear war). Between 1952-59, net national output, measured in constant prices, rose by 20%, yet personal consumption rose by 25% (and for 'youth' an even larger per- centage). Personal disposable incomes rose by 28% in real terms. Incomes varied considerably in their rate of growth in the 1950s. Professional salaries, and the like, rose faster than wages and investment income rose even faster still. Incomes from equities and land, rents, *etc.* rose equally quickly and confirmed a trend in the period for *greater* inequality in incomes rather than the promised/anticipated levelling-out. As Parkin has argued (in *Class, Inequality and Political Order*), there was not really any question of successive post-War governments (especially significantly not Labour ones) attempting an equitable division of the means of producing wealth. What did take place was to set in motion a series of policies to provide a greater surplus from production, which could be divided up among the producers and the requirements of an ever-increasing sector of the public expenditure. Not only did the relative (and largely indiscriminate) post-War improvements in standards of living not threaten the vested interest of the owning and ruling elite, but the lion's share of that surplus went directly, or indirectly, into the pockets of the middle class or the Treasury coffers. We have seen the consequences of this uneven distribution of the 'goodies' in the recent bitter arguments over pay policy. The Labour governments of the 1970s, basing themselves on the monetarist policies of the Treasury, have argued that high wage costs had 'caused inflation' But suspicion exists in the British labour movement that this is not a wholly satisfactory explanation of *recent* practices. After all, as Shonfield suggested in 1958 (in *British Eonomic Policy since the War* (Penguin): "Since Sir Stafford Cripps' bargaining experiment with the trade unions in 1948, when they agreed to hold the wage level stable so long as the government held the price level, a mood of acute suspicion has settled upon British labour." (p.15). However, economic crisis was around the corner, due perhaps to Britain's duel role of ensuring full employment and prosperity at home and as guardian of one of the two reserve currencies.

When, in the mid-1970s, Anthony Crosland, as Secretary of State for the Environment, announced that: "The party is over", he set the seal on an era of great significance in British cultural history. Crosland, as a senior minister in the third Labour administration in ten years, was stating flatly that the post-War expansion in public expenditure had come to an abrupt end. It is familiar ground to argue that Conservative administrations look at cuts in public expenditure at times of economic crisis. They had, after all, had a series of 'stop/go' throughout the 1950s. Whenever the economy boomed at home, inflation followed, costs rose, imports soared over exports, there was a balance of payments deficit and a run on the pound. To safeguard the economy, deflationary measures followed. Why then, was 'the party over'? Was it because the period of post-War reconstruction was over? Was the residing Labour leadership satisfied with social progress to such an extent that a stop could be put to growth? Not so. Crosland, as an important representative of the 1970s policy, was saying that the notion of upward and onward public expenditure in a 'Welfare Statist' society was seriously under question.

It was Crosland, who in *The Future of Socialism* in 1956, had expressed the intellectualised belief of the social democrat/Fabian majority in the Labour leadership that the economy of post-War Britain would continually expand. This gradual, but regular growth in the economy (6% per annum in the National Plan of the 1964 Wilson regime), would 'pay for' the continued expansion in public expenditure, which would, in turn, see continued improvement in living standards for all, save a very small minority of pathologically hopeless cases. The building of the Welfare State was developed on such an ideology. So long as industrial production and output was high (including greater and greater productivity) and the economy strong and growing in relation to world markets, this progress could be translated into concrete social benefits. In the 1950s, the major problem of the economy, and its organisation, was seen to be the issue of the distribution of the 'goodies' once they had been created. Social justice was to rest on the issue of a more equitable distribution of the products of an industrial society in full employment and full swing. Little was argued about redistributing the existing resources of society, or the proportions held in some quarters; major improvements were seen to come via additional resources. The demands of the working people and the Labour movement for full employment, a national health service, state run industries, personal social services and, above all perhaps, greater access to a reformed educational service, could be met out of the economic growth of a State influenced, corporate managed, bureaucratically planned and technocratically rational 'mixed' economy. And all of this within, for most protagonists, a free enterprise market system. Crosland's 1950s thesis, and Gaitskellite revisionist policies, emphasised that the preconditions of social and cultural degradation, in the inter-war years, were absent in the 1950s. They argued that a new era of consensus politics had replaced the overt antagonisms of the pre-war years. They *argued* that 'socialism' would be reached gradually through the evolution of British social and cultural life over time. The 'right atmosphere' for these changes would be created by a sound economic base, on sustained growth and expansion, upon which the superstructure of society could be embellished. Clarke, Hall and Jefferson have pursued these issues in particular relation to the development of a culture(s) of youth in the post-War period (refer to Introductory essay in *Resistance through Rituals*, edited by Stuart Hall and Tony Jefferson, Centre for Contemporary Cultural Studies). They outline three themes that dominated post-War ideology, *viz.* affluence, consensus and embourgeoisement. These are seen in particular relation to post-War standards of living and a changing way of life. It was argued extensively in the 1960s, that living standards, especially for the working class, had risen. This 'news', related to a recognisable reality, took on an even more important context, when it was argued that an even more dramatic change had taken place among youth. Their relative position had improved most significantly. The youth were seen, in general, as a (*the*) new high-spending, acquisitive, consumers, able to exercise choice over a wider and wider range of goods and services. This view, which became a 'conventional wisdom' in many ways, confirmed and legitimated the idea that, 'youth' could be seen as a homogeneous classless group in society. Any societal division would typically exist between young and old, *i.e.*, a generation gap.

This 'gap' was emphasised that, as the newly-liberated con-sumers (more demanding, less discriminating?), they con-sumed quite distinctive goods and services to those consumed by 'them', the older generation. The products of the rock and pop industry are obvious examples.

But, of course, this consumption thesis says nothing about the fundamental *needs* of youth, those similar to any other persons in British society; a home, food, transport, extended education, a job. Consensus was as much about the general acceptance of such a situation as anything else. The agencies of ideology of the period; media, advertising, *etc.*, stressed that these 'goodies' were there for the taking, so it is hardly surprising that young people's appetites were whetted and expectations raised. The dominant ideology of consumerism explained the value-free nature of this consumption. Ideas that 'the market' may have been part contrived (*i.e.*, tastes manipulated) got little or no discussion. Not only had a new era of classlessness been achieved in some people's minds, but it was agreed that even if classes continued to persist, it did not matter any longer, as mobility (contest and sponsored) existed and could be seen to cut across the rigid social dimensions of pre-War years.

So, if all things being equal, it is possible to talk about a degree of improvement in the post-War standard of living, it is then necessary to stress the relative nature of this improvement. If we are to argue that this relative improvement existed, then it could never have been more relative than the differences between most of the south-east of England, say, and the Merseyside area of north-west England.

Merseyside, like other enclaves, pockets of economic underdevelopment in Britain, has been characterised by a social development obviously and typically English, but yet forcefully idiosyncratic.

What view of Liverpool has existed in the years since the War? Consider all the writing on The Beatles, a good deal has been said about Liverpool. Some of the assessment has come from North America, for example, from James Morris:

> "To most English people, not so long ago, Liverpool seemed the back of beyond - a great port and not much else, a vast, dingy Victorian mess of a city, whose only excitements were apparently provided by ships, riotous Irishmen and drugged Chinese and whose proper symbol seemed to be the enormous, smoke-blackened insurance block that dominated its pier head. Liverpool! The very name was a heavy joke and stood for all the ham-handed and unimaginative Philistinism of the English north - nobody of taste or spirit, it seemed, lived in Liverpool: no grace or colour illuminated its heavy streets. In fact, Liverpool is, and always was, not only one of the toughest, but also one of the boldest cities in Europe. It is a sailors' city, wide open, full of marvellously ornate gin palaces, gambling joints,

blue-nosed comics, noisy young thugs and blustering winds off the Irish Sea. It is a city that has always thought big, and intermittently embarked upon crazy and gigantic enterprises. . . It has large Irish and Welsh minorities, together with many Chinese, and a shifting population of seafarers, and the standards of the bourgeoisie have never ruled the place. Long before its Cavern Club became famous, Liverpool had its hundreds of shebeens, dives and cellar clubs, with a guitar down every other alley. It is a very stimulating city, with a dreadfully high crime rate and a manner of instant and open-handed response."

(Written in 1966 and quoted in
'From Metterwick to The Beatles',
Edited by Richard C. Lukas, Mentor Books,
1973)

But we need not rely on impression and opinion from across the Atlantic. A surprising amount of material has been produced on Liverpool (and Merseyside) over the last four or five decades. What picture do we get from these accounts of the development of Liverpool?

A good deal of emphasis has been placed on the fact that Liverpool was (and is) the major transatlantic port. Mike Evans, writing in the *Story of Pop* series in 1973, outlines this issue in a typical way:

"So emerged the 'Cunard Yanks'. . .these were the lads that worked the Cunard and Blue Star lines to New York and the eastern seaboard down to New Orleans and came home looking real flash, like a million dollars...they were the lads to contact if you wanted anything in the way of ciggies, clothes or records - the supply, in this way, of otherwise unavailable records proving to be the most significant part of this strange transatlantic export of a subculture.

Even at the height of the mid-50s Rock and Roll madness, the record companies only released the most obviously commercial material from the States, and much important music, especially in the field of black rhythm and blues records, was only available to those who could get it direct. This situation got worse towards the end of the decade, as fashions once more began to wallow in the more traditional syrup of Tin Pan Alley. At this time there were no shops selling imported records (except for highly specialised fields such as jazz or folk music...), so the consequences of the 'Cunard Yank' trade was that there was a whole wealth of material fairly easily available in Liverpool that simply wasn't to be found elsewhere."

(p.300)

The importance of sibling activity is obvious here. 'Big' brothers at sea were not merely a source of records, *etc.*, they were also participants in musical styles creating a Merseyside reality that was a distinctive, and dominantly male working class, alternative to what was happening elsewhere. I will develop my discussion of this musical and culture *milieu* in my section on 'The Beatles'.

As well as discussing the cultural inputs to the Liverpool matrix, I would like to suggest that within the economic and social context, even the *physical* environment of Merseyside was important to particular cultural developments.

Post-War Liverpool was a mixture of suburban affluence and development and inner-city mess and underdevelopment. No doubt it appeared patently clear to the municipal authority that a substantial renewal programme was necessary to reconstruct the city. Or perhaps people believed that the new city could be a great improvement on anything that had been seen since the 19th century? However, the post-War reconstruction of a city like Liverpool involved more than the organisation of a few plans in council offices. Walter Bor, in his book *The Making of Cities* (1972), outlined the political framework for such redevelopment. He emphasises the individualistic nature of the planning process in the US compared to the UK. Bor argues that there exists a framework of legislation and an atmosphere of the acceptance of such intervention in the UK. To some degree, of course, this is quite true in that the intervention of the State, in the UK, into city planning, renewal, *etc.*, is understandably extensive given the nature of State intervention in general over the last eighty years particularly.

But does Bor overestimate the value and success of this comprehensive intervention? He argues, for example:

> "The whole of the country is covered by an all-embracing planning legislation and the renewal of slums and worn-out areas is an integral part of a continuous planning process."
>
> *Bor (p.55)*

Is this really true? In practice has the urban renewal programme been so comprehensive in its sphere of activity? Bor certainly indicates that the *needs* and the opportunity were there in some degree, due to the. . .

> "...unusually high degree of dereliction coupled with extensive municipal ownership of land in the city centre."
>
> *Bor (p.141)*

It is worth commenting here that, perhaps due to the physical growth of Liverpool, it has a city centre that is comparatively small and concentrated around the central dock area. It was here that the traditional 'clubland' and 'shebeens' developed - an area of particular musical focus in the post-War years. David Muchnick, in a study of urban renewal in Liverpool, published in 1970, did, however, offer a view of the planning process somewhat different.

> "Since the earnest resumption of slum clearance nationally in 1954, the design of Liverpool's renewal policy has rested with a number of municipal organisations. Never has it been the sole responsibility of a single agency. Over time, varying degrees of understanding, power, interest

and involvement have left their marks on both the participants and the programme. Initially, the effort was almost exclusively the demolition of slums and their replacement by new dwellings. Other components of a renewal strategy were conspicuously absent by today's perspective for, at the time, there was little awareness of their need and, accordingly, few tools for their execution."

[Presumably, Muchnick means little awareness among planners and policy makers?]

"During the next decade, new information and fresh ideas became available to Liverpool's policymakers. New groups became active in the endeavour. The comprehensive nature of renewal has now been debated . . ."

(Urban Renewal in Liverpool; Occasional papers on Social Administration, number 33, p.26)

Muchnick seems to be suggesting here that simply replacing old housing stock by new was not sufficient to combat social deprivation. That other factors, for example, unemployment, lack of adequate schooling, the lack of cultures, of expectation, *etc.* carried a great deal of importance in relation to the overall quality of people's lives on Merseyside.

Robert Steel, in his Preface to *Merseyside - Social and Economic Studies* (1970) edited by Lawton and Cunningham, raises a number of relevant illustrations to the arguments I have elaborated. Firstly, he outlines the decline of the area after the relative loss of status of Liverpool as a Victorian port of considerable significance:

"Such matters were the concern of the Merseyside Social Survey which, under the leadership of D. Caradog Jones, produced in the 1930s a notable social survey of the Merseyside region.

"During the war years, studies of Merseyside were continued in the University [of Liverpool] in anticipation of the expected post-War reconstruction and a hoped for economic revival, they included, for example, those by Wilfred Smith in industrial location on Merseyside. The prospects were hopeful, for the port of Liverpool had regained something of its former prosperity under a war economy while the basis for industrial revival had been established on the foundations laid by the Corporation, aided by the Government, in the new industrial estates. The times were, moreover, favourable to regional planning and economic reconstruction."

(pgs v and vi of Preface)

It is a certain irony that, had the central area clearance of Liverpool been carried out more quickly by the Corporation, no doubt 'improving' the City's appearance and commercial standing, the venues for most of the music clubs would have been lost in a welter of concrete and plate-glass. However, city centre renewal was slow to pick-up, as Steel suggests:

"However, the post-War years showed that many of Merseyside's fundamental problems remained. The high rate of natural growth of population could not be absorbed by the local labour market, the poor lost ground, relatively, as commercial emphasis continued to move to south-east England, wartime bombing had added to decay in creating a severe housing problem. The need to strengthen and diversify an ill-balanced economy remained."

(Preface to Lawton and Cunningham - pgs v & vi)

It is possible to feel the restrained understatement of Steel's academic analysis. Others, less used to carefully selecting their

119

words, would have said it was a 'fucking mess'. Others, not prepared to use such a politically sanitised analysis as Steel, would have said, 'Merseyside' was the sound of thousands on the dole and slum housing conditions (for example the *Daily Worker*). Bor himself had commented on the appalling housing situation as late as 1965.

> "The Merseyside and Manchester conurbations between them have the most serious problems of obsolete housing in the country. In Liverpool alone some 60% of the city's 205,000 dwellings, date from before 1920, and in 1961, approximately 79,000 of these were unfit."

Muchnick illustrates what Bor seems to have been arguing as Liverpool's planning officer, namely that localised jealousies and the desire to meet piecemeal demands by local politicians, prevented a comprehensive reorganisation programme coming about. Kathleen Pickett (in Lawton and Cunningham) also emphasises the nature of inner-city housing in that even by 1961, Liverpool contained a very high proportion - nearly 12% of persons - living on density greater than one-and-half per room (p.87). Vauxall, for example (in the late 1960s to become the focus of a Community Development Project (CDP) action research team) had 36% of population living at one-and-a-half persons plus per room in 1961.

Muchnick (in his 1970 paper) quotes a Liverpool Labour Party Councillor on the sad history of neglect and missed opportunity combined with political and administrative incompetence. "Lack of emphasis was given in 1930 to clear slums. [In the] 1930-60 period, there has been thirty years of procrastination. It was also significant that Liverpool had a Labour controlled council in the 1955-61 period. However, the Labour Party leadership was 'old-schooled in opposition' and unprepared to meet the problems of governing the city." *(p.33)*.

The two years of Tory party rule that followed, 1961-63, paved the way for city centre commercial development. Muchnick illustrates the plight of those seeking a housing solution in the numbers of local authority houses provided in the late 1950s and early 1960s:

1956	2,569
1960	1,711
1961	1,579
1962	2,136
1964	3,217

When Steel suggests, for example, that one of the major factors in the decline of post-War Liverpool lay in the shift of 'emphasis' to the south-east of England, he is touching on a critical issue: The 'emphasis' that shifted was capital investment, capital outflow itself from regions like Merseyside, and the eventual movement of the young and the skilled. The 'emphasis' that Steel raises as a factor is the chronic, and deliberate, underdevelopment of regions like Merseyside. Despite the successive attempts by the State to redirect capital to such areas (with all the frustrating twists and turns of successive government policy for 'regional planning'), these areas were, and have remained, pockets, enclaves of underdevelopment. Even when 'regional planning' policies have created a 'Skelmersdale', with new houses and jobs for Merseysiders, the dream has often become a nightmare (Skelmersdale was developed in 1961 and by 1979 had an unemployment rate of twenty-odd per cent, due to the sudden closure of some major employers encouraged into the scheme by government policy and handouts on a massive scale.).

Development area status was granted to Merseyside in 1949, descheduled in 1959 (on the crest of the 'You've never had it so good' boom) and returned to development district status in 1963. Interestingly enough, Employment Exchange areas were used as the boundary lines for the 'development' area.

Steel suggests that, in fact, 'good progress' was made in the 1950s and 1960s and a considerable improvement on the situation reported by Wilfred Smith in the 'Scientific survey of Merseyside' in 1953. But Steel goes on to reflect on a certain complacent neglect in the 'good years' of the late 1950s and early 1960s.

"Yet there were no general studies of the economic changes of the 'fifties', let alone detailed investigations of their significance with the advent of the motor industry on Merseyside."

(See H. Beynon, 'Working for Ford', 1973, on this)

"A new phase of even greater promise and change seemed at hand, although unemployment remained obstinately high and many social problems remained. There were pressures on land from both housing and industry and an urgent need to reshape the central area, much of which had changed little in its essentials over the previous fifty years, yet the depression seemed a distant memory, and confidence, as well as prosperity, in the region seemed high: was not Liverpool, in a special way, a symbol of the swinging sixties?"

(Lawton and Cunningham op. cit. p.VI)

Liverpool was a potent symbol indeed. For, by the 1960s, it reflected the inherent contradictions of a national economy, within which most of the people of Liverpool could find only a superficial respite from hard times, exploitation and neglect. Kathleen Picket reflects on the 'trap' for many of Liverpool's people, for example, the higher than average family size with resulting high ratio of dependant-to-working population. This contributed to the chronic situation for juveniles, usually unskilled, in the late 50s and early 60s. The evidence seems to suggest that what economic development took place in the 1950s up to 1963 only kept pace with the needs of population growth. As a degree of new jobs were created, so more and more jobs in the traditional sectors; docking, shipbuilding and the like, were lost. Ironically, not even some of Britain's post-War expansion industries, for example, the continuous-process chemical industry, maintained their growth into the 1960s. There was, in short, little *sustained* growth in the area.

The images of Liverpool that were created in the 1950s, and 1960s especially, have reflected these very contradictions discussed above.

The veneer of the late 1950s prosperity, and the early 1960s hedonism, glossed over massive cracks in the social structure of that community. Lawton concludes his analysis (in 1970) thus:

> "The Mersey sound which roused the sixties has reverberated into the 'seventies': it must not be permitted to die away into a mere echo of what it was."
>
> *(p.495)*

The images relayed of Liverpool as the 'swinging city' were always a mixture of conscious and unselfconscious processes. More Liverpudlians were clearly surprised by the strange mixture of images of them and their city, replayed via the media, *etc.* Liverpool, in the 1950s and early 1960s (as now indeed), was caught in the contradictory grip of the past successes and failures and the current malaise, uncertainties and promise. Hunter Davies touched on this in the introduction to his biography *The Beatles* (1969):

> "All those great ships and railways, all those funny comedians, even all that fighting and football, have paled in importance. In the minds of millions who had never heard of Liverpool before, and even to those who had, Liverpool is now known as the place our four heroes came from."
>
> *(p.17 of Mayflower, 1978 edition)*

What an irony this is. . .

Youth

WHAT IS IT about vast numbers of young people that makes them a fascinating combination of innovation, tradition, bravery, conservatism, scepticism - and revolt?

I do not intend to go into a lengthy analysis of the rise or place of youth in modern industrial society. What I would like to do is offer a view of the significance of youth in the creation of post-War British society and illuminate some of the contradictions that accompanies this presence.

For those brought up in the post-War years of austerity, the years of social and economic reconstruction that had significant consequences for politics and culture, a great many changes have taken place. A life that spans the 1940s to the 1970s, encompasses the epoch of greatest technological change in the history of the world (and importantly one of the fastest rates of economic growth in British history). Many writers, in the years since WWII, have attempted to define the essence of this epoch. These contributions, from Hoggart, to Orwell, to McLuhan, to Williams, to Marcuse, to Burgess, to Lennon and McCartney, have all, in their way and mode, offered a slice of social reality, a relative truth. Significantly enough, precious few of them have been sociologists.

We have only to look at those decades since the end of War in 1945 to see that *times* and *values* have changed in important ways, while retaining significant elements of tradition, custom and practice within British culture.

Young people in the 1950s and 1960s, not only had to come to terms with the time in which they lived, they also had to come to terms with themselves as both receivers, carriers and *creators* of culturet. The epoch of the 'Gutenberg galaxy' may well have been replaced by the epoch of electronic media, but it was not so self-evident among young people that they had their fingers nearest to the starter button. (I am often reminded here of of Thom Gunn's collection of poems *The Sense of Movement* (1957). A line from the poem 'Elvis Presley' comes to mind: 'We keep ourselves in touch with a mere dime' [*i.e.*, in the jukebox].

The sense in which the impulse of the moment, the spontaneous expression, may become the byword of a social category, is important in understanding 'youth'. So much of the everyday lives of young people, now and in the 1950s/1960s, is set within a framework of typicality and likelihood: family, neighbourhood, peer group, school, youth clubs, law and order, media, workplace, romance, *etc*. These, and other aspects of a young person's life, both liberate and circumscribe. Nor are they just the inheritors of custom and practice. It would also be wrong to suggest that they face existing, perhaps dominant, culture and have to absorb that culture as part of their socialising. The accumulation of knowledge of ways of life is more complex than that. We are all, young or old, both seekers of knowledge *and* Knowledge. How we *see* what we encounter is going to, very largely, depend upon what we already are as people. We carry with us 'theories of the world', and *us* within *it*. Whether we can articulate these theories particularly well is another matter. However, they do exist and social life becomes a reality for us. We articulate it through the use of our perspective.

Richard Hoggart's description of his cultural environment in a working class *milieu* is an apt example of the point. *The Uses of Literacy* is not only a piece of reflective description; it is also a programme of change. The text is about social development and the place of the individual as recipient and creator of culture.

At the centre of Hoggart's concern is what he sees as the intensification of alienation in the widest sense (*à la* Marx) in that the individual/community are constantly being drawn away from their known common ground into the unknown, untried, and - perhaps - undesirable. The intensified *reification* of human relations under the pressure of new forms of social organisation highlights forms of social change that are essentially seen as problematic. In the field of popular culture, in the post-War epoch, Hoggart underlines Marx's view that the economic relationships of capitalism means that moral relations are constantly being replaced by 'cash' relations. The everyday 'product' of the working class and their community structures in the form of popular culture is more and more turned into a commodity form which fits into the Marxian theory of value and, in turn, adds to the reification of that popular art/culture itself.

Ray Connolly's screenplay for *That'll be the Day* created an atmosphere of the place of youth in the 1950s and 1960s that often rang true (for me anyway); this is largely because it offered a picture of an era of change, and youth circumscribed by social conditions and yet breaking out, and contributing to something new. So many of the activities of youth, particularly Rock and Roll, reflect the central characteristic of great literature in that they offer an account of what exists, what social relations are like, but then goes beyond this and suggests a range of futures that transcends that. Geoff Mungham and Geoff Pearson highlighted this point in their introduction to *Working Class Youth Culture* (1976) in a discussion of 'Mods':

> ". . .There was more to being a mod than the outward insignia of clothes, scooters and neat hair. As with the earlier teds and the later skinheads, it also involved a distinct approach to life. As an outraged mod correspondent put it in one of the popular magazines of the period, he was tired of the magazine's stress on clothes and records: 'Mod isn't something you can just walk into a shop and try on. It's an attitude of mind.' "
>
> *(p.6)*

Then again, the cultural artefacts of the 'Mod' attitude of mind (for example) were focused upon by entrepreneurs who attempted, successfully or otherwise, to make that *distillation*, and version of things, available to a wider section of youth. This process of adoption, adaptation and exploitation by the commercial nexus, not only made certain styles accessible, they also made the producers and entrepreneurs substantial profits. However, youth styles also seem to be one jump ahead of the producers and today's *attitude of mind* artefact is tomorrow's cultural imperialism.

Over the years since 1945, many observers have recoiled from a picture or image of youth that they have held to be true. The resistance to the emergence of certain musical and associated styles was commonplace in the late 1950s and early 1960s. Not the least of these concerns has been reaction created among some middle class and authoritarian circles to the arrival on the stage of history of The Beatles.

The 28th February 1979 marked the fifteenth anniversary of Paul Johnson's infamous *New Statesman* article: 'The Menace of Beatlism'. Johnson savagely attacked the notion that The Beatles were worthy of the contemporary idolatry they enjoyed. He went on to suggest that: 'The Beatles phenomenon' had its origins in the craziness of the commercial exploitation of such commodities as

'The Beatles' and the nature of the adult/youth relations in the early 1960s.

> "The growing public approval of anti-culture is itself, I think, a reflection of the new cult of youth. Bewildered by a rapidly changing society, excessively fearful of becoming out of date, our leaders are increasingly turning to young people as guides and mentors. . . whatever youth likes must be good."

The central thesis of Johnson's article was that he was concerned lest we not halt the degeneration of some adults and youth to the levels of ...

> ". . .the least fortunate of their generation, the dull, the idle, the failures."

He seemed to be obsessively concerned to show that the really important youth of the period were, like him, destined for better things:

> " . . the core of the teenage group, the boys and girls who will be the real leaders and creators of society tomorrow, never go near a pop concert. They are, to put it simply, too busy. They are educating themselves. They are in the process of inheriting the culture which, despite Beatlism or any other mass-produced mental opiate, will continue to shape our civilisation."

It always struck me that Johnson had got some of it right and most of it wrong. His approach seemed 'Janus-like' in the confusion of contexts and issues; perhaps he was equally bewildered by a rapidly changing society?

Johnson noticed that the post-War attempts to use certain reforms (*e.g.*, educational ones) to alleviate the excesses of stratified society, and bring about greater social justice for all youth, had failed. He recognised that some values had changed in post-War society, not the least significant of which was an increased concern about the status of youth in society.

It is interesting that Johnson, writing in 1964, could not foresee the cultural and political upheaval that was to erupt within 'European civilisation' from the mid 1960s on. The seeds of that social change had already been sown long before 1964, and ironically, the very conditions that could create a context for 'The Beatles' were inherent within many industrial societies, without, apparently, the 'Johnsons' on the right of social democracy, identifying these same conditions.

It is ironic that higher education, with the limited post-Robbins expansion of the late 1960s, should act as the foci for so much upheaval. Of course the expansion of higher education in that period was essentially a middle class and aspiring working class phenomenon. It strikes me that the relative affluence of the mid to late sixties, coupled as it was with a continuing belief in the reality of social policies of continually expanding public and welfare services, provided middle class youth with some space. This space, a period, and initially at least atmosphere of, reflection, criticism and optimism were significant for a number of reasons. Despite the questioning that engulfed so many at that time there was rarely any question that the participants could not later 'settle-down', find themselves some interesting, intellectually demanding and financially worthwhile place in social life. But what were working class youth doing in the mid- to late-Sixties? Well, most of them were at work. People, like Johnson's less fortunate school-leavers, were fitting themselves into the world of work, getting on with recognisable life, and more or less following along the well-trodden paths pursued by thousands of others since the end of the war, in a reconstructed Britain.

The 15-16 year-old school-leavers (who so disconcerted Johnson in 1964) are now middle-aged men and women. Where are they doing now? What are the present generation of 15-16 year-olds doing? Anything so very different?

The overt political nature of so much of middle class youth's activities in the 1960s has since been dissipated. The main foci of political activity among youth today appears to be working class. This reality is a good deal more uncomfortable for ruling elites than the often abstract, intellectualised and essentially ephemeral character of middle class activity. Working class youth now finds itself more and more alienated from the security, albeit superficial, of ten years ago. Working class youth now finds itself at the frontiers of a period of frightening *uncertainty*. The oft-referred to 'Leap in the Dark' of the school-to-work transition has an edge to it now. The majority of middle class youth, admitted to further and higher education, seem increasingly concerned with getting themselves a viable niche in the professions or the like. There seems to be a greater concern now with securing a place on the career ladder and maintaining an appropriate status, with consequent 'freedoms'. A noticeable political shift seems to have taken place.

The political activity of working class youth is not all of a kind. It varies in nature and intensity. Certainly, the overt political behaviour of many has been reflected in increased membership of a number of political organisations, ethnic based and other 'youth' movements. But, also, there is the uncompromising (in most cases) posturing of especially working class youth creating and, associated with, aspects of popular culture in the 1970s. Black and white urban working class youth are, in fairly large numbers, engaging in, for example, grassroots Reggae and Punk Rock. The enthusiasm for certain musical forms, and the ambivalence towards social rule breaking, may well have its origins in the 1950s and 1960s, but it strikes me that the *political* character of context and content seems somewhat heightened. I am certainly not suggesting that working class are responsible, exclusively, for the creation of 'reggae' or 'punk', but many members of the class may be using it as a vehicle for their enthusiasm, discontents, hedonism or revolt. Just as, a generation earlier, many working class youths both developed and used the rock of the early 1960s.

In this section of my study of 'The Beatles phenomenon', I do not want to repeat what has been said in the previous part. Indeed, what I have argued there is that it would be foolish to hive off the study of youth (let alone an explanation of behaviour, *etc*.) from a general view of the culture of post-War British society. What I have said in this chapter is an attempt to focus on what I see as particularly interesting and significant characteristics of youth as part of an overall notion of post-War British social development. Sociology has, by its very nature, been primarily concerned with the question of social change in relation to social order and stability. Perhaps it is because of this, in some respects, that much attention has been focused on youth in the last three decades. I have a copy of a widely circulated photograph of a section of an early Elvis Presley audience. Sections of the audience are 'freaking out' as a consequence (perhaps) of what is going on, on stage. At the side of the photograph is 'a Cop'. The expression on his face tells all. It is not exactly horror or hostility, more sheer amazement at what he is seeing. His expression suggests that he is transfixed while looking at the arrival on earth of three-headed, nine-legged green aliens. I also have a photograph of a similar situation at a Beatles gig in 1963. What seems to be happening here is a degree of separateness that reflects the different behaviour of people in a certain situation, but more particularly, perhaps, the way in which these events are symbolic of differing world-views. For those in the know, the situation is quite comprehensible: "You don't need a weatherman to know which way the wind blows" bears some relation to the statement once made in the *Times Education Supplement* that:

> "Lennon and McCartney's lyrics represent an important barometer in our society - sentiments are shared by pupils in every classroom in Britain."

Nothing very sensational in itself, unless perhaps those same sentiments, then, representing different world views as they do, come into conflict with what already seems to exist and what, in conventional wisdom, normative order, terms, appears appropriate. Lennon once got into 'hot-water' for expressing this sentiment:

> "We're more popular than Jesus Christ now. I don't know which will go first, Rock and Roll or Christianity. Jesus was all right, but his disciples were thick and ordinary. It's them twisting it that ruins it for me."

Now clearly, post-War youth have not been a homogeneous grouping. Despite the enthusiasm of many writers in the 1960s to offer us a view of the 'generation gap', it is fair to suggest that the view of the relation between youth with adults in post-War industrial society, is very simplistic. Yes there are, as I have suggested, distinctive differences. Peter Berger, in his phenomenologist way, suggests there has been, and will always be, divisions between generations and that these divisions are deepened in modern industrial society because of the complexity of social change. It is an empirical fact that there exist youth cultures to which young people belong, and that they are, to some degree, *exclusive*. Whether by accident or design, is an interesting question. Musgrove, in Britain, and Berger, in the USA, have both suggested that the ambiguity of role and status of youth leads them to form (and establish, maintain and destroy) their own norms and patterns of behaviour. Berger, like Mannheim, has also asked whether the world views of youth are "a permanent settlement or a way-station?" Now here we might find more evidence of the cultural contradictions inherent in the situation. Roszak, for example, offered what seemed a very relevant view of post 1945 youth in his notion of the 'counter culture' of west coast USA. (*See* T. Roszak's *The Making of Counter Culture*, 1969).

He was describing what he saw, *i.e.,* that significant numbers of youth were rejecting the dominant values of that community (generally speaking, the WASP - White Anglo Saxon Protestant - values). However, most of these developments were mid- to late-60s and reflect perhaps the related consequences of The Beatles phenomenon. Where have all the young people gone to now? What happened to all the Hippies? I am sure many of them are still related to the same value systems and world-views, and find some niche or enclave within western industrial life. The process of responses to the pressures towards conformity may well have allowed many young people in Britain, or elsewhere, to *negotiate a place* in social life. Frank Parkin (in *Class, Inequality and Political Order*, 1971) suggested a three part typology of response by the working class in general that has been adapted to the situation of youth by Clarke and Jefferson (Working Paper: 'Working Class Youth Cultures' - 1973, Centre for Cultural Studies, Birmingham). Here they suggest the consciousness of the working class in response to subordination of that class is 'dominant', 'negotiated', or 'oppositional'. Here, then, Parkin reflects the notion held among sociologists of youth that only a relatively small section of working class youth, let alone youth in general, see themselves in opposition to the dominant (or dominating) structure of social relations, values, *etc.* Most youth seem likely to support, replicate or perhaps even legitimate the dominant order of social life. It has always struck me that a very significant section of post-War upper working class and lower middle class youth have negotiated, in their own terms, a situation of peaceful co-existence with the dominant order. Those generations of post-11+ grammar school pupils in the late-40s to mid - 60s seem a good example. Many pupils of the grammar schools found themselves in an unfamiliar setting to say the least. What they needed to do, perhaps, was to work out or negotiate a position within that system that was tolerable. Perhaps they then, like so many middle-range people in the education system today, were bored, frustrated, by constraints on them, and often confused. However, they did recognise, and realise (quite literally), the necessity, in their terms, to operate within a general framework of acceptance, while perhaps innovating as much as possible in some aspects of their life. Surely the development of grassroots musical styles has got something to do with this? It may have been one, perhaps the only, worthwhile and viable vehicle for sections of post-War youth. The youth of The Beatles phenomenon were essentially *negotiators* of their social and cultural worlds, experience and experiment, a bit here and a bit there, and that somehow, suddenly, apparently out of nowhere, something momentously distinctive appears.

Now, I do not mean this simply in the sense that some kind of mediation goes on in the cultural superstructures of society. Though it *is* more than merely emphasising (as invariably discussed in 'Marxist' explanations of culture) that the base of productive forces is so *determining* in relation to everyday social life[1]. What I would like to develop here is a view of incorporation and hegemony that allows us to see post-War Rock and Roll culture as one area of youthful activity, as an aspect of social development in a continual process of contradictory structure and change. 'Marxists', like Gramsci and Raymond Williams, in their own era, offer us a view of hegemony that incorporates their ideas. They stress that 'Marxist' cultural analysis has been much better at discussing the building and active career of ruling class hegemony in epochal terms (*e.g.*, Aristocratic to Capitalist domination), than

---

[1] I have already posed this reservation in the section on Society and Culture.

it has at analysing historical relations *within* Capitalist society, say. What we need to do is acknowledge the significance of hegemony in offering a really total view of how people come to see life. Why, within any culture, people do see things in the way they do, seems to rest on an analysis which is much wider than merely a notion of social relations being manipulated and controlled by a ruling class or ruling elite. Edward Thompson, in the sphere of 'History', has also contributed his part to the development of such analytical tools. He, like Williams, has emphasised the necessity to attempt a recreation, in analytical terms, based on empirical study wherever possible, of how social life was seen *at that* time. What, in my terms, we may then have, are a series of images of post-War social life and social relations, set within an overall view of culture, an holistic perspective.

In the way I have (very inadequately) attempted to develop these ideas, I have said something of youth in post-War British culture, their role, their responses, reactions, negotiations and the like. What set of meanings and values actually existed among youth in general, and particular groupings, in the post-War years that contributed to the *creation* of The Beatles phenomenon?

Using Williams' typology of residual and emergent cultures (as elaborated in 'Base and Superstructure in Marxist Cultural Theory', *New Left Review*, 82. Dec., 1973), is it possible to suggest that Rock and Roll is clearly a feature of residual culture, incorporating, as it does, say, jazz, folk and rhythm and blues, expressions of pre-Capitalist industrial social structures and class conflicts, resulting in musical practice, carried forward into capitalist industrial-urban society? What then can we say of emergent culture? Are the peculiar elements of some - essentially post-1945, youth-based - Rock and Roll aspects of emergent culture? Is The Beatles phenomenon one of the clearest ex-pressions that we have, in the post-War years, of an emergent culture being developed and drawn out of certain aspects of a residual culture, while at the same time being essentially affected by the dominant culture? The agencies of dominant culture may well have known little of any such developments in its early phases and then, recognising the ambiguous and contradictory alternative and oppositional nature of the emergent youth-based Rock and Roll culture, moved towards and between attempts at both opposition and incorporation? Faced with such focus of attention, did the creators or carriers of any such emergent youth-based Rock and Roll culture remain iconoclastic, recalcitrant and remote, or attempt to negotiate a place of coexistence within the dominant musical production/consumption culture? Subsequent coiners of the emergent Rock and Roll culture may have calculatedly, self-consciously or unself-consciously, sought out a place in this negotiated space, within this incorporation and co-existence framework.

A substantial amount of writing appeared in the late 1950s and early 1960s, attempting, in its way, to explain the nature of youth and youthfulness in that era. Now, of course, these writers did set themselves the difficulty of assessing and evaluating the mood or tenor of youth empirically, 'in front of them', at that 'moment' and, as I shall indicate below, more than one of those writers has reflected critically upon their own remarks made at an earlier time. However, these critics, and I am thinking of Nuttall (*Bomb Culture*), Mays (*The Young Pretenders*), Fyvel (*The Insecure Offenders*) and Musgrove (*Youth and the Social Order*), among others, were not merely attempting to discuss some aspect or other of post-War youthful attitudes and behaviour. They were, essentially, offering us a view of youth as an aspect of post-War British society and culture as a whole.

I now aim to illustrate this by reference to these texts, and in so doing suggest the significance of the attempt of these writers to offer us, not a partial, but an overall, view of the nature of post-War youth as part of society and their explanations for such a state of affairs.

John Mays' *The Young Pretenders - A Study of Teenage Culture in Contemporary Society* was published in 1965 (Mays being, of course, Eleanor Rathbone Professor of Social Science in the University of Liverpool - one feels this is not a coincidence, perhaps). From the very first in the book we get a feeling of a general critique of modern social life into which context we can place 'the problem of youth' and particularly inter-generational conflicts. Mays quotes Tawney:

> "...the first duty of youth is not to avoid mistakes, but to show initiative and take responsibility, to make a tradition, not to perpetuate one."

and sets the tone for his essay, which, from the outset, considers post-War youth as a largely homogeneous body within a consensus framework. He suggests, for example, that youth are often perplexed by the range of choices they have to make, without, in my opinion, spelling out quite clearly that the range of choice may vary considerably, especially perhaps for Liverpudlians?

He begins with accepting, unproblematically, the conventional wisdom of youth and the 'generation gap':

> "The current adult image of youth, if we may judge by newspaper reports, is one of comparative irresponsibility, hooliganism and disrespect for established authority. It is a picture, which can only be described as a cari-cature, and one which most young people, naturally enough, resent very strongly.

> "Probably at no other time in the nation's history has there been so much adverse criticism of youth as there is today, and so little under-standing also, of what really is its role and function in society. So much so, in fact, that there is a very real danger of something like inter-generational alienation developing and spreading in the future. If this should happen, the social consequences will be very serious indeed."

> *(p.15)*

One must assume that the consequences will be dire in general and not for one generation or another. Equal casualties will be inflicted in this head-on clash of cultures. Mays goes on to elaborate his notion of early 1960s' youth culture, using this prognosis as his starting place. He does, however, underestimate the historical extent of inter-generational conflict, or perhaps to be more accurate, the way in which, within many (if not most) societies, certain sections (usually adult and/or most powerful) of the population set about the recalcitrant youth of their era. We have to recognise that, there has never been a 'golden age' of completely harmonious relations between generations. We can trace an unbroken line back to Plato, of a carping and a moaning about the state of youth. And, although I do not want to evoke the work of Mannheim here, we need to recognise that the special focus placed upon youth in the mid-20th century is tied up with the emergence of the quasi-scientific notion of adolescence on the one hand[1], and perhaps the development of much more pervasive mass media of communications on the other, coupled with a historically re-cognised decline in the abilities of modern industrial society (particularly capitalist ones) to solve fundamental questions of economics and politics. Is it not interesting, for example, that the sub-title of Mays' book is changed from 'A Study of Teenage Culture in Contemporary Society' to 'A Study of Adolescence in Contemporary Society' between the first edition of the book in 1965 and the Sphere paperback edition of 1969? With what we know of the development of a quasi-scientific 'biological ring' to the concept of 'adolescent', should we not be a little cautious? (It is also interesting that the front cover of the 1969 Sphere edition of *The Young Pretenders* carries four photographs of 'youth', very characteristic of the dominant image of middle class youth in revolt: long hair, beards, moustaches, NHS/Trotsky/Lennon! spectacles, *etc.* - images quite out of keeping with the early- to mid-1960s text.)

Mays poses a pretty unequivocal view of the manner of *salvation* for adolescents. Then, having successfully put notions of the interrelation between *youth* and social structure behind him, he moves on to the question of maturity:

> ' The concept of maturity, thus envisaged, is both psychological and physical. Physiological and psychological elements intermingle and re-invigorate one another. Neither must be stressed to the point at which the other is relatively excluded. Moreover, the whole process must always be seen as taking place *within* a social context."

---

[1] For an interesting discussion on the evolution of adolescence see Manning & Truzzi - *Youth and Sociology* (1972).

[My emphasis to heighten the integrative nature of the 'social context'.]

> "Thus a mature individual is one who succeeds in resolving the problems presented to him by the particular culture in which he happens to live."
>
> *(p.139)*

Despite what reservations Mays may have of the ideal mature adult, he does leave us the notion of having to come to terms with life *as a whole*. I find this very difficult to take. On the one hand, Mays seems to be offering us a view of the adolescent in society, with all the evolutionary-psychological concern that he musters. On the other hand, he strips the society of a human-made (even by the young!) culture and, therefore, seems to devalue any notion we may have of youth being creators as well as carriers of culture. His notion of the person is that of the individual, a singularly one-dimensional creature, who manages, all things considered, to compete successfully in the mature adult world once having got there. I suspect that Mays was, is, not alone in this view of youth and culture and social structure and social process and development.

Time and time again, Mays returns to a fundamentally popular theme of the early sixties. The failure of communications between the generations:

> "We have seen, however, that the so-called youth problem, is not confined to young people and that it is intimately associated with the whole life of the community. It arises from ordinary social processes and trends in contemporary western civilisation and cannot be evaluated in isolation. We live in a highly complex society, subject to strong pressures and influenced very often by impersonal forces, which we neither perceive nor control nor understand. The result is that, the vast majority of us are merely bewildered at what is happening."
>
> *(p.165)*

This is, of course, very close, in analogy, to dominant notions of 'the problems of the workplace' and the 'problems of race' in terms of conflict situations. The Industrial Relations and Race Relations industries grew in similar ways in the 1960s to the 'youth relations' industry. In all these consensus politics exercises, we see the integrative systems model, *viz.* the strangeness of new, destructive, and powerful sectional interests, come face-to-face with the old, familiar and established power base. The argument went that, if the 'new' and the 'old' could be educated about each other *within* the existing social context, then the existing and potential conflict could be 'nipped in the bud'. Mays sums up his prognosis so:

> "It is well to remind ourselves, once again, that the great majority of young people are comparatively passive and conformist, often to the point of dull mediocrity. Perhaps the brightest and more interesting youngsters are those who, while generally accepting the values of the community into which they are born, nevertheless evidence some degree of protest and criticism and so offer a challenge to the establishment. They probably comprise the future teachers of society, the brighter sparks from which the future will draw its warmth and dynamism. They may be the ones who, in the ultimate analysis, will justify our concept of democracy to history."
>
> *(p.171)*

If Mays' offering is typical of one overall synopsis of the young in the post-War world, the views of Jeff Nuttall are something else again. Very few books published in the 1960s could have been so widely read as *Bomb Culture* (1968) Nuttall was thirty-five years old in 1968, and had served a vicarious apprenticeship of kinds in the English 'Underground' - well before his fame spread. Many post-War writers have risen to popular acclaim on the backs of young people's cultural activity. Many of them have been optimistic. If this is hardly the case with Mays, it certainly is the case with a prophet of doom like Nuttall. To understand the hedonism and nihilism of much middle class youth 'revolt' in the late-Sixties, we need to grasp the notion of culture located within the consciousness of the Nuttall generation. Thus:

> "Culture, being the broad effect of art, is rootedly irrational, and as such, is perpetually operating against the economic workaday structure of society. The economic structure works towards 'stasis' centred on the static needs of man. It is centripetal. Culture forces change centred on the changing appetites of man. It is centrifugal. The effect of culture has never been so direct and widespread as it is among the international class of disaffiliated young people, the provotariat. Consequently art itself has seldom been closer to its violent and orgiastic roots. What has happened is that the pressure of restriction preceding nuclear suicide has precipitated a biological reflex compelling the leftist element in the young middle class to join with the delinquent element in the young working class for the reaffirmation of life by orgy and violence. What is happening is an evolutionary convulsion rather than a reformation. Young people are not correcting society. They are regurgitating it."
>
> *(p.9)*

For a more elaborate discussion of the new *appetites*, and generally an interesting middle class view of the 1950s and 1960s, see Christopher Booker *The Neophiliacs* (1969). So, having laid his foundation, Nuttall sets off on a 'ghost train' journey, pulled along on a set track, assailed on all sides by the diabolic; growled at, touched-up, and eventually, perhaps, shot out into the jeering and day light of realisation that it was all a rather nasty experience:

> "Let's not wait for those cripples in the administration to hand out money or land, and let's not wait for them to grant us the future that they owe us. They won't. They can't. Let's start

thinking in terms of permanence now and build
our own damn future."

(p.255)

Oh, where have all the Hippies gone? Along the way, Nuttall
offers a positive view of the development of Rock and Roll:

"The students and the mods cross-fertilized,
particularly in Liverpool. Purple hearts appeared
in strange profusion. Bell-bottoms blossomed
into wild colours. Shoes were painted with
Woolworths' lacquer. Both sexes wore make-up
and died their hair. The art students brought their
acid colour combinations, their lilacs, tangerines
and lime greens from abstract painting. The air in
the streets and clubs was tingling with a new
delirium. The handful of art-student pop groups
appeared, with louder, more violent music, their
cultivated hysteria, their painful amplifiers, The
Rolling Stones, The Pretty Things, The Kinks,
The Beatles. 'Kinky' was a word which was very
much in the air. Everywhere there were zippers,
leathers, boots, PVC, see-through plastics, male
make-up, a thousand overtones of sexual de-
viation, particularly sadism, and everywhere,
mixed in with amphetamines, was the birth pill."

(p.36)

This view, not a partial, but an overall one, is so hysterical in its
tone, that Nuttall, the observer, becomes Nuttall the frantic
masturbator. Contradiction is heaped upon contradiction. Considering Nuttall's general level of pessimism, I would have expected to see him refer to oral contraceptives for women as the
'death pill'. More than this, though, he overlooks the fact that
among the more overt disciples of the demonic mode in pop was
Arthur Brown ('Fire', *etc.*) - one of his contemporaries in the
London 'Underground'. Nuttall here also underlines his belief in
the manipulative, but somehow extraterrestrial, influences over the
young. What of the independence, vitality and choice of youth?

The view offered of post-War youth in *Bomb Culture* (albeit only the partial section of youth mentioned by Nuttall) is an overall one of youth possessed from without. An international tribe of now gibbering, now passive, now violent, now doped, youth, whose belief system, terms of reference, Gods, are 'Hiroshima-ism', whose high priests are the Hell's Angels and whose end is near at hand. Any similarities with American protestant fundamentalism are purely accidental!

In many ways though, a much more influential book of the *early* 1960s was T. R. Fyvel's *The Insecure Offenders: Rebellious Youth in the Welfare State* (first published in 1961). *Influential* because Fyvel was within the post-War institutionalism ethos that helped create and shape the Welfare State that he was so concerned about. Later on (*New Society* of 20-7-79), Fyvel offered a retrospective view of this study and the prognosis he put forward there. It is interesting to put together and juxtapose what he wrote of youth, especially inner-city working class youth in London in the late 1950s, and his comments now. Initially, let me present a piece of the 1961 analysis, where we see Fyvel offering another version of a post-War manipulative culture dominating youth. In this instance, it is a culture of consumerism, a crass, vulgar, bright lights and non-discriminatory culture, that youth seem part engulfed by, and part drawn towards, almost hypnotically, by the neon and the plate glass of the shop window and the disembodied strains of dance hall melodies:

> "It was. . .not hard to see the basic defects of their link with the new culture of the streets. It was not so much because the latter was primitive, but because, by 1960, it had become so many degrees more commercialised and deceptive and artificial, so that it seemed dangerously easy for young minds, cut off from other influences, to see all society in terms of caricature: that is, a society where newspapers were concerned solely with sex, sensation and betting, where television dealt only in violence and get-rich-quick quiz programmes and the popular film was a gangster film; a life of recurring boredom where nothing mattered but

> money and the smart thing at all times was to
> give as little as you could for as much as you
> could get; in short, they saw it as a distorted
> materialist society without purpose. On this soil,
> luxurious visions could flourish, where fact and
> fancy were apt to mingle."
>
> *(p.12)*

If you sense echoes of Eliot and Leavis, give yourself nine out of
ten. The pessimism is there. The admonishment of the bourgeoisie
for failing is there. Where Fyvel differs, of course, is in his
commitment to putting the matter right by a programme of
institutionalised resocialisation. What Fyvel finds centrally con-
fusing and disturbing is that, despite post-War affluence,
consensus politics, and the development of welfare policy and
practice (*i.e.*, the Welfare State), youth has rebelled. Youth is
lawless. Youth is recalcitrant. Youth is less easily *manageable*
than was assumed would be the case. Having been given
everything (within reason), youth has turned its back (or back-
sides, perhaps) on the Brave New World of post-War liberal
democracy.

Now, his retrospective comments in *New Society* convey a
sense his bewilderment:

> "I wrote of disquiet over juvenile crime figures
> rising steadily, despite rising social welfare ex-
> penditure. I described the gang-fighting, peacock
> -dressed Teddy Boys of the time, as a 'working
> class cultural subgroup', seeking its place in the
> consumer society. And I linked the sharp rise in
> juvenile earnings with a decline in parental
> authority and a rise in juvenile defiance and
> lawlessness."
>
> *(New Society, p.128, 20.7.79)*

Despite the influences inherent in the institutionally inspired social
structure of post-War industrial-urban Britain, the integrative
tendencies assumed in socialisation and unproblematic role
adoption were not taking place. Youth were indeed, being more,
indeed exclusively, influenced by destructively deviant sub-

cultural norms. Delinquency among youth was not a fact of life, it was comprehensively a way of life. But why was this *amazing* phenomenon existing at all?

> "What I saw as finally crumbling by the fifties was the classical bourgeois capitalist society dominated by the urban upper middle class. This society consolidated its status in the 19th century and was based on exclusive upper middle class economic privilege, buttressed by domestic servants. It was filled with institutions and patriarchal figures embodying moral authority."

(New Society, p.128)

But methinks he doth protest too much. A fundamental weakness in Fyvel's historical sketch is that it is itself a caricature, a partial truth. Those very streets in central London where Fyvel witnessed the 'surprising' deviance, defiance and degradation of youth in the late 1950s were likely the same streets where sections of the working class demonstrated in the late-19th century, for franchise reform, for improved pay and conditions, for trade union rights, for republicanism, *etc*. Fyvel's view of a dominant order in the late-19th century omits the constant, albeit 'ebbing and flowing', responses of the industrial-urban working class to their situation. These streets, where Fyvel witnesses the disaffiliation of post-War youth, are the streets referred to by Cecil Rhodes in his enthusiasm to argue for colonial (particularly African) expansion, to take pressure out of the industrial-urban environment of the late 19th century. While *overemphasising* upper middle class domin-ance and hegemony in the late-19th century situation, Fyvel underestimates the extent to which privileges continued to exist in post-War life.

> "Before the new onrush of mass consumption, mass advertising and mass entertainment, *the whole system* of upper middle class exclusiveness, with its large houses and servants, was simply swept away."
>
> *(New Society, p.128 - my emphasis)*

This is simply not the case. The evidence of the Diamond Royal Commission on Income and Wealth (1975) serves to illustrate the point that I have stressed elsewhere in this essay, namely, an element of the surpluses from post-War economic growth and production was distributed and redistributed among the working class. However, this was much larger than any major concessions wrung from the privileged sections of the population. The consequences of the upper middle class's falling share of the return on capital have been more complex. The British working class may have taken a greater share of that wealth, but one of the consequences has been for the investors to put their money into overseas enterprise and not into British industry. This may have contributed to the decline in the ability of British industry to re-equip, reduce unit costs and compete, *etc.*, but it does not appear to have seriously dented the privileges of those with capital to move around the markets.

Fyvel, then, merely reproduces (*c.* 1979) the mistakes he made in 1961. He supports his view of change in social order and status, by arguing that, the young of the late-1950s were 'caught up in' unreflective, even unselfconscious, deviance. Youth 'lost' its deference for traditional, benevolent, dogmatism and opted for a vicarious, hedonistic way of life that merely replicated the slide into consumerist mediocrity. Fyvel clearly deposits the 'problem' of youth in post-War Britain, in the 'insecure' nature of that youth. Fyvel offers us a standard 'pathological' view of individuals, which, ironically, might - in his terms - be a lot closer to the realities of life in a highly competitive and individualistic society.

In reading through the literature of, and about, the 1950s/1960s era, I am struck by the absence of a coherently coordinated statement by the young and particularly working class members of British society. The 1950s was certainly not a decade of writing by the working class about themselves in the way in which accounts of life were produced in the inter-War years say. We could now turn our attention to the likes of Alan Stillitoe, who, by the late 1950s, was producing a series of stories and novels offering a relative account of working class life. In *Saturday Night and Sunday Morning* and *The Loneliness of the Long-distance Runner* collections (published in 1958 and 1959, respectively), he offers us a rare literary view of the young working class in the 1950s:

"Arthur walked into a huge corridor, searching an inside pocket for his clocking-in card and noticing, as on every morning since he was fifteen - except for a two-year break in the army - the factory smell of oil-suds, machinery and shaved steel that surrounded you with an air in which pimples grew and prospered on your face and shoulders, that would have turned you into one big pimple if you did not spend half an hour over the scullery sink every night getting rid of the biggest bastards. What a life, he thought. Hard work and good wages and a smell all day that turns your guts. The bright Monday morning ring of the clocking-in machine made a jarring note, different from the tune that played inside Arthur."

('Saturday Night and Sunday Morning', p.22-3
of Pan edition)

And again in 'war' and love:

"Arthur sweated at his lathe, worked at the same fast pace as in winter to keep the graph-lines of his earnings level. Life went on like an assegai into the blue, with dim memories of the dole and schooldays behind and a dimmer feeling of death in front, a present life punctuated by meetings with Brenda on certain beautiful evenings when the streets were warm and noisy."

(op. cit. p.110-111)

In Sillitoe's 1959 short story, *The Loneliness of the Long-Distance Runner*, he offers us an insight into working class deviancy, not a 'way of life' (as so often stressed by functionalist theorising and positivist criminology), but as a 'fact of life' for many:

"As soon as I got to Borstal they made me a long-distance cross-country runner. I suppose

they thought I was just the build for it because I
was long and skinny for my age (and still am)
and in any case, I didn't mind it much, to tell you
the truth, because running had always been made
much of in our family, especially running away
from the police."

(p.7)

And again, summing up the ex-army, *Daily Telegraph*-reading
Governor:

"He's read a thousand books, I suppose, and for
all I know he might even have written a few, but
I know for a dead cert, as sure as I'm sitting here,
that what I'm scribbling down is worth a million
to what he could ever scribble down. . .I know
when he talks to me and I look into his army
mug that I'm alive and he's dead. . .Maybe as
soon as you get the whip-hand over somebody
you do die."

(p.12-13)

And maybe again, this is an aspect of the 'willing suspension of
conformity' that make urban working class youth in particular
seem to be part of:

"I didn't think about anything at all, as usual,
because I never do when I'm busy, when I'm
draining pipes, yaling locks, lifting latches,
forcing my bony hands and lanky legs into
making something more. . .When I'm wondering
what's the best way to get a window open or how
to force a door, how can I be thinking or have
anything on my mind? That's what the four-
eyed, white-smocked bloke with the notebook
couldn't understand when he asked me questions
for days and days after I got to Borstal."

(p.23-24)

Despite the efforts of a few Sillitoes, the 1950s and early-1960s was not a period when much was to be written by, or about, the young working class. This may be because they, particularly, seemed to epitomise the conventional wisdoms of post-War affluence, consensus and embourgeoisement. There is a certain irony to be found, therefore, in a back-cover review of Sillitoe's novel *Key to the Door* first published in 1961, this, in my 1963 Pan edition: "Bitter and vivid - what an eye-opener for a generation brought up in an era that has 'never had it so good' . . .".

However, we might want to suggest that post-War working class youth was to find its 'voice' in other ways, by using other media, for example, through music and song? What the post-War young working class male had to express may have been more appropriately transmitted in a musical, rather than in a literary, idiom. I attempted to bring the concern to the fore in an essay I wrote on The Beatles in 1972. The title of that essay was, 'The Beatles and the *musical* manifestations of adolescent revolt' [my subsequent emphasis]. That title may now seem very didactic and heavy handed, even iconoclastic in its tone. However, I offered it then in all good faith. I was not, of course, implying that 'The Beatles' had set out on a programme of political activity, or embarked upon a campaign to radicalise society. John Lennon may have become overtly political in his posture after 1967, say, but that was fairly late on in the history of things. What I was groping towards in my 1972 essay was a recognition of my conviction that young people often, even typically if they are working class, repressed within a social structure with dominant elites, ideas, *etc.*, respond. I suggested in that essay that, the development of musical cultures, like The Beatles' version of Rock and Roll, is an aspect of the now self-conscious, now un-selfconscious, resistance and attempt to mediate and negotiate.

It seems to me that, in attempting to understand the culture of post-War Britain, we look at what is offered up to us from the past. Existence and consciousness have to be considered. I have elaborated these ideas in the chapter on Society and Culture of this essay particularly.

Finally, in this vein, I must mention Musgrove's *Youth and the Social Order* (1964). Again, we see the way in which an academic (like Mays, say) puts forward an overall view of youth in post-War British society. I could do worse than to quote directly from the fly-leaf of the book, which gives an outline of Musgrove's orientation:

> "This book deals with the status of youth and the unequal conflict between the generations; it is concerned with the strategy - and arrogance - of the mature in protecting their position. Dr Musgrove argues that our social arrangements, and not least our educational system, are based on gigantic myths concerning the needs and nature of 'the adolescent'. Formal education and training are discussed as means of disabling, as well as enabling, the young; youth clubs, university halls of residence and other segregated age-grade institutions as means of creating 'adolescents' where none naturally exists.

> "The status of the young is related to their earnings and their education. A close connection is traced between the power of the young and their conservatism. The relatively high - but precarious - status of youth today is seen as the basis of their contemporary dullness."

So, yet again, we have a pessimistic view of culture, with youth fairly and squarely 'trapped' within it. Two major concerns emerge from Musgrove. On the one hand, there is doubt about the wisdom of extending formal education in British society. He argues, quite rightly in my opinion, that the economy does not require a continuously expanding, articulate and skilled workforce *en masse*. We have seen the contradiction here. On the one hand, the post-War schooling system has perpetuated an ideology that holds out rising standards of education related to high levels of achievement and upward social mobility. At the same time the changes taking place in the relations of production have pointed to a notion of greater equality, even democracy. However, the management of the forces of production have not created a situation where both the acquired skills and aspirations of post-War youth could be comprehensively utilised. Indeed, I would be persuaded by the argument that most jobs in the manual *and* non-manual sector of

150

the economy could be adequately carried out by a workforce that ended its formal education at thirteen or so. Why is this, I wonder? I suspect that despite the ideology of expanding opportunities within an increasingly open society, the reality is somewhat different for the young. What they seem to experience in great numbers, perhaps even, ironically, more so in the past five years or so, is a vital disjuncture between what is promulgated in terms of schooling and what actually are the requirements of a capitalist economy in a desperate state of flux. There is, to be sure, a real shortage of skilled craftsmen in industry at the present time, but I see that that is more to do with the combination of governmental incompetence and short-term greed by employers. Certainly, if we look at the demands of the existing economy, then Musgrove's prognosis was valid. But, of course, restricting ourselves to such a pragmatic view of the relation between youth, schooling and the workplace, is a cornerstone of a pessimistic prognosis of the future of youth. It assumes that youth will, more or less un-questioningly, accept the prevailing Social Order. If we adopt that view then, we seriously undervalue the non-conformity of youth. In adopting a view of 'the problem of youth', while seeing the Social Order - economic, political and cultural relations - as unproblematic, is injudicious to say the least. In that light, there seems no answer to schooling being a despotism in society in a desperate state of disequilibria. I simply cannot accept the view that post-War youth was ever as pusillanimous.

Before passing on to look at some alternative, indeed opp-ositional, views of youth in post-War British society, I must say a word or two about sex. One of the very few areas of everyday life that post-War British Sociology has discussed sex, is youth. Indeed, I would go as far as saying that *most* writing about youth in post-War society has seen sexual activity as *the* major 'problem'. This obsession has been reflected in the media, in postures struck by politicians, teachers and other pundits. But why? Is it merely a reflection of the increasing sexual promiscuity among the young? I fear not. I do not doubt that many sections of society, certainly in the late-1950s and early 1960s, perceived matters in that way. But perhaps it was the pundits who were more 'out of step' with everyday life than the young? Perception is vital, of course. The meanings placed upon everyday social phen-omenon by actors are going to be relatively important in the creation of their own sets of theories about society, culture and youth. It seems to me that many observers saw, or thought they saw, all kinds of changes in the values and behaviour of the young in post-War society. The meanings placed upon such perception, elevated from the typical to the conventional wisdom, surely helped to create a social reality that incorporated sexually promiscuous youth? However, that aside, I do sense something much more interesting and culturally complex. The actual and believed sexual attitudes and behaviour of the young from the fifties on, has been seen as a diabolical plot to undermine the social order. The extent to which commentator after commentator has over-dwelt on the unbridled lust and abandon of the young, has left the former, flushed and breathless. The 'art of the voyeur' has surely never been so enthusiastically taken up, as under the auspices of post-War social scientific accounts of youth. Could 'youth' resist the opportunity?

"No one will be watching us, why don't we do it in the road?"

When The Beatles were fooling around with their formative years, Cliff Richard was singing 'The Young Ones', epitomising, as it did, ephemeral youth. Later on in the 1960s, Roger McGough was under ining this with "Let me die a young man's death," *etc.* (From *The Mersey Sound*, Penguin Modern Poets 10, 1967).

Youth, like the weather, is always with us.

The Beatles

IN THIS SECTION of my essay I would like to outline a few ideas about The Beatles, as people, as a rock band, as Liverpudlians, as carriers and creators of culture. I want to especially concentrate on the decade from the mid fifties to the mid-1960s. I hope, in sketching a social history of The Beatles, to offer a sociological insight into the creation of 'them' and pointing-up some further considerations of 'The Beatles phenomenon', in post-War British society and culture. I would like to see The Beatles as part of the social structures and social processes that I have already elaborated in this study. This is, then, is the sharp end of my study. How am I going to relate and inter-relate the account, speculations, I have offered of post-War British society and culture, and the presence, activity and consequences of 'The Beatles'?

The temptation would be to put on one side the comments and analysis I have made to date and pass on, to write a biographical sketch of 'The Beatles'. This approch would, no doubt, prove highly entertaining and diverting, and would miss the point. As I have already suggested, in the first part of my essay, this has been the dominant tendency in the accounts of The Beatles, or John, Paul, George and Ringo, over the years.

I hope to avoid this 'trap'. How successful I will be must largely rest with the reader.

At the outset, I would like to see 'The Beatles' within a social matrix. What aspects of Merseyside culture, and youthful culture particularly, need emphasising in terms of the development of them? However, I would want to add two important, constraining, and yet liberating influences on their development: on the one hand, the nature of a post-War musical culture in their lives; and, on the other, the notion that the development of The Beatles was taking place, while, throughout Britain, other young people were inheriting, carrying and creating culture. Their lives, their music, their place in post-War British society are well documented. Their contribution to British culture is widely acknowledged. However, their prominence obscures the acknowledged contribution of many, all essentially a part of that society and culture.

I am looking at a photograph of 'The Beatles'. The image is from 'The Hamburg days' (1960-61) and shows Pete Best, George Harrison, John Lennon, Paul McCartney and Stuart Sutcliffe in their pre-Epstein style. Remnants of the Teds, plus 'Rocker' gear, plus 'winkle-pickers' plus DAs and quiffs, plus an unselfconsciousness that is quite striking. It is much like photographs of 19th century workers caught vicariously by the itinerant photographer seeking ethnographic material to prove his or her art rather than the particular qualities of those photographed in their anonymity. They are just another averagely good band; getting what work they can, living on their wits and promises. Knowing that they can't go back; not knowing where their futures may be. It reminds me of Lennon's story about playing in Liverpool on their return from Hamburg. Lennon claims that he overheard some of their audience agreeing that, 'That German band speak good English'. Like 19th-century journeymen, they are carrying the tools of their trade: four guitars plus drum and sticks. The faces are youthful and yet they carry a feel of lost innocence, in the sense that experience is etched there, in the faces, in the clothes, in the postures.

Now I am looking at a photograph taken of Ringo, John, Paul and George 'on stage' during the first American tour in February 1964. The different line-up is in obvious contrast from the first image: Ringo, veteran of Rory Storm and The Hurricanes and Butlins, has replaced Pete Best; Stuart Sutcliffe has gone, forever. However, there are other contrasts, which are more telling. These are 'The Beatles' being photographed in full swing; they are adopting their successful, earth-shaking and self-conscious faces. They are older and yet, compared with the first image, they *look* younger. They are each wearing the same hair and clothes. They have become a corporate image. They are not surprised that they are being immortalised on films, on tape, in time and space. They *know* it. They are surrounded by thousands of idolatrous young people; they are also surrounded by a ring of police, for their own protection, of course. When they returned to Britain, the Prime Minister called them, 'Our best exports'. The corporate image reflects in the reification into commodity status.

Now I am looking at a third photograph, quite a different image from the first two. For a start, it is in *colour*! It is from the finale of *Magical Mystery Tour*, the TV film produced by The Beatles in December 1967 - only six months after the release of 'Sergeant Pepper', their high-water mark in artistic credibility. The film was panned by the critics as obscure, witless and blatant rubbish. Paul, John, George and Ringo are dressed all in white. White morning suits; each with a button hole. They are singing in unison; they are self-consciously entertaining by way of pastiche. Hair styles are longer and irregular; Harrison and Starr are moustached. Here we witness four young men, older and more experienced in the ways of all flesh, wealthy and indulgent, able to act out their fantasies in public, albeit from a very privatised distance. Not a guitar or drum set in sight. Between the release of 'Sgt. Pepper' and the release of *Magical Mystery Tour*, Epstein had died, The Beatles had sung 'All You Need Is Love' to 150 million viewers, and the Maharishi was setting up shop in Wales.

I juxtaposed these three images on the cover of my (earlier) essay 'The Beatles and the musical manifestations of adolescent revolt' (1972). It seemed to me that these images were potent, not just that they carried 'The Beatles', but represented moments in a cultural history.

However, I must be cautious. Photographic images, no matter how potent they may be in their mediated way, are attempts to make history stand still. As I have already suggested in the first part of this essay, a great deal of post-War popular culture and popular music, history, has been attempted through 'static' images of this kind. They certainly evoke a nostalgia; but they do, of course, require an interpretation. One reading of these images may seem quite different from another, and any attempt to analyse the nature of social structures and social relations as social processes must include a sense of movement. What is the dialectical process that creates the moment for such situations to be created and for such images to be constructed? What, in fact, lies beyond the emulsion? There is also the question of the idealisation of the process whereby the musical phenomenon is produced. By carrying these idealised images with us through life, returning to them as we do, we can *forget* the blood, sweat and tears that make up the production process of The Beatles music, *etc.*

However, I should say that my choice of these three images is not random or idle. They do represent, to me, images from the three distinctive phases in the career of The Beatles.

First phase: the years between the mid-1950s and 1962, when they, in turn, topped Liverpool's *Mersey Beat* popularity poll (reported in *Mersey Beat* Vol.1 No.13, January 4-18, 1962), were successfully managed (by Epstein) to a recording contract with EMI and a musical arrangement apprenticeship with George Martin, and made the UK top twenty charts with 'Love Me Do' and created the environment for 'Please Please Me' to reach number one in the top twenty in January 1963.

Second phase: the years between 1962/3 and 1967. These were the years when the corporate image of **The Beatles** was first created and established. The first tour of the USA, ten consecutive 'instant' number one records (the run ending with 'Paperback Writer'), world tour, awards of MBE, and last live performance in Britain (at Wembley in May 1966), marriages, ends of marriages, drugs, films and exhaustion. This phase culminated, in my mind, with the death of Epstein and the ending of the *raison d'être* for the corporate image to be maintained any longer, faced, as it was, with all the contradictions.

Third phase: the years after 1967. The 'rise and fall' of Apple Corp. The ending of the partnership, musical and otherwise, of Lennon and McCartney. The 'fall and rise' of Lennon and McCartney (and Harrison and Starr) as musicians and performers - in all manner of ways, in their own right. The coming back to Abbey Road to end it all, and in May 1970, the release of the film *Let It Be*, when fans came to praise Caesar, not to bury him, but The Beatles, by proxy, buried the corporate Caesar, not knowing what to praise. McCartney said: "I didn't leave The Beatles. The Beatles have left The Beatles, but no one wants to be the one to say the party's over." Which reflects what he had suggested long before, "The thing is, we're all really the same person. We're just four parts of the one." (See Wilfred Mellers on The Beatles as 'Earth, Fire, Air and Water').

I will endeavour, in this section of my narrative, to assess these phases and to consider and evaluate the material written on The Beatles over the years. A good deal of the 'evidence' is contradictory where, clearly, the perceptions of the various biographers differed, often it would seem, to the extent to which those biographers felt liberated or let-down by The Beatles.

I would like to start with a look at the 'youth culture' scene in Liverpool in the 1950s. At that time, most pop music, recorded material and 'super stars' came from across the Atlantic or Tin Pan Alley. Even if, like Dickie Valentine and Frankie Vaughan, they were 'home-grown' varieties, they still carried the mark of showbiz that came from their association and promotion by Tin Pan Alley, as well as their acceptance of that cultural route to success, fame and fortune. Despite the popularity of these entertainers and their counterparts, they were a world apart from the ordinary day-by-day experiences of the young. This was not a participant culture as such, it was one where the groomed product was consumed or not, as the case may be.

As the decade unfolded, however, *musicians*, indigenous to Britain, began to develop a new, distinctively different, musical style, namely Skiffle. Lonnie Donnegan helped more than any other performer to establish Skiffle as a national movement. Skiffle, because of its *popular* nature, broke the mould of post-War British pop music. Almost any one (even me) could put a Skiffle band together, not necessarily for the local night club or Butlins or The London Palladium, but just for your own entertainment, amusement and perhaps even kudos. Indeed, all that was needed were some acoustic guitars, bought or made, a tea chest for a bass, and enthusiasm tempered with lack of inhibition. Skiffle did not create for the first time the notion or possibility for 'home-grown' music, but it did create the environment in which a whole range of musical seeds could take root and germinate away. The flowering of British R & B and Rock and Roll in the late 1950s and early 1960s, may have been humble compared with the American varieties, but it was no less significant in its hybrid nature and its awe-inspiring qualities. It certainly *got at* John Lennon:

> "It gets through, it got through to me, the only thing to get through to me at all, things that were happening when I was fifteen. Rock and Roll then was real, everything else was unreal...You recognise something in it which is true, like all true art."

> *(From 'Rolling Stone Interview', Rolling Stone, 7-1-71, p.33)*

John Lennon was 15 years' old in 1955/56.

I can recall, from my own experience, that Skiffle was essentially a peer group activity. It was your mates that shared the music and the laughs and the fantasies and the realities of everyday life as a teenager. Lennon 'put together' a Skiffle band while in the fifth form at school, Quarry Bank Grammar School, and called his band 'The Quarry Men'. Billy Shepherd's account of The Beatles in 'A Tale of Four Beatles' in the monthly 'The Beatles Book' illustrates the point.

> "So the Quarrymen came into being. John was a fifth former at the time and lots of homework and studies clashed pretty hard with rehearsals and arrangements for the group. 'I thought we had big problems in those days,' he says now, 'but it was all terrific fun at the same time...I was on a battered old guitar, which hadn't cost much. A bloke named Rodney was on banjo, Pete Shelton was on washboard, I think Eric Griffiths was on another guitar and Len Gary was on box bass.' "

(The Beatles Book, No.2, Sept 1963)

Never mind the 'fanzine' gush; the issue is sound enough. Lennon met McCartney, so it is claimed, on 15th June 1955, while the Quarrymen were doing a gig at Woolton fete. We have some evidence of gang activity among the young on Merseyside in the 1950s and early 1960s. Colin Fletcher produced a study 'Beat and Gangs on Merseyside' in 1964 (reproduced in *Youth in New Society* edited by T. Raison in 1966). I realise that it is not very acceptable among sociologists to see youthful activity as 'gang activity'. Indeed, apart from Fletcher's essay and the work of J. Patrick in Glasgow ('A Glasgow Gang Observed', 1973), there is precious little published material where the notion of 'gang' plays a large part. However, I still feel that Fletcher's essay of the mid-1960s was, and is, valuable, if for no other reason than it attempts to interrelate peer group activity in general and emergent musical cultures like Skiffle and Rock and Roll in particular.

Fletcher suggests that the gangs self-consciously guarded their territory, and involved themselves in leisure activities, for example, self-made, homegrown entertainment. Of course, any collective notion, like 'gang', needs supplementing with a cautious view of the person. They may surrender a certain amount of themselves to the overall ethos and identity of the 'gang', but according to Fletcher, there were desirable and distinctive 'types' within the peer collective:

> "The 'musical' type was latent. In the Park Gang there was a boy who played a good harmonica, the one who was adept at a rhythm with knitting needles on a lamp post, the singer who never smiled and two harmonisers who picked up tunes readily, but could never remember the words. There was a similar motley talent in the Holm Road Gang, but they shouted more and took entertaining the gang far less seriously."

(C. Fletcher, p.152 of 'Youth in New Society')

Merseyside youth had been first 'infected' by Rock and Roll (American style) through various sources. Media played a major part in the conversion. Both cinema and TV began to promote the 'new' music from Stateside. Rumour and local reportage also played a part in popularising the new trend. News about Bill Haley and the film *Rock Around the Clock* had reached most gangs on Merseyside well in advance of the film itself. Despite early attempts to ban the film, it eventually went out to adolescents. Colin Fletcher's impressions of seeing the film in Liverpool are much like my own reflections from seeing it in a south coast city cinema.

> "Gangs filed in and filled up row after row. Unlike most of the films, this one had commanded an almost entirely adolescent audience. When the music started it was infectious, no one managed to keep still. It was the first time the gang had been exposed to an animal rhythm that matched their behaviour. Soon couples were in the aisles copying the jiving on the screen. The 'bouncers' ran down to stop them, the audience went mad. Chairs were pulled backwards and forwards, arm rests uprooted, in an unprecedented orgy of vandalism."

(Fletcher, p.153)

As Fletcher describes it, the passing of the music onto the young was infectious. Habits of long standing were changing. BBC television's '6.5 Special', with budding pop stars such as Tommy Steele, put back Saturday night gang time from 7pm to 7.30pm. Television played a major part in showing the provincial youth the development of London based Rock and Roll talent. McCartney was affected like anyone else in the circumstances.

> "I watched The Shadows backing Cliff Richard one night. I'd heard them play a very clever introduction to 'Move it' on the record, but could never work out how they did it. Then I saw them do it on TV. I rushed out the house straight away, got on me bike, and raced up to John's with me guitar. 'I've got it.' I shouted. And we all got down to learning it right away."

> *(Quoted from "The Beatles' by Hunter Davies,*
> *p.62)*

According to Fletcher, the music, like the conscious habit of roughness, soon became 'them'; it was their new idiom. The girls especially helped to change habits within the peer group. Whereas the 'romantics' in the gangs usually brought their girls along to be shared out, the girl's enormous interest in pop and pop singers began to change things. The girls were 'real-gone' on the new musical dimension; the romantics needed little encouragement to stay away from some other gang activities (fights, petty crime, *etc.*).

Instead of the usual gang meetings, small groups of boys and girls would go off to someone's home to listen and dance. All of these events gradually distilled into the notion and desire to form a rock group within the gang.

Fletcher emphasises that there were many strands that were pulled together in the formation of the gang's group. The girls were often prepared to turn their hand to making suits. Some teachers encouraged the boys to make crude acoustic guitars at school. The 'criminal' element in the gangs soon lost what passing interest they had in the group idea. Their recalcitrance only added impetus to the efforts of the potential musicians.

The groups initially entertained themselves within the gang. They became a totem for the gang; something other than territory to be proud about and, if necessary, fight over. The groups sung about the cares and woes of being a down-trodden black (by proxy) and an insecure, yet adventurous teenager, with equal conviction. "If I fell in love with you, Would you promise to be true," etc. ('If I Fell' from 'A Hard Day's Night' LP, Lennon and McCartney, 1964). And again: "Love, love me do, You know I love you", etc. ('Love Me Do', Lennon and McCartney, 1962)

Is that posed naivety and directness ever to be recaptured in later years?

> "That's what we want to get back to, simplicity. You can't have anything simpler, yet more meaningful than, 'love, love me do'. That's just what it means. I think I slagged off school to write that one with John when we first started."

> *(Paul McCartney, quoted in 'The Beatles Illustrated Lyrics', Vol.1, edited by Alan Aldridge, p.92)*

The involvement in the groups became strong motivation in these young people's life. Everything else had to take second place. Even such mundane things as jobs after leaving school seemed irrelevant when compared to the needs and demands of the 'new world' of Rock and Roll. Horizons opened up that had not existed before. Here, perhaps, was an avenue that would lead beyond the usual humdrum life. The groups, rock as a job, may lead to freedom from the constraints of factory, dockside, office and dole. This was the perspective that many enthusiastic beginners had before their hopes were dashed. Some survived the various crises of doubts and difficulties. Parents often assumed an unsympathetic tone and at least were circumspect.

> "...'But I wanted him to stick in at school and get a good job,' says Mr Harrison. 'I was very upset when I saw he was so mad on the group. I realised you had to be good in show business to get to the top and even better to stay there. I

couldn't see how they were going to get anywhere. My other two boys were well set up,
Harry as a fitter and Peter as a panel beater. I
wanted George to do as well."

(Hunter Davies, p.59)

Harrison senior was a bus driver; George Harrison was an
apprentice electrician after school. But, of course, the young
people that made up the groups were just a cross-section of the
teenage population. They had certain traits and tendencies that
became extended. They were mostly not at all 'talented' in school
terms (or could not be persuaded to concentrate their latent
potentialities within the school context). Within themselves, however, they were a huge fund of talent, skill and innovation. The
emergent culture was becoming stronger, more buoyant, more
articulate.

"If there is such a thing as genius, which is what,
what the fuck is it? I am one, and if there isn't, I
don't care. I used to think it when I was a kid,
writing me poetry and doing me paintings. I
didn't become something when The Beatles
made it, or when you heard about me. I've been
like this all me life. Genius is pain too."

(John Lennon quoted in 'The Rolling Stone'
interviews, p.30)

Lennon believed in himself, even if others didn't. The groups
believed in themselves; their peers believed in them. Fletcher
reminds us that the groups went through several stages of em-
ancipation from the peer groupings and indigenous environment as
such. As their playing experiences multiplied from club to pubs,
socials, dances, competitions, *etc.*, to eventually touring, they
moved further away from the original ties. Even so, the groups still
had to take all manner of hurdles in their stride.

"They were doing more and more engagements,
still earning only a few bob, playing at working

men's clubs and socials. But as the beat group
boom took over Liverpool, little teenage clubs
slowly began to spring up. They were basically
coffee clubs, on the lines of the hundreds of
coffee bars serving expresso coffee amidst lots of
rubber plants and bamboo, which had arisen all
over the country. The Liverpool ones occas-
ionally put on live shows for the teenagers,
which gave the hundreds of beat groups somewhere to play. The beat groups could never get
into the traditional sort of clubs, like The Cavern,
which had always had live groups. They were for
jazz fans and jazz bands, which was considered a
much higher art form. The beat groups were all
scruffy and amateur and Teddy Boyish. It was a
working class art form, full of electricians and
labourers."

(Hunter Davies, p.66)

Many of the club premises were 'homemade', as, for example,
with 'the Casbah', in Liverpool. 'The Quarrymen' joined forces
with Pete Best, a drummer, to convert the cellar of Best's mother's
cafe into a club. The group had turned up with their guitars and
were given paintbrushes. The cafes and 'chippies' of the early
coke-sipping days gave way to the coffee bar and the juke-box.
Here, for the price of a coffee or two, was warmth, reasonable
comfort, the chance of a 'pick-up', a chat about latest trends and
above all, perhaps, a jive to the latest top twenty on the 'juke'. A
sanctuary from the home, the school and the street. A place to
speculate about the future of rock and beat. Something of an
enclave, somewhere set apart from the world of 'them', the people
who did not, or could not, comprehend just how important it all
was. "Well, she was just seventeen/ You know what I mean," *etc.*
*(*from 'I Saw Her Standing There' - Lennon and McCartney, Long
Tall Sally EP).

The groups were dynamically affected by what was going on
around them. The media expanded its interest in general. As
Lennon and McCartney have said, their particular style was
created in large part by whatever was going on around them at the
time. Their music evolved by listening to Chuck Berry, Carl

Perkins, John Lee Hooker, Presley, The Shadows, The Everleys, Buddy Holly, and so on. They were great adventurers; they listened, copied, translated, and modified. The process of mediation included the ebb and flow of self-expression through music and musical performances. It was "a life-style" (as people now would say). Perhaps a good many of the Merseyside young, in this situation, were like teenagers elsewhere, essentially a mixture of optimism and pessimism about their future. It was very much a 'grass roots' popular musical movement in the way in which the local acceptance and local accolades were accorded and carried in a local *milieu*. At some subsequent point in time and space, these same young people, contemporaneous with their audience, might become *commercially* successful and move away, become distanced, remote, and mythical. On the other hand, they might not even leave, or as in many cases, might get 'exit visas' from Merseyside, but come, or drift back, for one reason or another. But this did not start or end with Merseyside, Merseysound, or The Beatles. In a book by Burchill and Parsons, *The Boy Looked at Johnnie - An Obituary of Rock and Roll* (1979), this point is raised in relation to the events of another youth phenomenon (of that time):

> "In the UK, punks are prepared to pay out hard cash for expensive albums by bands who could just as easily have been standing behind them in an audience. Kids like themselves, the fact that they were musicians almost incidental, who, maybe just a month ago, had been standing next to them at the bar 'down the Roxy'. Kids who had followed these bands long before they had signed six-figure recording contracts (with companies that would have laughed at them had it not been for their hard-core, ready-made 'market') not only felt like peers, but also like campaigners."
>
> *(p.66)*

This is a rare insight in an otherwise pretty awful book, but I would see a useful analogy here with Merseyside in the late 1950s and early 1960s. Substitute the Cavern and the Jacaranda say, for

165

the Roxy, adjust the album/single contract and contract figures and we have the same phenomenon. I want to come back to commercial nexus in a while, and to certainly consider the roll of Epstein and others in the promotion of The Beatles and the 'Merseysound'.

Before that, however, I must return to accounts of 'Liverpool life' and turn first to Billy Shepherd who was commissioned by 'The Beatles' monthly to write 'A Tale of four Beatles'. This account was serialised in *The Beatles Book* between Issue 2 in September 1963 and issue 9 in April 1964, up to, in fact, the chart successes of the 'Please Please Me' single and LP. Shepherd later translated this serialisation into book form as *The True Story of The Beatles*, which was published by Beat Books in 1964. Beat Books were the publishing company for 'Beat Monthly', a glossy monthly covering 'top' commercial pop and the 'monthly' books like *The Beatles Book*. It was not only Dickens that was to go from popular serialisation to more successful and commercial book form; Billy Shepherd achieved a considerable readership for *The True Story. . .* It also reads like myth, an account based on remembering truth, conjecture and hearsay. It has all the characterisation necessary to take the story out of the ordinary, everyday world of the teenager and yet leave enough nitty gritty there to be clearly and closely identified with, even from afar. Shepherd successfully, in commercial terms, created an account of development and success that can appeal to young people throughout Britain; his is one of the first examples of up-rooting The Beatles out of their Merseyside cultural environment and posing them as *déclassé* and delocalised. Let me illustrate this social pathology of 'The Beatles' that Shepherd offers: "Like every other great world seaport, Liverpool has seen many famous names pass through its docks and streets ... Liverpool is a tough city of some three-quarters of a million people situated about 200 miles north-west of London. . .The Liver-pudlians are noted for their humour under difficult conditions. It's something that the youngsters pick up when they are very small and it usually stays with them all their lives." (*The True Story of The Beatles*, p.7). This 'tourist guide' for the less than disc-riminating national, London orientated, audience is followed by an opening note on 'The Beatles' that attempts to stress the importance of the four individuals, ironically not even mentioning Pete Best, which somewhat undervalues the influence of the local culture in the most contradictory way.

> "John, Paul, George and Ringo were no different from any other boy in their city. Quick to laugh, ready to fight for themselves, loving to take a risk, which would make their parents hair stand on end if they could see them. But at the same time forming the very individual characters that were going to make them continue fighting to succeed long after most others would have given the whole thing up as completely hopeless. Refusing to be beaten, refusing to accept that their ideas and dreams were impossible. Trying and trying again until Lady Luck decided that they'd earned their place at the top."
>
> *(p.7/8)*

This is amazing fanzine PR material. What is particularly significant about this 'history in reverse' is that this was to become the well-cultivated, dominant image of The Beatles: the image on which much of 'Beatlemania' was successfully constructed by the growing team of 'associates and helpers' of the band. It was the image that was replicated throughout the media, with very few exceptions. An image that gave The Beatles, culturally, a corporate virgin birth in *c.*1962. Shepherd ends his story on this note:

> "The boys take stardom with an *un*-story like attitude. They don't want to change - and as long as they are all there to curb any changes they note in any of the others, they surely will not change.
>
> There's so much yet to come from this talented foursome. The critics are convinced of that.
>
> They have made a great deal of money already, though it is impossible to work out precisely how much. They spend little. For they remain shrewd lads who will never forget the days when they

had to struggle for every pound note and when they often had to make do with a stale bun instead of a good meal when on tour.

Their future is the biggest question mark in the entertainment world today. Will any of the Beatles get fed-up and leave the quartet? Will they continue to hit the top with every record? Can they stand the pace of being the hottest property in show business?...The questions are endless. The answers are locked up in their heads alone. Only The Beatles themselves can say what they are going to try and do in the future. But whatever happens, their place in history is secure. The era of Beatlemania will be remembered for a long, long time as one of those incredible phenomena that can only happen in show business."

(p.223-224)

Now, this is not an extraordinary account at all. It is, in fact, the most typical, ordinary form of 'analysis' that is to be found in relation to popular culture in the post-War western world. It is, for me, the antithesis of what I feel needs to be said about the relation between culture and social being. I have outlined my thoughts on this relation (particularly in the introduction to this study) and I want to reaffirm them again.

It is all too easy to write the sort of 'history' that Shepherd and many others have done. I do not particularly begrudge them their share of the 'gold mine'. That kind of 'cultural prospecting' is no less innocuous than a good deal of what masquerades as a professionalised sociology. However, I just do not feel that it does justice to the subject. It does not, ironically, value The Beatles or their cultural environs; it reduces the discussion to a veneer of hyperbole that is, in a sense, the real world turned upside down. It is an idealism that reifies cultural relations and processes.

I will return again to this point. For now I would like to add more to my view of the 1961-64 period. It seems to me that one of the most difficult questions to consider is, why, among everything else, was it *The Beatles* that achieved such prominence in that period? Were they *that* extraordinary? I suspect not. I suspect that, despite their qualities, it was much more likely that they emerged as they did because of a complicated cultural process whereby they came to represent, even *symbolise*, the emergent culture. I intuitively draw back from saying, 'the process of myth'. I need to consider that problem more. I want to know what happened to them between late-1961 and 1964. What cultural processes and personal relationships were they part of, created, maintained, carried and destroyed, and I want to draw on some more evidence from that period as well as offering assessment to the situation.

British Rock and Roll became big business. Despite the new regional flavour of the recipe, the entrepreneurial 'pie' was still cooked in London as Britain's over-dominant musical centre. Brian Epstein was traditional and shrewd enough to eventually gain acceptance for The Beatles when he took their tapes with him to London to see the moguls. Once the news was around, everybody cashed in:

> "Epstein himself tried to stop the boom from getting out of hand. He signed up only those in whom, usually correctly, he suspected some staying power and he tried to avoid overexposure and too much close identification under a Liverpool label. If he failed, it was because others were less scrupulous. As he told me, at the height of the 'Pool mania', agents were getting off the train at Lime Street Station and signed up each other; while, at the Cavern, it was difficult for a press photographer to get a shot which didn't include another photographer on the other side of the room."

> *('Revolt into Style', George Melly, 1970,*
> *p.76/77)*

This reminds me of what Stanley Cohen has called the Midas touch in reverse: 'Everything that is gold you touch'.

As Melly stresses, the Merseyside boom was over by 1964. Mainstream rock and pop had turned the R & B (rhythm and blues) corner. The Beatles escaped this crisis, but many did not.

"There were so many groups in Liverpool at one
time that we often used to play just for each
other. It was a community on its own, just made
up of groups. It was all nice. Then the record
companies came up and started signing groups, it
wasn't so friendly. Some made it and others
didn't."

*(Ringo Starr quoted in 'Rolling Stone', No.20,
26-10-68, p.15)*

To escape the crisis of regional pop, it seemed The Beatles had to
permanently move to London. They had to turn their backs on the
Merseyside community of groups, their own origins, and concentrate on a newer, higher level, of isolated life, as national
celebrities (The Beatles farewell performance at the Cavern was in
August 1963). They were required to become mobile, ageless,
synthetic, shiny packets of people. They went on by not saying no.
Some Merseyside agents, like Alan Williams, were bitter about the
turn of events.

"They let Liverpool down. That feller Epstein
took them to London along with all the other
good groups and that killed the scene here."

*(Quoted in McCabe and Shonfield - 'Apple to the
Core').*

Williams' 'sour grapes' attitude seems somewhat static with the
benefit of hindsight. Perhaps he should have been more optimistic
about the lasting success of locally and regionally based rock and
pop. The provincial centres could not compete with the international show-business machine that already existed in London.
Groups were compelled to launch or re-launch from there if they
were to reach the 'big time'. "I asked a girl what she wanted to
be/She said baby can't you see?" *etc.*, (From 'Drive my Car',
Lennon and McCartney, 'Rubber Soul' LP)

Fundamentally, different people had a different vision of the
'Mersey Sound'. Whereas most outsiders saw something 'fab',

'gear', romantic or outrageous about the sound, local reportage was more authentic in the main.

One of the key features in the development of Rock and Roll on Merseyside was the high quality of local reportage. 'Grass roots' musical innovation does, of course, come to be known about through eye-witness accounts, but a local press, orientated to the music of youth and run by participant observers, can be a vital factor in the creation of an emergent culture. *Mersey Beat*, the paper produced by Bill Harry from July 1961, is such a factor in The Beatles phenomenon. I would like to draw from the pages of *Mersey Beat* in this section of my study. I feel it will help to illustrate points being made about the development of The Beatles. But it is also important to see the paper as part of the cultural matrix that created the 'environment' that Rock and Roll bands on Merseyside could develop in the way that they did. The pages of *Mersey Beat* are open to those fortunate to have access to them, and many photographs of The Beatles used for the first time in *Mersey Beat* have been reproduced time and time again. However, a very interesting slice of *Mersey Beat* was re-produced in book form: *Mersey Beat: The Beginnings of The Beatles* (1977), edited and with a short introduction by Bill Harry. The selection in this 1977 book is, understandably, heavily slanted towards The Beatles. However, in selecting the issues of *Mersey Beat* to include (in ninety-six pages), Bill Harry has chosen significant issues from the months between the first issue in July 1961 and The Beatles chart success with 'Love Me Do' in October 1962. This may not seem a very long period, but the Rock and Roll scene developed rapidly from the late 1950s, and The Beatles' activities even more so. The pages of *Mersey Beat* do capture that process and that feeling of excitement. These early issues are significant because they are not totally dominated by The Beatles. Indeed, until January 1962, The Beatles are just one of many aspiring Rock and Roll revival bands on the Mersey circuit who are covered by Bill Harry. Nor are the early issues so parochial as the post 1962, post 'Please Please Me' issues. The turning point is, in my opinion, issue number 13 from Vol.1 for January 4-18, 1962. This is the issue that carries a well-known photograph of The Beatles on the front page; they, having been voted top of the *Mersey Beat* Popularity Poll for the top group throughout 1961. The four members of the band are still in their black leather gear, this being pre-Epstein days. Pete Best is there, of course, and McCartney has his name spelt wrongly as usual. But let us consider the rest of this front page of 'Merseyside's own entertainments paper' at 3d a copy. There are a number of adverts, all in their way indicative of a growing 'grass roots' music culture, emerging from a local culture traditionally strong in self-made musical entertainment. There is an advert for Cranes, a local electrical and musical business. There are adverts for clubs, jive halls, an audition service and, at the bottom of the page: 'Welsby Sound Recordings'. Their advert is headed: 'For the ambitious group - Have you cut your first disc yet?'. Welsby offer a service for recording, producing and publishing 'your' record, 'whether 1, 100 or 1,000 copies.'

In his 1977 introduction, Bill Harry makes several interesting comments about his association with The Beatles phenomenon:

> "I began to hear more of the group that John was with during the following months because they were appearing regularly at our own Art College dances and were considered, by some, to be the college band. This was around the period when the proposal came up at the Union Meeting to buy a PA system which the group could use in exchange for them being available to perform at our dances.
>
> I began to frequent a local coffee bar, The Jacaranda, where I met various people from the music scene who drifted in from time to time and I began to gather information about the local scene as I was co-editing a local music magazine for Frank Hessy, the local musical instruments dealer. . . It was evident that the members of the groups had no conception of the scope of the scene they were involved in. One group would know two or three venues, another half a dozen, someone else a couple more. . .I began to work on the lines of a local paper covering the Rock and Roll and general entertainment scene."

(p.6)

One of the intriguing features here is the indication by Harry that the emergent music scene in the Liverpool of the late 1950s was not as homogeneous and consciously integrated as the popular image. *The* Mersey Sound became the dominant image projected after 1962. As I have already indicated, this dominant, PR stimulated image created a situation where myth was heaped upon myth, which, in turn, reinforced and helped to replicate the dominant ideology. A musical culture may have existed that had a uniqueness and style, but I suspect that the culture was a very cosmopolitan and heterogeneous one. This is not to deny that the nature of an emergent Rock and Roll musical culture 'on Merseyside' was fundamentally seminal to The Beatles. On the contrary, it seems to me that, The Beatles, like other bands, inherited and created. A process of mediation took place. That mediation may, however, have been significantly localised and personalised.

> "When I first became involved, a main reason why Liverpool Rock and Roll bands had such a strong repertoire of excellent US material was due to the fact that Bob Wooler played his rare collection of American Rock and Roll discs at many of the venues."
>
> *(Bill Harry, p.7)*

Mersey Beat was very popular from the start among a wide variety of young musicians and their associates. Bill Harry was in very close contact with Stuart Sutcliffe and thereby with Lennon, *etc*. Both Lennon and McCartney contributed to the early issues of *Mersey Beat*, adding, no doubt, to their local reputation. *Mersey Beat* was certainly a useful vehicle for The Beatles in 1961 and 1962, and much of the reportage of them must have helped to give them a wider audience. It was certainly through Bill Harry that Brian Epstein came into contact with Lennon, McCartney, Harrison and Best. Epstein contributed record reviews to *Mersey Beat*; that is, at a time before his management of The Beatles *et al* began to 'eat up' his life.

Bill Harry suggests the major reason for The Beatles' unique success was the combined song writing talents of Lennon and McCartney. He reflects other contemporary evidence that, well before 'Love Me Do", Lennon and McCartney had written a great many songs. Harry puts the figure at eighty, information obtained from Lennon and McCartney themselves. What is evident is that Lennon and McCartney were excellent re-writers and arrangers within their *milieu*. They had been able to use their innovative skills to good effect in transposing American Rock and Roll standards. They were, however, influenced by the Oriole - American, Tamla Motown records. These influences can be felt throughout their early 1962-1964 recordings. Not only did they create their own music from such a tradition, they also re-recorded some of their favourites, in the process paying a 'debt' to that tradition, acknowledging those seminal influences.

Bill Harry also reflects upon the scene of Liverpool overcome by 'Beatlemania'. If we survey the many accounts of The Beatles' progress through the 1962-1964 years, we confront the 'Beatlemania' phenomenon. Bill Harry is certainly not the only analyst of that era to suggest that concept or process. There is no doubt, however, that the origins of the concept 'Beatlemania' lies with the national press. The concept emerged as part awe-struck wonderment, part titillation, part sensationalism. But what are we supposed to understand by it?

> "Beatlemania was very descriptive of the fanatical fervour that swept in their wake, first in Liverpool, then throughout the country and eventually the world. Merseyside in particular seemed to be in a state of ecstasy."
>
> *(Bill Harry, p.14)*

Certainly, the civic receptions that they received can have only been equalled by Liverpool FC and Everton FC 'mania', VE day, VJ day and the like; these are spectacles of civic bonhomie, idolatrous in their welcoming home of the conquering heroes, the explicitly popular, *local* heroes. A more speculative, even more injudicious approach to 'Beatlemania' is to be found in the Phoebus *Story of Pop* account: 'The Beatle Story' edited by Jeremy Pascall (1974).

> "To catalogue Beatlemania exactly for anyone who wasn't there would be impossible. Even the

memory is pale in comparison with reality, and if it happened again now, it would still amaze everyone all over again. Spend a day looking through newspaper files, watch a week of news films, read a dozen of the thousands of books they inspired and you won't begin to know the half of what it was like. Travel back in time and live in the midst of it and it's a trip into bedlam. Not just a few screaming girls, but the whole world seemingly gone mad."

(p.16)

So the past is closed to us? The process of historical analysis cannot offer us any hope - or insight? I hope, then, to have proved that view to be incorrect. But if we look at 'Mania', what do we have here? My dictionary tells me the following: *Mania: 1. Mental derangement marked by excitement, hallucination and violence. 2. Excessive enthusiasm.*

It is true that many people became enthusiastic about The Beatles' music and persona. Much of that attachment might have 'gone over the top' and landed the devotees in hospital, in the clink or kept at home. Many of those who idolised The Beatles screamed themselves hoarse, cried, wet themselves or masturbated in their excitement. However, it is clear that one of the interesting characteristics of The Beatles as a rock band was their appeal to both sexes. Most contemporary accounts of 'Beatlemania' are levelled at hysterical girls. This, even if it were a relative truth, was hardly the whole picture. Many boys became excited by The Beatles; perhaps they even identified with the (musical) success of the band, and then looked to replicate that side of the phenomenon in their own musical enterprises.

I do not feel happy to consign the enthusiasm (even love) for The Beatles to the psycho-physiological. I am not convinced that the career of The Beatles caused a degree of violence that was even over and above the typical 'breaking out' behaviour of the young at that time.

Indeed, to suggest that the 'Beatlemania' phenomenon, located by conventional wisdom in the 1963-67 period, is a major contradiction in the respect of 'violence'.

The rock career of The Beatles, before the change of direction in 1962, initiated by Epstein, was - typically enough - bordering on the aggressive and vicariously violent in its mode. The image of The Beatles, in their pre-1962 days, especially their Hamburg activities, is well in line with what George Melly identified as the central characteristics of Rock and Roll, music and practice.

> "Rock, initially at any rate, was a contemporary incitement to mindless fucking and arbitrary vandalism; screw and smash music. To us in the jazz world it seemed a meaningless simplification of the blues with all the poetry removed and the emphasis on white, and by definition, inferior performers. Fats Domino or Little Richard we could, with reservations, accept, even Presley, in his earlier records, showed some feeling for the blues, but Bill Haley was a source of mystified repulsion. Why should anyone prefer this unsubtle, unswinging, uncoloured music to the real thing?
>
> What we failed to recognise was that the whole point of Rock 'n' Roll depended on its lack of subtlety. It was music to be used rather than listened to: a banner to be waved in the face of 'them' by a group who felt themselves ignored or victimised."

> *(George Melly, 'Revolt into Style', p.36)*

Shades of folk devils and moral panics!

However, even here, with Melly, we have partial truth. He both underestimates Rock 'n' Roll and overstates the conscious 'revolt' of performers and audience alike. Did The Beatles feel ignored or victimised? Did I? Did you? I don't think so, to the extent that we could isolate such factors in a sense of causal alchemy.

I would suggest that most of 'us' got 'pissed off' with school, home, parents, peers, adults in general, jobs, employers, *etc.* from time to time. But this was part of our cultural environment, whether we consciously realised the structures permeating our lives or not. It was not something 'tacked-onto' the outside of our existence. It was, in a very real way, central to it in other ways and under other, mediated, conditions. The use of music - Skiffle, Rock, Beat, *etc.*, - to express ourselves was part of a complex cultural process, not a simple adoption of a 'new suit of clothes', at the behest of a new idol, or entrepreneur. This is not to underestimate the enormous stylistic influence that The Beatles had from 1962-3. Bill Harry reminds us of that in terms of Liverpool in 1963:

> "The entire city was Beatle-mad. All the clothing stores had window dummies holding guitars, Beatle pictures and posters were on display by the thousand and the range of Beatle merchandise included Beatle boots, Beatle wallpaper, Beatle caps, Beatle mugs and Beatle cakes. The latter were produced by a local confectionery firm, Sayers."
>
> *(Bill Harry, p.15)*

Despite such influences, we are not looking at a simple or vulgar notion of production and consumption here. Firstly, because within capitalist relations, such 'simple' relations do not exist. Secondly, because it is absolutely necessary to reinforce the conviction that an arrangement of cultural values and practices has to have been created before it is possible for such events, phenomenon, to come about. The selling of Beatles cakes, like the emergence of Rock and Roll, is not something 'out of the blue'.

Before moving away from Bill Harry and Melly and Liverpool, in their terms, I would like to quote Melly to reconfirm an important point about clubs and the emergent (Merseyside) Rock and Roll culture and commercial exploitation:

> "Each successive pop music explosion has come roaring out of the clubs in which it was born like an angry young bull. Watching from the other side of the gate, the current Establishment has proclaimed it dangerous, subversive, a menace to youth and demanded something to be done about it. Something is. Commercial exploitation ad-

vances towards it holding out a bucketful of
recording contracts, television appearances and
worldwide fame. Then, once the muzzle is safely
buried in the golden mash, the cunning butcher
nips deftly along the flanks and castrates the
animal. After this painless operation, the Establishment realises it is safe to advance into the
field and gingerly pats the now docile creature
which can then be safely relied upon to grow
fatter and stupider until the moment when
fashion decides it is ready for the slaughter house
…I don't mean to suggest that there has ever
been a conscious arrangement drawn up between
the Establishment and the entrepreneurs of pop.
It is simply that their interests happen to
coincide.

The Establishment wants order. The entrepreneurs want money and the way to make most
money out of pop is to preserve at least a
semblance of order."

(George Melly, p.39)

Melly's long metaphor is very attractive and very nearly right.
But, methinks, the man doth protest too much! He allows, quite
understandably, his relations with 'The Establishment' and the
entrepreneurs to cast a very deterministic tone over the proceeding
of commercial exploitation and an ideological formulation and
incorporation of 'pop'. It is too easy to represent a stereotype of
The Establishment, distanced but in touch, and the Entrepreneurs,
in touch but distanced. It is a sociological truism that post-War
popular music, and the resultant artefacts of that emergent culture,
have been commercially *and* politically exploited to suit powerful
minorities in society while offering ephemeral pleasure and
involvement to the rest. It is true that the commercial and political
exploitation has been part of the relations of culture production
that existed before, during and after 'The Beatles phenomenon' as
such. It is true that 'what happened' to The Beatles and their
contemporaries looked straight-forward, commonsense and unproblematic in that it maintained the illusion, created ideologically

and *recreated* time and again through a replication of such cultural processes as exploitation and incorporation, that this was the natural way in which things happened. It seems to me, that we need to locate our discussion of exploitation in a two-sided way, in what Marx sees as the distinction between 'phenomenal forms', the surface forms of everyday life, and the 'real relations', those underlying processes, which need to be understood to explain the superficial forms. Marx raises this throughout *Capita*. For example, in the section on 'The Sale and Purchase of Labour-Power':

> "The secret of profit-making must at last be laid bare.
>
> The sphere of circulation or commodity exchange, within whose boundaries the sale and purchase of labour-power goes on, is in fact a very Eden of the innate rights of man. It is the exclusive realm of Freedom, Equality, Property and Bentham. Freedom because both buyer and seller of a commodity, let us say of labour-power, are determined only by their own free will. They contact as free persons, who are equal before the law...Equality because each enters into relation with the other, as with a simple owner of commodities and they exchange equivalent for equivalent. Property, because each disposes only of what is his own. And Bentham, because each looks only to his own advantage. The only force bringing them together, and putting them into relation with each other, is the selfishness, the gain and the private interest of each. Each pays heed to himself only, and no one worries about the others. And precisely for that reason, either in accordance with the pre-established harmony of things, or under the auspices of an omniscient providence, they all work together to their mutual advantage, for the common weal, and in the common interest.

179

When we leave this sphere of simple circulation or the exchange of commodities, which provides the 'free-trader *vulgaris*' with his views, his concepts and the standard by which he judges the society of capital and wage-labour, a certain change takes place, or so it appears on the physiognomy of our *dramatis personae*. He who was previously the money-owner now strides out in front as a capitalist; the possessor of labour power follows as his worker. The one smirks self-importantly and is intent on business, the other is timid and holds back, like someone who has brought his own hide to market and now has nothing else to expect but - a tanning!"

(Marx Capital Vol.1, Pelican edition 1976,
p.280)

What I would want to emphasise in relation to The Beatles phenomenon is the way in which the exploitation ran very deep indeed, and yet, at the same time, was there on the surface of everyday life. One such example was the calculated replacement of drummer Pete Best by Ringo in August 1962. *Mersey Beat* covered the story when it first emerged:

Mersey Beat Exclusive Story: The Beatles change drummer!

Ringo Starr (former drummer with Rory Storm and the Hurricanes) has joined The Beatles, replacing Pete Best on drums. Ringo has admired The Beatles for years and is delighted with his new engagement. Naturally he is tremendously excited about the future. The Beatles comment, 'Pete left the group by mutual agreement. There were no arguments or difficulties and this has been an entirely amicable decision.'

On Tuesday, September 4th, The Beatles will fly to London to make recordings at EMI Studios.

> They will be recording numbers that have been specially written for the group, which they have received from their recording manager George Martin (Parlophone)."
>
> *(Bill Harry, p.36)*

The move of Ringo seriously undermined Rory Storm. Pete Best moved to 'Lee Curtis and the All Stars' and into oblivion. Epstein and Martin convinced Lennon, McCartney and Harrison that Best had to be replaced; for the very best 'production' motives, of course.

Later in the year, Bill Harry wrote an article in *Mersey Beat* - *'The Rat Race'* *('Mersey Beat' Vol.2, No.35, Nov 29-Dec 13 1962)*:

> "They no longer called Liverpool 'The Rocking City'. Her reputation as a leading, lively, happy centre of Rock and Roll has been smeared. Stained by gossips and rumour-mongers, acid tongues which would put backyard muck-spreaders to shame.
>
> FORGET 'THE ROCKING CITY' - THE NAME IS NOW THE RAT RACE...
>
> Who are the casualties in this Rat Race? Well, people are saying that new groups aren't getting the breaks they used to. Others say that the scene is becoming a closed shop - in which only the top groups are getting the breaks. . .Johnnie Sandon hinted at it in a recent 'Meet the Singer' article in which he stated: 'The friendliness and com-radeship between different groups seems to have lessened. . .Members of different groups used to meet quite frequently in certain Liverpool pubs and have a laugh and a drink together. . .All that seems to have gone. . .'
>
> '...Too many groups are deliberately spreading rumours to cause dissention among groups in

competition with themselves . . .for their own personal gain. This does not only apply to groups, but to drivers, managers, promoters in general.' - Jim Turner, Manager, The Odd Spot Club.

'Some groups are like puppets - they should change their names to the 'pawns'. - Bob Wooler, Compere."

(Bill Harry, p.48)

In later years, John Lennon was to reflect upon the way he had become sanitised and exploited and had, at one and the same time, been encouraged to take part in furtherance of the process of exploitation.

"We're a con as well . . .we know we're conning them, because we know people want to be conned. . .They've given us the freedom to con them. Let's 'stick that in there,' we say, 'that'll start them puzzling.' "

(Lennon quoted in 'Rolling Stone', No.20, 26-10-68, p.18)

And again, after the break-up of the band, and the corporate image was finally shattered:

"We all dressed up, the same bastards are in control, the same people are runnin' everything. It is exactly the same. We've grown up a little, all of us, there has been a change and we're a bit freer and all that, but it's the same game."

(Lennon quoted in 'Rolling Stone' 4-2-71)

True to form, people did start puzzling from 1963 onwards. The educationists, the music critics, the pundit and intellectuals all started to scratch their 'egg-heads'. Huge assumptions have been made about the motivation behind arrangements and lyrics.

Competition was keen to import the definitive meaning into the songs of Lennon and McCartney and the role of The Beatles in society. Pop idols were increasingly placed among the hierarchy of society; despite small falls from grace here and there, the liberal-bourgeois elite and political opportunists in the Establishment were det-ermined to 'absorb' the new heroes.

I can remember well the televised spectacle of Mick Jagger (who had recently been remanded for a drugs offence) arriving in the grounds of a country house by helicopter. He was dressed in a white suit and walked across the spacious lawns to join in discussion, three - or was it four? - eminent members of our society. There was a Bishop, the Editor of *The Times*, and some other illustrious types whose faces slip my memory. It was truly an awe-inspiring spectacle. Jagger must have laughed all the way back to his Rolls Royce.

The Beatles have all said that they just wanted to be Rock and Rollers, but, because of the external forces exerted on them, they turned out to be 'Marks and Spencers'. In later years, the capitalisation into Apple seems to have been their final blunder. The problems got bigger than the pay-offs. "Let me tell you how it will be/There's one for you, nineteen for me", *etc.* (George Harrison 'Taxman', Revolver LP)

After 1963-4, the 'exploitation' took on some paradoxical forms. Rock and pop culture was taking on some flesh. The painters, poets, *etc.* of the post-War rock generation were carving a niche for themselves. They have the musicians to thank for opening that particular door. Ironically enough, the limelight created by the essentially working class bands fell kindly on many middle class 'artists' of one kind or another. Their work was prepared and progressed under the same umbrella. Rock culture was an emergent culture that was potentially a liberating force personally and sometimes even colle-ctively.

Songwriters became important, illustrators became important, people diversified, all manner of people became hippie-philosopher-poets. The big divide was not so much between youth and youth culture, but between Us and Them; not simply a generation gap, more of a lifestyle and values gap to a great extent. This quest, this tournament between the 'light and dark forces' of our society, as seen through rock culture's eyes, runs through much of Lennon's work. The film interpretation of this concept, in

Yellow Submarine and, less acutely, in *Magical Mystery Tour* unified many of the Homeric idyll aspects of this tendency. Without over stressing this point, it is relevant to the development of the, The Age of Aquarius idea and the expression of a new enlightened age of love, peace and inner harmony. It marks an important level of consciousness in the rock culture of the mid to late-1960s. "Without going out of my door/I can know all things on earth", *etc.* (George Harrison, 'The Inner Light'.)

Lennon's deliberate, openly self-conscious protestations of his overt political development followed on from his demands for world peace through music. The 'musical revolution' was at hand, at least in the minds of many writers and performers and carriers in the culture. There was nothing that could not be done, if the machinery was first oiled with love. Love, love, love; all you need is love.

So, having made this chronological digression to make a point about ideological commitment in the process of certain signifying practices, I would like to return to the 1962/63 period for a moment.

Many writers of 'pop history' in the post-War years in Britain have confirmed that the initial phase of American-led Rock and Roll had gone flat - as early as 1957. George Melly (in *Revolt into Style*, for example) argues that, between 1957 and 1961, the charts reflected this flatness. The first 'Rock 'n' Roll generation' had hung up their 78s and bootlaces, got married, and moved onto other things, *etc.* Ian Whitcomb in *After the Ball* (1972) makes a number of references to this period directly relevant to the discussion of entrepreneurial activity in rock and pop exploitation. Particularly interesting are Whitcomb's comments on one of the most important 'front men' of late-1950s rock and pop, Jack Good. In many ways, Good represented both the best and the worst elements of emergent British, albeit London-based, Rock and Pop in the mid- to late-1950s. Good was an arch manipulator of style and form. He took budding young rock performers and created, from their brash naivety, a brand of British Rock and Roller, that, although highly parochial, did open many hearts, eyes, doors and, in less good taste, thighs.

Good was involved in the BBC's first attempt to put order into Rock, namely '6.5 Special' (which ran from February 1957) and, although it may now look very tame, it created an enormous impact on its Saturday tea-time audience. Good was responsible for most of the precocious developments and went out into the coffee bars and clubs (of London in the main) to 'grab talent' - Wilde, Faith, Joe Brown, *etc.* He turned local 'hillbillies', like Harry Webb into Cliff Richard, all drooling epigone of 'Elvis the Pelvis'. He also brought in 'big name' stars from the USA to give the show an authentic, time-served feel about it.

Eventually, Good became cramped by the BBC and moved over to commercial television to produce 'Oh Boy!' (from August 1957) and quickly won audiences away from '6.5 Special'. Good went on to produce 'Boy Meets Girl and 'Wham!' among other ventures. By 1962, Good had tired of the British (London) scene and gone to America. It is worth mentioning, in passing, that in 1958 Jack Good and Larry Parnes (Marty Wilde's manager, and an aspect of The Beatles' development) were always 'falling out'. In late-1958, it was over competition between Marty Wilde and Cliff Richard on 'Oh Boy!'. However, in early 1959, Good and Parnes made up their quarrel and Marty Wilde returned to 'Oh Boy!' after 'appearing' in the Robin Hood panto at the Hippodrome, Stockton! (I mention this here because of Parnes' and Wilde's later association with The Beatles.)

Earlier in this section of my study I raised what is, to me at least, a fundamentally important question: namely, how did The Beatles establish themselves so firmly and so dramatically in such a short period of time, between mid-1962 and early-1964? In that period of time, they moved from obscurity to being top Liverpool/Merseyside band to being top band in *Britain* and, eventually, to *top band in the world.*

I feel that one of the crucial factors in this phenomenon is their saturation of the domestic popular music scene in 1963. It is worth reminding ourselves of such events in their career (*see table over*).

Nothing on this scale had been seen in Britain since the impact of Buddy Holly at the end of the 1950s.

Also during that year, their 'personal' appearance took on a different dimension. In May 1963, they topped the bill on a national tour for the first time, with Gerry and the Pacemakers and Ray Orbison in support.

In October 1963, they appeared on 'Sunday Night at the London Palladium'.

12-1-63	'Please Please Me'	Single released. Becomes their first Number One.
11-4-63	'From Me To You'	Single released. Number One.
Also in April	'Please Please Me'	Long Player record. Number One.
23-8-63	'She Loves You'	Single released. Number One.
Sept. 63	'The Beatles Hits'	Extended Play released

[Includes: From Me To You, Thank You Girl,
Please Please Me, Love Me Do]

| Also Sept. 63 | 'Twist and Shout' | Extended Play released |

[Twist and Shout, A Taste of Honey, Do You Want to
Know a Secret?, There's a Place]

| 29-11-63 | 'I Want to Hold Your Hand' | Single released. Number One. |

(First major success in USA)

| Also Nov. 63 | 'The Beatles No. 1' | Extended Play released |

(I Saw Her Standing There, Misery, Anna, Chains)

| Also Nov. 63 | 'With The Beatles' | Long Player released |

In November 1963, they appeared on 'The Royal Command Performance'.

In December 1963, they made up the 'jury' for BBC's 'Juke Box Jury'.

In December 1963 into January, their first Christmas Show (in London, of course).

Also during February 1963, Northern Songs Ltd. was launched as The Beatles' private song publishers, which went public in 1965 (for a fuller view of The Beatles' portfolio: see *The Observer* Colour Supplement of 1-9-68).

Additionally during 1963, The Beatles became established securely in the Popular Music Press in particular, and in the National Press in general. As 1963 progressed, the tone of the reception of The Beatles becomes more and more idolatrous.

One of the more interesting facets of The Beatles hit parade records of 1962-63 is their continual reference to, centrality of, love and sexual relations. Were these words and titles spontaneous? Were they carefully engineered to both reflect and replicate what seemed to be the pervasive concerns of youth? Youthful 'careers' and preoccupations are 'captured' and played back via - 'Love Me Do', 'Please Please Me', 'I'll Get You In The End', 'She Loves You', 'From Me to You', 'Thank You Girl', 'I Want to Hold Your Hand', *etc.*

I would contend that a great deal of blood, sweat and tears was put into 1963; not just by The Beatles of course, but by a growing corps of PR men, A & R men, front men, backroom men, agents, road managers, DJs, journalists, and so on, and so forth. The result was a massive campaign to first establish The Beatles on a secure foundation, and then to build layer upon layer of the popular image.

The reality of private everyday life for The Beatles often contrasts very sharply with the public persona. I want to explore some of that area.

Before I do that, though, I would mention Michael Braun's account of some events in 1963. On a trip to Liverpool with The Beatles, Braun, a journalist, meets and eats with Epstein. Epstein is reported as even then (1963) reflecting on the commercial pressures:

"He said he was having trouble with people who
were using the word 'Beatle' on their products.
... 'We have the copyright, but they always try to
get round it by showing a beetle or by using the
word Beetle.' "

*(Michael Braun 'Love Me Do - The Beatles
Progress', 1964)*

In the early part of his book, Braun confirms the significance of
1963 in The Beatles' career:

"On the drive back to London they listen to the
Top Pops on Radio Luxembourg. 'And now,'
says the radio, 'You've guessed it. The Beatles -
I Want To Hold Your Hand.'

'They wanted to know if we were slipping,' says
George to their recording manager, George
Martin, who is accompanying them, 'just because there was only 400 fans outside instead of
1000.'

Eight of the Top Twenty songs that week were
Beatle numbers.

'They asked me if I was crackin' up,' says Paul,
'Crackin' up? They must be soft....'

Over the radio, Dora Bryan sings the week's
number twelve song, 'All I want for Christmas is
a Beatle.'

The Beatles spent the last week of the year
preparing for their show at Finsbury Park. One
hundred thousand people had bought tickets
before the first curtain rose. In celebration, the
London Evening Standard put out a special
supplement headed: '1963: the Year of The
Beatles'. Under their picture, it said: '1963 has

been their year. An examination of the heart of the nation at this moment would reveal the word BEATLE engraved on it . . .'

Under the heading: 'Why we do Love them so much: Because. . .Because. . .Because...' columnist Angus McGill said that, 'like well-bred children, they are seen and not heard.' The paper's pop music writer, a usually acute young woman called Maureen Cleave, could only conclude, 'Everybody loves them because they look so happy.' "

(Michael Braun, p.64/65)

As Braun and others reflect, the general tone of response to 1963 was equally banal and mystifying. Far from attempting to analyse why it was that The Beatles were so very popular, the mainstream media coverage was a confirmation of the 'beyond the need to ask why' status. An amazing conventional wisdom overcame the media, DJs, politicians, and the like: that The Beatles were undoubtedly the greatest, they were British, they were consensus politics, they were an epitome of the open society. There were, of course, some sharp reactions to this, for example, that of Paul Johnson in 1964, which I have already mentioned. I'm sure Johnson spoke for a silent majority who saw The Beatles as low status and high risk, rather than the high status and low risk posture adopted in so many quarters.

The year 1963 consolidated and confirmed the entrepreneurial arrangements for the proliferation of popular (and particularly youth-orientated) music in Britain. The 'ringing of cash registers' followed The Beatles increasingly throughout 1963. (Talking of shopkeepers, it is worth drawing a comparison over time with Epstein and McLaren - of Sex Pistols fame - both shopkeepers with very useful merchandise on their shelves?).

If we want to seek out why The Beatles were *so* successful, it would be injudicious of us not to reflect upon the prospect in all quarters of a great deal of money being created out of a new boom in the pop music and artefact industries, at a time when some of the golden calves of the 1950s were tarnished and going lame. John Heilpern (in an article on Epstein in *The Observer* Colour

Supplement on 1-9-68) suggested that Epstein had signed up a considerable number of Merseyside bands and solo singers as a means of 'keeping the pot boiling'.

Let me now turn to a key witness to the events of The Beatles phenomenon, Cynthia Lennon. In her book, *A Twist of Lennon*, she offers her own version of 'life with the lions' from the earlier times up to the Yoko Ono era of the late-1960s. The 'Lennons' met during their student days at Liverpool Art College, and were married in August 1962. Cynthia gives an interesting insight into the pre-1962 development of The Beatles, focusing particularly on the hard times they shared. Although Cynthia Lennon came from a fairly respectable background, like Lennon, McCartney and Co., she found herself increasingly involved in the seamier margins of Merseyside's clubland, drawn in, and along by, the musical obsessions of her husband to be. One of the most fascinating aspects of this saga is the degree of sincerity that she puts into the account of her day-by-day involvement and participation in just about everything that was going on in the early-60s career of The Beatles. Fascinating, because, in Allan Williams' account of the same period (Allan Williams and William Marshall *The Man who Gave The Beatles Away* (1975), she is (effectively) *never* mentioned. Allan Williams comes in for plenty of coverage by Cynthia Lennon, though, and one can only speculate as to the exclusion of her from Williams' account. If Cynthia Lennon is right, and she was there, Williams' effective removal of her from his 'picture' and 'history' is comparable in its way to the removal from 'history' of Leon Trotsky and other leading Bolsheviks by Stalin and his associates.

Most of Cynthia Lennon's story is of charming domestic detail, life and love with Mr Lennon. However, now and again, the outside world is allowed to penetrate the narrative. In the winter of 1962-63, she observes of the intrigue:

> "While the boys were becoming more and more of an obsession with the British record-buying public, I had been very delicately advised that it would be wise to keep a very low profile. It would be to everyone's advantage if the marriage to one of The Beatles was kept a secret. I must admit, I didn't relish the thought of publicity."

(Cynthia Lennon, 'A Twist of Lennon', 1978,
p.81/82)

And again, in early 1963:

> " 'Please Please Me' was a Number One hit, a
> phenomenal success. The Beatles were on the
> crest of a wave. Publicity photographs were
> taken of the four, fresh-faced young innocents,
> grinning with embarrassment. It must have been
> embarrassing for John to grin. The mean and
> moody was out and the wholesome boy-next-
> door image was fast taking over, much against
> the grain with all of them. Professionalism was
> the name of the game and the stakes were high. "

(Cynthia Lennon, pp.82/83)

In her account, then, Cynthia confirms the conventional wisdom
that The Beatles were *managed* to acceptance and pop success.
Part of that success was the pressure to move to London. Lennon
and wife rented an apartment in Kensington. Cynthia Lennon
describes how she was delighted at spending with no limitations:

> "I found the transition from the quiet life that I
> had been used to, to a world brimming over with
> exhilarating speed, excitement and interesting
> characters very much to my liking…Money was
> really flowing into the coffers by this time with
> two hit songs already chalked up and one more
> in the pipeline. They were really big business."

(Cynthia Lennon, p.95)

If *she* did write this, and she meant it to come over as it does in all
its commonsense banality, then a good few Beatles' devotees
would have many an illusion shattered. Was it really like *this*?
Was the greatest Rock and Roll quartet of all time spending 1963,
their first year of success, like this?

One of the ever-present themes in this part of Cynthia Lennon's account of 1963-4 is the Lennon's relation with fans, especially the doorstep variety. She is far from complimentary in response to fans, in themselves exploring The Beatles phenomenon.

> ". . .[It was] when the fans found out our whereabouts that life became unbearable. We were trapped like caged animals. Girls of every shape, size, colour, creed and nationality would sit on the steps of the building in all weathers, clutching autograph books in their hands...Every time John or I ventured out we were pounced on. The screaming hysteria would deafen us, hands would grab, stretch out and touch, pull at our clothes."

> *(Cynthia Lennon, p.96)*

Harrison, McCartney and Starr had moved into Knightsbridge with Epstein, and were apparently experiencing similar difficulties.

> "George, Paul and Ringo were also having fan problems and in such a high-class area it just wasn't on. The neighbours were paying a great deal for the privilege of living in Knightsbridge and were not going to put up with the scruff of the land camping outside their property."

> *(Cynthia Lennon, p.98)*

These few extracts epitomise a view that is generally expressed in Cynthia Lennon's book as elsewhere: the process whereby rock and pop 'artists' and their associates become enmeshed in the commercial nexus of everyday economic relations in a society like Britain. However, the process of this phenomenon is expressed in a commonsense and unproblematic way, in a way that suggests the process is *natural* and not, in fact, to do with the complicated, now exposed, now hidden, explicit and implicit relations that give the phenomenon its form.

Cynthia Lennon's account, like many others, does not go beyond the 'face value' of the process of cultural production. I have attempted, in this study, to underline what seems to me to be crucial in understanding the way in which a *commercial* phenomenon, like The Beatles, could (and can) come about.

Meanings placed upon products (in this case The Beatles musical product) are not *only* a cultural form; they are also crucially important in the process of providing a suitable market for the continued production of commodities to take place. The Beatles' *artistic* success is part of a larger, intrusive, system of financial mechanisms, which we might, for convenience, call capitalist relations. The success of The Beatles *per se* was accidental, perhaps; the fact that their success took the form and direction it did could hardly be held to be accidental. The development of popular music in the western world since the mid-1960s has followed a similar pattern because of the complex network, indeed matrix, which makes up the commercial exp-loitation of artistic products in such a society. I would stress, therefore, that the *conditions* for The Beatles'commercial success predated and post-dates them.

An aspect of this phenomenon is contained in Allan Williams' account of the early years of The Beatles. The very title of Williams' and Marshall's book *The Man Who Gave The Beatles Away* is an indication of the commodity status of The Beatles corporate, and exploitive, entity. This issue is touched on throughout the book. For example, in Williams' story of The Beatles when they were contracted to work in Hamburg. He recounts a discussion with Brian Epstein that led to managerial 'interest' in The Beatles being transferred from the somewhat bitter Williams to the optimistic Epstein. This particular account is, of course, the moment on which the whole point of the book turns.

> ". . .I had to tell him what had happened between The Beatles and me if he was this serious.
>
> 'Well, Brian, be bloody careful. Look what they did to me in Hamburg. They wouldn't pay my commission, a lousy fifteen quid a week. Me, after all I'd done for them. They wouldn't have been anywhere without me.'

I called them a few choice names. Brian winced visibly.

'Okay, Allan, should I take them over or not? Your honest opinion?'

'My honest opinion, Brian, is this: don't touch them with a fucking bargepole.'

'Do you still want to be associated with them?' asked Brian.

'No, thanks. Anyone can have them as far as I am concerned.'

There, I'd one it. Cut the mental bonds. They had been under exclusive contract to me. Now I was saying to Brian, and anyone else, to do what the hell they wanted about it. Take The Beatles and good luck. Yes, if you like, I was giving them away. . ."

> *(Allan Williams and William Marshall,*
> *'The Man who gave The Beatles Away',*
> *p.212/213)*

One of the interesting aspects of The Beatles phenomenon commercial nexus is the increasing tendency towards 'corporatisation'. In a sense this 'came to a head' and was epitomised by the events around the shift from Nems Enterprises (Epstein's original company) to Apple. After Brian Epstein's death, Clive Epstein took over at Nems, but he eventually gave way to Stigwood. The relation of Nems to Apple, and both to The Beatles, took a distinctively sour turn in 1969 when Allen Klein and New York solicitors Eastman and Eastman took hold of matters at Apple. There seems little doubt that The Beatles very own company was in a perilous state. From a narrow commercial point of view, *i.e.* taking into consideration all the conventional wisdoms of how to run a business, Apple was anarchic and on the verge of collapse. . .

However, McCartney upset The Beatles 'apple cart' by his association with the Eastmans, and particularly with Linda Eastman, daughter of Eastman senior. Apparently, McCartney had suggested that the Eastman company take a greater share of control in The Beatles' affairs, let alone in Apple. It seems that Lennon had misgivings; and, since he was personally heavily committed elsewhere, he was not so much in touch with McCartney and Co. Lennon was outraged when he discovered that, without telling the others, McCartney had heavily invested in Northern Songs' shares.

Lennon in particular thought that McCartney had acted independently and in bad faith for the first time. Relations between them, financially and otherwise, were never the same again.

When we look at the reality of that time, it seems naïve of Lennon to have assumed that they would not come to see matters in different ways. Lennon and McCartney had long since stopped writing songs as a team, and their interests and affairs had grown dramatically apart since the 1966-67 days.

Whatever the details of who said what and what was expected by the individuals concerned, it is clear that The Beatles found themselves divided by money interests. It would be injudicious to say dogmatically (à la Marx) that, 'All relations were reduced to cash relations', but after the events of early 1969, the writing was on the wall. The artistic achievement of The Beatles, their close personal and professional relation over many years was, after all, only one aspect of The Beatles phenomenon. It would be naïve to suggest that they could have lived and worked through that period without some serious consideration being given to financial relations. Perhaps they collectively felt that money matters were not that important. Maybe they still identified themselves with times when either they had no money, or when such concerns were taken out of their hands by Brian Epstein and Nems?

Their differences over financial control even affected their artistic production, for example, with the dispute over whether McCartney's solo album ('McCartney') should or should not be released at the same time as the 'Let It Be' album. In May 1971, the final split took place, The Beatles, as an on-going artistic venture, ceased to exist.

Later on, Lennon and McCartney talked with each other, but who knows if those old wounds were ever healed - or re-opened open from time to time?

Some bands of the 1960s era seemed to escape such horrendous internecine struggles, but there were precious few. I would suggest that this aspect of The Beatles phenomenon is not so surprising if we consider the general level of business ethics in British society and the exploitative music industry in particular (which surrounds such artists).

In passing, I would also observe here how so many rock musicians of the 1960s era met with an early death. Many died at their own hands, or in circumstances that were largely attributable to their lifestyle and *milieu*. I have often reflected that, on looking back at the mid-1960s in particular, I am surprised that Lennon survived.[1] With his background of emotional upheavals, and his personality, he always seemed to me to be a likely candidate for the growing list of dead heroes (Janice, Jim, Jimmi, *et al*). Perhaps he was fortunate in being able to use his music as a conduit, over a very painful period in the late-1960s and early-1970s, to work through the problems associated with his very unusual situation.

Before passing onto other matters, I would like to return to the question raised on the creation and production of an image that is then related to the continued commercial production of that commodity. Very briefly, I am struck by three examples of this phenomenon and quite an arbitrary choice. *First*: my daughter once insisted upon having 'Muppet Talc' bought for her. The meaning she placed upon *this* product was clearly crucial in her judgement and association. *Second:* people buying a new car are often told, in effect, that 'This is not a car for Mr & Mrs Average.' Is this a mere sales gimmick, or does it rest within a cultural context that is highly significant in the way we view and consume products? *Third:* the advert for milk that juxtaposes two young persons, late teens or early twenties, of opposite sexes, one black and one white. Now, am I merely being told that milk is fun, or that milk is good for me? Clearly not. This kind of advert is not only using race relations and youth as a way of selling milk; it is making a social and cultural point that is clearly, to me at least, ideological.

---

[1] Eerie to read this now that we know of Lennon's eventual demise at the hands of Mark Chapman in 1980 (*after* this text was first produced).
- *Ed.*

Are these examples such a long way from Rock and Roll? A long way from The Beatles phenomenon? I think not. The culturally created meanings placed upon such production and products is part and parcel of our notions of consumption, personal freedom, private property, status, power, *etc.* This is then, I would argue, ideology at work. It may not be explicit most of the time. Nor may it be as clearly ideological as the overt signifying practise of so much of mid- to late-60s Rock.

I would add here that we do have a methodological problem in addressing ourselves to *such* cultural studies as I have outlined above. Sociology, as such, does encompass a great deal, but even so, the essence of many real problems in the analysis of cultural production and reproduction may continue to be very diffuse. It is not only the Dewey library system that often, so it seems, arbitrarily sectionalises bodies of knowledge.

Go into any large-ish bookshop organised for the academic and your own epistemological eclecticism might well be offended by the way the books are categorised and allocated to the shelves. You may feel, as I often do, with what odd bed-fellows books offering a sociological analysis of culture are to be found; 'Sociology', 'Literature', 'Literary Criticism', 'Anthropology', 'Social History', *etc.*

The problem of location of the studies of culture (and perhaps even more concretely, Cultural Studies) is central to many of the difficulties I feel we face. The problem, however, is not one of mere practice, it is also, essentially, one of theory.

The very way in which we might organise our studies, use the language we do, is, in the context I have outlined above, ideological. Certainly we have difficulties in our analysis of the complex cultural processes that go to make up The Beatles phenomenon, say. I would say, from my own studies of popular cultural phenomenon, that the more I move towards some answers, the more complex the issues become and the more questions that I come up with. This is not to offer a sloppy relativist context, but points to the complexity, over time and in space, of the cultural factors being considered.

In turning our attention to the nature of ideology as discussed in this chapter, it is worth using a concrete example of the phenomenon, in this case, the way in which significant cultural meanings have been invested with the idea of *freedom*.

One of the dominant themes of the 1960s' Rock and Roll musical culture is that of freedom. Freedom from what and from whom is not always explicit or well defined, or consistently and logically argued. However, the theme, the nuance, is strong and characteristic. Lennon, particularly of all The Beatles, epitomises the tendency to raise questions about freedom within his work. In the early-1960s, the issue is dealt with, blatantly, in terms of boy and girl socio-sexual relations. In the process of creating their version of the 1960s, Lennon, especially, sharpens his critical faculties on the issues of the day. By the 1967-68 stage, Lennon is overtly politically motivated in his artistic and private 'career'. This emphasis is notable from the production of the 'Revolver' album (1966) period onwards. The Beatles were able to play a part in the creation of that aspect of the emergent culture. They also fed from that culture and, in their different ways, exploiting their own freedom and constantly adjusting their position within everyday social life.

The American experience in the post-1966 period of Rock and Roll is particularly exciting and complicated. Exciting in that the rock writers and musicians, *etc.*, increasingly felt the need, freedom and opportunity to address themselves to political questions in their private and public lives. They also found an audience that was sharing this process demanding and receptive. It was complicated because the production of an 'Underground' and/or 'Progressive' rock culture was full of contradictions.

These contradictions manifested themselves in terms of the ontological and sociological dimensions of the phenomenon. Something we might expect within society and culture that is so heavily imbued with notions of individuality and private property on the one hand, and collectivism in the face of problems of organisation of everyday life on the other. More fundamentally, perhaps, the contradictions manifested themselves in terms of the ability of even the rich and famous, The Beatles *et al*, to *escape* the cultural strictures of their epoch.

We have here a central problem and concern in the discussion of ideology that I offer in this study. How, in fact, do we relate the questions of material existence, conditions of and for everyday life (for example, as elaborated in the chapter on post-War Liverpool) to the level of understanding, awareness, action and consciousness expressed as The Beatles? Eve Brook and Dan Finn addressed themselves to a complementary concern in an essay published in 'Working Papers in Cultural Studies', No.10, 1977 (Centre for Contemporary Cultural Studies):

> "...material conditions, of course, exist at the level of everyday class experiences and class practices. These experiences and practices differ, not only between classes, but also within them - generating occupational or local class fractions. Thus, it is not only ruling class ideas that are put to the test in working class experience, but just as importantly, we would suggest, class practice generates its own kind of consciousness and culture. Thus the contradictory nature of working class consciousness reflects the difference between the real experience of capitalist production and the phenomenal forms of the market, reflected in the superstructure. The collective, lived experience of capitalist production, gives alternative sets of practices and organisations em-bodied in working class structure."
>
> *(p.128).*

I have already dwelt on this problematic in the chapter on Society and Culture. If, for example (and the choice is arbitrary) I take the film *Easy Rider*, I can illustrate some concerns. The film, made by Dennis Hopper with Peter Fonda, was released in 1969 and made, in every respect, a great impact on its audiences. I remember seeing the film with a number of friends; the sense of distance from the precise American experiences, yet close association with the *feel* and concerns of the film, was lasting. Much of the music was already familiar, and yet, placed into the context of the 'morality tale', it assumed a different dimension. A logical coherence and collective, purposeful, intent, that emphasised their part in so many people's lives and consciousness, typified the songs.

If, say, we listen to Steppenwolf's 'Born to be Wild' or Hendrix's 'If Six was Nine', or Roger McGuinn's 'It's Alright Ma (I'm Only Bleeding)' and the 'Ballad of Easy Rider', we discern one dominant theme. This theme is also to be found in the work of

John Lennon, namely that there is a fundamental contradiction within the emergent political and politicised rock culture. A contradiction arises in the relation between the demands for personal freedom, demands for collective freedoms, and the constraints of the dominant and residual cultures on everyday life and social development. To me, the most significant consequence in this process was the way in which the awareness of these contradictions, the inherent *cultural* contradictions, imposed and impressed themselves upon people. Often the outcome was a pessimism that I feel is there in, say, *Easy Rider*. Despite this, however, there remained, indeed remains, a heartening optimism that, while increasingly sceptical, is not cynical. "How does it feel to be/One of the beautiful people? (Lennon and McCartney, 'Baby You're a Rich Man'. 1967)

In terms of cultural production in the 1960s, for The Beatles and for their contemporaries in rock, the very technology involved in their enterprises was important. I would suggest that a good deal of the 'freedom', illusory as much of it might have been, was due to the development of electronics in the 1960s, certain electronic music production, and recording technologies. Access to these technologies was possible for The Beatles. When we turn our attention to the impact of 'Sgt. Pepper', say, we can begin to see (and hear) the significance of the process through which that aspect of The Beatles phenomenon could be culturally produced and reproduced over time.

Many writers/critics of the mid- to late-1960s commented upon the interrelation between developing technologies and the 'musical' product. One such writer was Joan Peyser. Her essay 'The Music of Sound'; or, indeed, 'The Beatles and The Beatless' (to be found in *The Age of Rock* edited by Jonathan Eisen) is an interesting example. In her essay, she strives to give an historical account of the development of electronics in music:

> "The explosive electronics of the pop field has diverted attention from the fact that technology came to art music well before it came to rock. As early as 1922, the French-American composer, Edgard Varèse, declared that composer and electrician would have to labour together to produce new media of expression. Rejected by

musicians and critics alike during the thirties and forties, when accessibility of music was the keynote, Varèse's views began to gain recognition in the 1950s and American universities and European radio stations built well-equipped laboratories to experiment with electronic techniques in sound. This gave rise in Europe to the works of Pierre Boulez and Karlheiunz Stockhausen and in this country, to the construction of machines such as the RCA synthesizer, a complex, costly apparatus which generates its own sounds... "

(Eisen, p.128)

What Joan Peyser is emphasising in this respect is that the development of certain kinds of technologies creates a situation for innovation. What I would add is that - increasingly so through the 1950s and 1960s - musicians placed greater and greater demands upon the technologies at their disposal, thereby creating further innovations in the technology itself.

Peyser reminds us that, during the early-1960s, The Beatles considerably developed both their musical and music production knowledge. They learnt, increasingly, to understand *how* to do this and that, rather than 'just' *doing* this and that. This marked an important liberating side to their music. Peyser quotes McCartney on this:

"I used to think that anyone doing anything weird was weird. I suddenly realised that anyone doing anything weird wasn't weird at all and that it was the people saying that they were weird that were weird."

(Eisen, p.130)

The tautology is no doubt amusing, but what McCartney says does reflect a changing consciousness among The Beatles, *et al*. The more they produced within their expanding *milieu*, the more they came to test out the limits, the analytical framework if you like, of their musical theory and practice.

However, as Joan Peyser reminds us, we should not suggest that the technology took over:

> "Despite the careful handling of so many diverse musical tools, the legend of how Beatles music is made persists: Lennon whistles to McCartney and McCartney whistles back to Lennon. "
>
> *(Eisen, p.130)*

We need to be reminded that, as The Beatles progressed, they changed their recording habits. The early albums (long players), took something like twelve hours to record. 'Sgt. Pepper', on the other hand, occupied six months of The Beatles' lives, albeit not day after day. There was also a developing tradition of working in the studio from 7pm to 2am. The change in their approach might have been frustrated or ill-advised if The Beatles had not had the ready market for their products. George Harrison summed this up well enough:

> "There's much more going on in our minds. There are things past drums and guitars which we must do. In the last two years [1964/66] we've been in a good vantage point in as much as people are used to buying our records...we can do things that please us without conforming to the standard pop idea. We are not only involved in pop music, but all music and there are many things to be investigated."
>
> *(Quoted in Eisen, p.130)*

Joan Peyser reminds us, quite rightly, that the nature of electronic rock makes the performance of it crucial. It would be very difficult, to say the least, to capture the nuances of 'Sgt. Pepper', *etc.* on sheet music. What is immobilised on the tape and record is history in the making. However, we also need to remember that music, like all such 'artistic' signifying practices, is going to have created a reception for them. Not only is the production of the music a cultural and a social activity, its *reception* is likewise. And although there is a tendency away from the compositional tradition, inherent in-post Renaissance western music, towards an oral tradition, the development is not a linear one. Certainly rock has been part of, and instrumental in, the democratisation of artistic production. We can see this process elsewhere, and it reflects the changes that have, and have not, taken place, as well as legitimating the existence of notions about freedom and an open society.

There is more than a hint of political exploitation in The Beatles phenomenon as well. I have already touched on the way in which politicians of both major political parties, and both sides of the General Elections of 1964/66, attempted to use The Beatles phenomenon to their own advantage. There is a sense in which the success of The Beatles in particular, and the revitalised British pop business in general, epitomised the economic and political revival and optimism of the early 1960s. No doubt many people, even politicians, saw these successes, and so saw the value of youthful activities in this field in general (also thinking of fashion, design, arts in general, sport, *etc.*) as an aspect of post-War economic success, political consensus/progress, and cultural diversity well inte-grated with social harmony.

I have already outlined some of these concerns in the previous chapters of this study, but it is worth emphasising them here. The popular viability and credibility of The Beatles is partially, at least, bound up with the meanings placed upon their situation and role in society. They were, after all, typical of resurgent youth, of an open society where social mobility of a diverse kind existed. They were seen to be both good British exports and ambassadors.

Now, of course, we need to be very cautious about these conventional wisdoms. They are important aspects of ideological processes at work in the post-War world. There is also a sense that these phenomena are part of a process of legitimisation-seeking, pursued by the ruling elites. These concerns, resting as they do upon my earlier comments about the process of hegemony in post-War British society and political life, assume some importance. It is not stretching our imagination too far to suppose that many sections of the ruling elites in Britain, as elsewhere in the world, will utilise an amazingly diverse, often bizarre, often contradictory range of cultural phenomenon, in the pursuance of their interests and the maintenance of their economic and political power.

All that mid-Sixties nonsense about 'Swinging Britain' and, more particularly, 'Swinging London', conned vast numbers of people, including many of the participant observers, into believing that life in post-War Britain really was egalitarian, socially just, open, progressive, permissive, liberal and humane, democratic, *etc*. There was a strong belief then that the 'bubble' could and would go floating on.

Greater emphasis was placed on this than on the prospect of major contradictory change taking place in the very short term. The 'bubble' burst, 'the party is over' prospect was not incorporated in the dominant, *public* view of how post-War British society might develop.

It strikes me that The Beatles were caught up in much of this. It seems quite a significant aspect of The Beatles phenomenon. The weight of Raymond Williams' work is here also:

> "We should look not for the components of a product, but for the conditions of a practice. When we find ourselves looking at a particular work, or group of works, often realising, as we do, their essential community as well as their irreducible individuality, we should find ourselves attending first to the reality of their practice and the conditions of the practice as it was then executed."

> *(R. Williams, 'Base and Superstructure' essay, 1973)*

If I read Williams right here, I would agree with him that, while not overlooking the importance or significance of The Beatles *per se*, we should be *more* concerned with the phenomenon as a whole. There does surely exist, for example, a political context for the development of technologies, rock music ones or otherwise. This politics is going to comprise of pressures for control and maintenance as well as demands for alternative or oppositional developments to take place.

We need to always keep in touch with, to keep in mind, such apparently commonsense associations as The Beatles and an advert for Vox amps in *Mersey Beat*, 12-26 March, 1964:

"Vox went The Beatles - USA -

Congratulations...Beatles, on your overwhelm-
ing success in the United States...and thanks for
phoning your appreciation of the new VOX amps
featured in your fine performances.

The Beatles, like Britain's other Top Radio, TV
and Recording Stars, feature VOX sound equipment."

Or again, the 1964-5 incorporation of The Beatles into the cinema
world (one of Brian Epstein's great desires). A diversification of
capital and talents? Certainly, a calculated move to reinforce the
development of The Beatles image as all-round performers:

"We asked George whether there were any plans
for another film as *A Hard Days Night* was
proving so successful. 'We'll be making another
film in February, but I've no idea what it'll be
about. I hope there are no songs in it. It was all
right getting songs in the last one because we had
an excuse; they worked into the film all right.
But I don't like these films where everyone
bursts into song for no reason and you have a full
orchestra blasting out from nowhere.' "

(Mersey Beat, July 30 - Aug 6 1964)

Despite that, The Beatles next film was, of course, *Help!*

In the *Rolling Stone* interviews published in 1971, John
Lennon was able to reflect upon the way in which their post-1962-
3 success dramatically changed their artistic role:

"The music was dead before we went on the
theatre tour of Britain. We were feeling shit
already, because we had to reduce an hour or two
hours playing, which we were glad about in one

way, to twenty minutes and we would go on and
repeat the same twenty minutes every night.

The Beatles music died then, as musicians.
That's why we never improved as musicians; we
killed ourselves then to make it. And that was the
end of it."

(John Lennon in 'Rolling Stone Interview',
7-1-1, p.27)

I have discussed elsewhere in this study the importance of
recognising post-War changes in values and taste. These changes
were to be found within popular music as elsewhere. The Beatles
phenomenon encompasses some of these shifts. Lennon was, for
example, articulating his belief in the nature of change very early
on in their corporate career:

"This isn't show business. It's something else.
This is different from anything that anybody
imagines. You don't go on from this. You do this
and then you finish."

(John Lennon quoted in 'Love Me Do:The
Beatles Progress', Michael Braun, p.52)

The cultural response to the shifts in values often took some
contradictory turns. The responses to youthful musical developments were often condescending in their tone, perhaps
reflecting the uncertainty that some sections of society had to the
changes taking place?

"Out of school, adolescents are enthusiastically
engaged in musical self-education. They crowd
the record shops at weekends, listening and
buying, and within the range of their preferences,
they are often knowledgeable and highly critical
of performance, and the technical performance of
the music they like is frequently high. They find

rhythm exciting. Some teach themselves, or each other, to play an instrument. From radio, television, cinema and concert hall, and for that matter, from the local chain store, music is making a continual impact. Here is a vigorous popular culture which is international in its camaraderie."

(Newsom Report, 1963, Para.412, pp.139/140)

The Beatles and their contemporaries knew about this. They realised in their own way the changes in values and tastes. They also had an eye and an ear for the response that their activities were making on others! "It's getting better all the time/I used to get mad at my school," *etc.* ('Getting Better' from 'Sgt. Pepper' album, 1967)

It is quite clear that the postures that young people strike are often related to their perception of how others perceive them. It may be in the response of their contemporaries, especially perhaps in the sexual dimension to everyday life. Media amplification of the activities of youth has, in its selective and pejorative way, identified postures, that has, in turn, encouraged others to participate. It may, predominantly, have been beaches from the early Sixties and football grounds from the early seventies. However, the musical focus in the everyday life of young people has always been 'eventful'.

More often than not, the range of adult responses to the music orientated behaviour of the young has been very 'Behaviourist', and has not acknowledged the fact that those young people are certainly perceptive enough to realise their place in this process.

When considering the changes in beliefs, values and behaviour taking place in post-War Britain, we need to pause for a moment, to consider the place of religions and more particularly, religiously orientated philosophies. One aspect of The Beatles phenomenon that is well known, and yet difficult to penetrate, is the embracing of the Eastern religious philosophy epitomised by the Maharishi. Between mid-1967 and mid-1968, The Beatles, to varying degrees, associated themselves with the Maharishi and Co. Lennon and Harrison (Harrison's album 'Wonderwall' was released in November 1968) were the leading lights among The Beatles, with the latter setting the pace, 'seeing' the essential relation (part of the whole in fact) between 'inner light' enlightenment and musical creation.

Whatever the ups and downs of The Beatles encounter with the Maharishi, the context of their association is more significant. Their part in this cultural episode of the life and times of post-War western civilisation epitomised the cerebral tendencies in most post-1966 rock music and artefact. The Beatles were part of a process, whereby they both produced and reproduced a culture that encompassed the long search for peace and truth, self-awareness and harmony of body and soul. This was, and is, pretty 'mind-boggling' stuff by any stretch of the imagination! But it does indicate an aspect of The Beatles phenomenon that underlines the cultural changes and shifts that were taking place in the mid-1960s. In this particular case, in the late-1960s. "Instant Karma's gonna get you, gonna knock you off your feet," *etc.* (John Lennon, 'Instant Karma', 1970. Single release, produced by Phil Spector)

The Beatles had used some of the space they negotiated for themselves in a way that most of their contemporaries on Merseyside would not have found acceptable. While the world-wide student-intellectual radicalisation was taking place, rock music, in its more 'progressive' tones, was striking a posture of oppositional intransigence to the world order. After *his* association with the Maharishi tendency, Lennon turned his attention to the 'aftermath' of the anarcho-syndicalist movements of the late-1960s and early-1970s. He spent some time 'there', with Yoko Ono and others. Caught-up in the events of the late-1960s were a significant number of the working class, who, despite being 'written off' by the likes of Marcuse (*One Dimensional Man, etc.*) and Mandel, among others, found it necessary to act in the face of worsening economic conditions and increasing State intervention in their lives. Even so, most young workers in the western world found themselves *in work*. Despite the stylistic alternatives to the normative order that they may have posed, they were, in the main, accommodated within the dominant cultural belief system that entertained the prospect of at least a job for most of them. What youth unemployment there was in the late-1960s tended to be concentrated in the traditional areas/regions of economic under-development in Britain, including, of course, Merseyside.

Here again, whether at work or on the dole, most of The Beatles' contemporaries would have been pushed to comprehend the mystic or intellectual mumbo-jumbo that their musical heroes had embraced in varying degrees. Certainly, The Beatles both produced and reproduced a cultural image in this later phase of their career. The image was, however, increasingly contradictory to that of the early 1960s. It was as if they had joined 'the other side'. Many of their fans found it increasingly difficult to relate to this aspect of The Beatles, which represents a turning point in The Beatles phenomenon. However, it was not only fans that found this phenomenon difficult to cope with, or be tolerant of. With the exception of George Harrison, The Beatles, more and more as independents, moved quickly away from this moment of heady-introversion to pursue other matters. McCartney and Starr did, by stages, attempt to re-establish themselves into the normative order, albeit the music and show-biz variety of that order. Lennon, as mentioned above, moved into a more overtly political phase and lent his name and music (and body) to liberationism, increasingly from an American base.

The careers of the four individuals seemed to reflect a dominant image of the late-1960s and early-1970s, namely that sides *had* to be taken, the era of consensus had been shattered by events and ideas interrelating and putting pressure upon the social structures, on the economic, political and social *relations* that made up those structures. A dominant image in those years became one of disaffiliation, society under stress, society as a despotism in a perilous state of disequilibria. A dominant image, not only of society at a juncture in post-War history, but exhibiting a major disjuncture in everyday affairs, social life and culture.

Lennon's lyric, from an apparently remote era, took on another, sharper significance, if reviewed in the light of events at the turn of the decade 1969/70: "Although I laugh and I act like a clown/Beneath this mask I am wearing a frown', *etc*. (John Lennon, 'I'm a Loser', given as Lennon and McCartney. 'Beatles for Sale' album, 1964)

The 'Beatles for Sale' album had been raggedly, hastily, put together and released in December 1964, in time for the Christmas market. The month before, their single release 'I Feel Fine' had made number one. The faces on the cover of the 'Beatles for Sale' album gave the lie to that line. They looked, and often sounded, far from fine! After having made and released the film and album, *A Hard Days Night* in the spring and summer of 1964, following their first US tour, they toured Europe, Hong Kong, Australia, New Zealand and the US again (doing 31 performances in 24 cities in the US).

The creation of the image was indeed done at enormous cost.

Some notes in conclusion

PEOPLE OFTEN SAY to me that they find the 1960s a more understandable, more complete and more satisfying decade than they do the 1970s. I wonder why? People comment upon the feeling of optimism that existed then. They draw on the dominant images they retain of life in the 1960s and use those images to illustrate the meanings they place upon that bygone era.

Human experience becomes an assembled entity which can be used to draw comparisons; often nostalgic, often fraternal, often disparaging, with the present or our view of the future.

But what are these reflections, these interpretations, these historical analyses offering us? One thing is clear, that is, that the era of which these people talk *does* require interpretation. The era does not 'offer itself up' as an entity for the taking. The choice of images to say this or that will be selective and idiosyncratic and yet, in vital cultural ways, there will be a typicality in these choices. Perhaps this is why so many people, 'veterans' of the 1960s, or otherwise, will select The Beatles to represent a whole series of dominant images, central, indeed perhaps essential, to their reading of that era?

If we take a long-term historical view of the post-War years in Britain, we must surely agree that it is an era full of contradictions. This sounds trite and could not be other than a truism in sociological terms. However, the post-War era is marked with a mannerism, a formalism, a decadence, that cannot easily be brushed aside. I have to ask myself, where does the artistic product of The Beatles come to be part of the culture of this time? I realise, for example, that what I have said in this brief study will be viewed sympathetically, even empathetically in some quarters, and with caution, scepticism and criticism in others. Whatever the response, it is clear that readers will have come to this study with their own preconceived notions. How then are we to understand The Beatles phenomenon? Should we identify with and admire the achievement of The Beatles themselves? Should we recognise in their artistic production a valuable contribution to our musical culture? We might also, or alternatively, identify with their purpose; what seems to have been their motives, their aims, their objectives?

If we take one aspect of this, say, in the form of 'All You Need Is Love', we may feel that, whatever the good intention, it was naïve to say the least. But to an important extent that does not matter. That naivety was, perhaps, part and parcel of their meaning, their situation in that optimism. If we take a detached, long-term view of The Beatles phenomenon, then the tendency is to stand outside of the culture in an attempt to produce analysis. But there are, of course, great dangers here, particularly perhaps in losing sight of the dialectical process by which these historical phenomenon, events, came about. If, however, we adopt a close-up, biographical approach, we encounter difficulties with placing too much emphasis upon *them*, The Beatles, losing sight of the overall passage of time and the overall significance of events, past, present and future.

In the Introduction of this study, I attempted to address myself to these methodological problems. Beyond that, I have offered a mixture of these two, but that seems very difficult to operate, to say the least. What I have attempted to do is say what is the significance, what are the significances, of The Beatles phenomenon? This is much more modest in its aims, in terms of how, in my opinion, the phenomenon has incorporated social change for a better, more humane, more just world. Perhaps it is inappropriate that I ask such questions of The Beatles phenomenon, but ask them I have.

This has an important relation with the nature of ideology. I have addressed myself to this problem as well. It is quite evident that some rock music, like other artistic production, can be overtly ideological, *i.e.*, we are left in no doubt about the message, about the ideas, we are being offered. This is as true of the reggae band 'Steel Pulse' today, for example, as it was of Lennon's song, 'Working Class Hero', before. However, this, even in terms of the later 1960s idiom, only represents a minority of the phenomenon. The vast majority of the rock phenomenon, certainly The Beatles, is - although ideological - essentially diffuse in its nature and form.

One of the most important aspects of The Beatles phenomenon, for me, is the way in which *I* have identified with them. What I have taken away from my encounter with and experience of The Beatles is, perhaps, very important for me, as for other persons, in that it has helped me to see social life that much better. How often have you and I heard a song, listened to a passage of music, seen a film, a picture, photograph, *etc.*, and thought, 'My God, that *is* right, that hits the nail on the head!'? Most of us have, in our association with The Beatles, *et al*, learnt truths that enhance, produce, reinforce, our consciousness.

It is clear to me that, from the many people who talk to me about The Beatles, cannot remember, even if they ever knew, this detail or that, this date or that. That does not seem anywhere near as important as the general impression, set of images and the like, that people have produced, or taken away, from their encounter with The Beatles. And there is the sense of having to and wanting to remind ourselves of monuments and signposts in our past. J. B. Priestly once remarked on this phenomenon when talking about a war memorial he knew. On one side of the memorial was inscribed, 'Their names will live forever', while on the other side was written, 'Lest we forget'.

I would not suggest that 'we' - all of us - wanted to be John, George, Paul or Ringo. Some people (such as Ray Connolly of *That'll be the Day* and *Stardust, etc.*) once argued that every boy wanted to be a rock star. I just do not think that is true, despite the fact that many young people, and others, have very closely identified themselves with The Beatles.

It seems to me that The Beatles phenomenon has been part comedy, part tragedy. It has been banal and dramatic, in short, contradictory throughout. For example, they were both carriers and creators of culture. But, for me, The Beatles phenomenon has epitomised the nature and importance of *popular* culture. It has also epitomised the discussions that I and others have engaged.

I would argue that The Beatles are undoubtedly suitable material for concerns and discussions about popular culture, especially if we look at both their popular esteem and the extensive knowledge of them and their music. This would include the popular nature of their origins, from the ordinary people, so to speak, the folk and their part in a folk idiom of the mid-20th century, Rock and Roll. But, of course, this is then unequivocally part of a much broader and deeper concern, study, of culture and society. That is where I have attempted to place my discussion of The Beatles phenomenon.

Let me then recapitulate on how I have attempted to reason out my analysis of The Beatles phenomenon and how this reasoning process is part of The Beatles phenomenon in my terms. This is, I hope, not arrogance, but the realisation, in both senses, of my study.

In my opening remarks, I have argued for an historical analysis of The Beatles phenomenon. I made great play with my own dissatisfaction with the tendency to consider The Beatles in a historical way on the one hand, or allow them to be submerged in a welter of meaningless Colour Supplement/PR writing on the other hand. I stressed that I would attempt to analyse the phenomenon with a view to how certain social relations are created, maintained and destroyed over time. This was tied up with an attempt to 'look through' rock images in order to facilitate a fuller understanding of post-War British society. In this study I have attempted to fulfil these intentions. In presenting the material on 'Society and Culture', 'Post-War Britain in Liverpool' and 'Youth', I have put forward an analysis of issues that has been related to an elaboration of how it might be possible to arrive at a view of post-War British social structures and the processes by which these structures came about, were maintained and have changed. I have then related these concerns to the specific material on 'The Beatles', in a way that enables my concern with ideas, issues and events to come to focus upon *them*, and then lead away to other, more general problems again. What I have attempted to do is produce a view of The Beatles phenomenon that includes an understanding of The Beatles *themselves* and yet, essentially, a view that does not allow the analysis to stay locked-into too narrow confines.

For example, I have addressed myself to the problem of The Beatles as idols and the issue of 'Beatlemania' coupled with idolatry. What we are faced with here is also a problem of relation between idol and hero. It strikes me that to talk of The Beatles as idols is not the same as to talk of them as heroes. Idol, the image of the deity, has a closed unquestioning sense to it. With hero, I would emphasise the sense of the character as subject of epic, the central focus of the story. The notion of heroes does suggest to me the *active* rather than passive association of people with these central characters in the epic story. Idol worship is virtually a thing in itself, whereas hero worship suggests a more open-ended relationship. These heroes are more as intermediaries between the ordinary folk and the Elysian fields; or was it *Strawberry fields*? There is a sense of representativeness here that is significant. This may seem semantic, but I offer it up as a reservation. Idols do not (cannot) ask for attention, ask to be listened to. Either they are, or they are not. Heroes can, and do, demand attention through their ideas, words and deeds.

In this sense, it seems to make more progress to talk of The Beatles as a reflection of, characteristic of, influential in and epitome of, an era. I have elaborated on this at some length in my study and I would only add here that I do feel they were, in many different and complex ways, all those things to some, many, people at some time and in some place. This again, in my opinion, becomes part of what I would want to call 'The Beatles phenomenon'.

I also addressed myself to the problem of how conscious The Beatles were, themselves, of their influence. At what moment in time and space did they recognise their contributions, large or small, in their terms? Cynthia Lennon relates the tale of how they were all on their way to the premiere of *A Hard Day's Night* in London. Lennon was amazed at the extent of the crowds that their car had to pass through to get to the cinema and asked if anyone knew what was going on. Who were the crowds waiting to see?

I have looked at the possible disjuncture between The Beatles and The Beatles phenomenon in such a sense. I feel this is important, because if, for no other reason, it would be injudicious to suggest that *they* were responsible for *it all*.

I have also argued that part of my task was to produce a 'way of seeing' The Beatles phenomenon that would be applicable for use *elsewhere*. One of the central facets of this perspective, this 'way of seeing' has been to argue for a grasp of culture in society *as a whole*. Of course I am not suggesting that what I have been able to do is produce an all-inclusive view of post-War British culture, a complete picture. That would, probably, be impossible. What I have attempted to do is acknowledge my own, and others', concerns about the production of cultures over time and how these cultures are not only a result of social structures and social processes, but do essentially, facilitate phenomenon to come about or not, *etc*.

Harold Rosenberg has touched on the problem I set myself. Writing in his collection of essays *The Tradition of the New* he has this to say:

> "Who ever undertakes to create soon finds himself engaged in creating himself. Self-

transformation and the transformation of others
have constituted the radical interest of our
century, whether in painting, psychiatry or
political action."

[And, in my terms, rock music as well.]

"Quite ordinary people have been tempted to
assume the risk of deciding whether to continue
to be what they have been or to exchange
themselves to fit a more intriguing role; others
have had self-substitution forced upon them.

Metamorphosis involves the mechanism of comedy and tragedy. Never before has there been
such wholesale participation in the secrets of the
ridiculous, the morbid and the idyllic. It is
through these, however, that the physiognomy of
an epoch must be recognised.

In such circumstances, criticism cannot divide
itself into literary criticism, art criticism, social
criticism, but must begin in establishing the
terms of the conflict between the actual work or
event and its illusory context."

*(Rosenberg, p.24 of the 1970 Paladin edition,
but first published in 1962)*

Now there is a tendency towards idealism in what Rosenberg has
to say about the nature of consciousness, *i.e.*, he places too much
emphasis on the autonomy of the consciousness of the person, but
even so, he manages to escape the trap. When Rosenberg wrote a
foreword for the Paladin edition, he comments further on these
remarks:

"To demand that criticism be *based* on principles
derived from a broad consideration of the
modern epoch amounts to insisting that the
special difficulties, already all but unman-

217

ageable, of judging works of art be compounded by the efforts to judge the quality and direction of contemporary *life as a whole*."

(Rosenberg, p.13. with my emphasis)

Rosenberg asks whether such an analytical posture is, from the outset, an act of sabotage of the critical enterprise? I would share the feeling with him that, although that enterprise is going to be fraught with dangers and difficulties, it must be attempted.

In this sense, I would raise an issue about the role of the critic or the analyst in these concerns. The development of science and scientists, and eventually, that of social scientists, has been an aspect of the development of the division of labour under the impact of industrialisation and industrial capitalism in particular. Prior to evolved capitalism, the thinkers were largely churchmen and scholastics; they were metaphysicians in theory and practice (except, of course, that they did not actually carry out their theories; for example, by walking through walls). However, the new set of relations of capital accumulation and manufacturing *etc.*, sealed the supremacy of the new ruling order. With their rational and positivistic (scientific) outlook, they produced thinkers cast in this mould and subservient, or at least accountable to, the new order of life and things.

One of the interesting and problematic (and therefore interesting?) aspects of this phenomenon is the inherent contradiction of keeping a dog and not barking yourself. Part of the social development of modern industrial societies has been the fact that when people, even lackeys of the State, begin to acquire knowledge, they become sceptical, they begin to reason about those societies. They begin to ask questions. Often these questions reflect upon their epistemology and that of others, and this may lead to questions about the very role of 'dogs' in everyday social life? Having let 'the cat out of the bag' (or at least been instrumental in that process), it is difficult to keep all the dogs under control. Most dogs have been well trained by their owners and keepers, but even so, the very nature of dogs and the dog-cat set of relations inherent in society, may provide a further set of contradictions and problems - for the owners and keepers?

218

The owners and keepers may decide to disassociate themselves from the vicarious activities of their domesticated charges, but then some other people, less fastidious perhaps, will continue to keep dogs. And anyway, there may be dogs on the loose, looking for cats to chase. Then again, dogs on the loose do have a tendency to be indiscriminate about whose heels they might snap at. . .

Or put another way, 'It's one thing to employ Humpty Dumpty, it's another thing to have egg yoke on your face every morning!'

But, of course, the extent of any particular social scientist's or critic's or rock musician's freedom is going to be related to a whole set of cultural and ontological factors. This is much like the problem as raised in Frederick Raphael's screenplay for Cukor's *Love Among The Ruins*. Olivier says to Hepburn, "Are you free?" She replies, "My dear boy, I am freedom's prisoner!".

The constraints on our everyday life, of course, may exist without our being fully conscious of them. I have raised this problem in my chapter on 'Society and Culture', especially the references to Hoggart's discussion in *The Uses of Literacy*. I am always reminded of J. B. Priestley's anecdote about the OAP in Leeds, who, on being told by a shopkeeper that she would *eventually* have to master the new decimal currency, retorted that it was not so, because she was moving to Wakefield next week!

One of the central issues of my chapter on 'Society and Culture' was the way in which young people may develop, take up, associate with, and produce popular culture. I moved my discussion through a concern about socialisation within society and culture, but also, clearly, the way in which fundamentally important aspects of any process of socialisation *are* cultural. This raises some very interesting questions about the extent to which a folk idiom or popular culture may have come about and be said to exist, and be on-going, and the extent to which this popular culture is then extended, become explicitly part and parcel of the activities of a very significantly large section of a population. This is not to deny the heterogeneity of that culture, nor is it my wish to suggest that that social process of adoption is evolutionary or linear. Clearly, it is not. But there is an important sense of the way in which this culture then becomes a *fact* of life for many, *i.e.*, it is there in the wider range of cultural experiences. It may then also become a *way* of life for many, in the sense that it forms a greater and greater *raison d'être* for social activity. This was undoubtedly the case for The Beatles and their contemporaries. They did increasingly identify themselves with this popular cultural *milieu* and, in one way or another, help to popularise it in turn.

An interesting elaboration of this problem is to be found in an essay by Zev Barbu, 'Popular Culture: Sociological Approach' (in *Approaches to Popular Culture* edited by C. W. E. Bigsby).

> "The fact is that the terms popular and popularised are often used in the same or similar contexts, and that this creates the impression that they belong to the same category. Now, whatever the methodological merit, such a position is based on a naïve, often unexamined, type of generalisation and as such constitutes a main source of ambiguity and confusion...While the former (popular) indicates an implicit state or condition, more precisely, a phenomenon which is widespread owing to some intrinsic or at least non specified condition, the latter (popularised) presupposes a specific process inside which one could discern a certain degree of autonomy, moreover, a certain degree of internal diff- erentiation between a set of initiating circ- umstances, on the one hand, and a final product, on the other."
>
> *(p.42)*

Now I would not want to go all the way with Barbu on this rather semantic point, for example, there is more than a hint of the Durkheimian preoccupations with definition and classification. However, Barbu does remind us of the importance of action, in his notion of popularised, even if he does tend to offer a somewhat *action-less* view of the popular.

There is always a problem about popular culture that I have touched upon above. Just how much, in quantitative terms, or the nature of, in qualitative terms, can it be argued that popular culture is really the creation, product of the people, the folk or the working classes (in the most usual formulation)? As I have speculated in this study, ideology might play a very significant role in the production of culture over time. It would be injudicious to look at the products of the working class in terms of *that* being working class culture, without taking into consideration, at least, that the long-term development of ways of life, values, ideas and even modes of behaviour, might have been significantly influenced by ideological intrusions by the ruling order? Clearly this is not to say that what has been seen as, or understood as, 'working class culture', is not in important ways a product of actions by members of that class. But that does not, of course, rule out my point of concern. We might also speculate about the extent and nature of influence of inter-class relations, or struggle, in the production of a working class culture. I have touched on such problems throughout this study and would see them as having here a diffuse, here a concentrated factor, in the relation, over time, of society and culture, of alienation and progress.

In viewing, and hopefully usefully using, Raymond Williams' typology of dominant, emergent and residual cultures, I put some stress on the multi-layered and dialectical nature of social change. Having argued throughout for a notion of cultural matrix, it is possible to suggest how this matrix might be drawn upon by a person or persons, in producing, creating, thinking and behaving. But as I have indicated, it would be wise to reflect upon the complex nature of this process. People, young and old alike, can become confused by changes in their everyday life. Explanations of one's own position in and relation to these changes may be difficult. Many discussions of post-War British society articulate the idea that ordinary people are bewildered by the nature of some changes, and that they may find it very difficult to relate these changes to their experience in a significant way. They may find it problematic to incorporate such changes. They may, in their own terms, or following a lead from others, resist such changes, especially if they identify the source of change as coming from a threatening, or despotic, or unjust agent? It would be possible to argue, as I have, that part of the attraction to Rock and Roll culture, or resistance to it, for and by, some people, is part of this process. The identification of The Beatles with certain changes in their own *milieu* certainly did lead them to adopt this posture and that, depending largely on their *reading* of the situation of that change. Part of The Beatles phenomenon is how this might have happened, but also how many other people, in their way, came to identify with The Beatles as agents of change. Whether The

Beatles were seen as agents of change for good or for ill is again part of my wider view of the situation of The Beatles phenomenon.

Now I have addressed myself to certain problems of the nature of ideology. What I have said in this study, and certainly above, is not a million miles away from the problems Althusser has addressed himself to. He has placed much emphasis on what he has called 'Ideological State Apparatuses', by which he seems to mean the way in which the dominant agents of ideology - family, school, media, law, *etc.* - the loci of the reproduction of ideologies. He argues that the *active* role of ideology is to reproduce time and again the relations of production, *i.e.* capitalist ones, those ensuring that the ruling order remains dominant. In the field of Literature, it has been Macherey that has attempted to use a relation between the ideas of Althusser and those of Gramsci. The latter was, of course, primarily concerned with how to destroy the structure of consent that the working class 'gave' to the ruling order. Gramsci was thus centrally concerned with what form the ideological struggles might need to take, if the working class were to see through the constant, if variable, ideological influence and role of the ruling order.

Gramsci was insistent that a proletarian hegemony needed to be produced to combat the ruling class. Gramsci did, of course, allocate prime importance to the role of intellectuals in this process of establishing an effective basis for struggle against the dominance of these ideological forces in society and culture. It has been interesting to witness the work of Anderson and the *New Left Review* collective in recent years, in an attempt to take up this challenge (with perhaps Anderson's essay in 1968 on 'The Components of a National Culture' as a seminal production).

I am not suggesting that my study here is in any way equal to such theoretical thrusts. Nor am I suggesting that I find myself in accord with it all. My own work owes much more to Goldman and Williams, and this will be apparent to the informed reader. I have said elsewhere that it has not been the intention of this study to critically survey theories and theorists, nor has it been my concern to champion this theoretical posture of that. My eclec-ticism and groping for synthesis will annoy some readers no doubt, but I did suggest at the outset that I was attempting to reason my way through this study.

I have already indicated that I see a history without a sociology as sterile, as a sociology is without a history. This is, of course, hardly an original epistemology. In the opening comments to this section of my study I ventured to make some observations concerning the problematic relation between a detached long-term view in history with a biographical approach. I find this concern present in the work of Leo Lowenthal:

> "The historian must depersonalise social relat-ionships in favour of an emphasis on larger events; at the other extreme, memoirs, auto-biographies and letters provide us with more personalized data, but the autobiographical 'I' fails to give us those generalised portraits that depend for their success upon holding the mirror of reality up to large segments of society. The fictional work, at its best embodying the general in the particular, combines the advantages of these two extremes: it presents the important theme as it is acted out and felt by the individual, and at the same time gives up a wealth of sociologically meaningful detail."

> *(Lowenthal 'Literature, Popular Culture and Society', 1968 ed., p.xiii)*

Although Lowenthal is concentrating his thoughts on literature, I would argue that we might usefully proceed with these concerns with popular culture in general, and certainly with my attempts to understand The Beatles phenomenon. I have said as much on a number of occasions in this study, and particularly in the section on 'Society and Culture'. Lowenthal expands his problematic, and I can share his methodological concerns:

> "In the end, of course, we should have to admit that our science is an historical one and that it suffers from the same lack of certainty as do all historical and, therefore, non-experimental scien-es. Also, only some of the subject matter of any science of man is self-evident. When our topic is

the living, full human being, with all his feelings
and attitudes, there can be no guarantees of
certainty there, as in psychology and sociology in
general, we can at best hope that, by a certain
finesse and an eye for probabilities, we can sift
out the valid and important from the misleading
and trivial in much of our data. Ambiguity is
inseparable from the study of man."

(p.xiv)

Hall and Whannel reflect on the concerns voiced above in their
work on the popular arts. They suggest that the rise of the
individual performer-communicator is particularly important
within popular art, within the development of modern industrial
society:

"Popular art…is essentially a conventional art
which restates, in an intense form, values and
attitudes already known; which reassures and
reaffirms, but brings to this something of the
surprise of art as well as the shock of
recognition. Such art has in common with folk
art the genuine contact between audience and
performer: but it differs from folk art in that it is
an individualized art, the art of the known
performer. The audience-as-community has come to depend on the performer's skills, and on
the force of a personal style, to articulate its
common values and interpret its experiences."

(S. Hall and P. Whannel, 'The Popular Arts',
1964, p.66)

What I have argued for The Beatles phenomenon is germane here.
I have already suggested that the relationship of the performer-
communicator is significant in ideological ways. If, as I have also
indicated, the line between the performer and audience is even
more flexible than even Hall and Whannel suggest, we need to
reconsider these relations. After 1962, for instance, The Beatles
became increasingly remote from their audience, even though the

extent of their recognition by the audience was greatly enhanced and modulated by the role of The Beatles *themselves (i.e.,* by the *posture* of Lennon, McCartney, Harrison and Starr). I have, therefore, attempted to navigate my way between a wide contextual view of The Beatles presence in society and a view of *them*, within this matrix.

In my concern to discuss the wider cultural context, I have certainly not suggested that The Beatles, or Rock and Roll, was a cipher. Far from it: a paradigm would be nearer the truth. A paradigm of cultural phenomenon and musical modes, form and meaning interrelated.

The material I have presented in this study of The Beatles phenomenon has been drawn from this diversity of fields and contexts, and yes, it may be ambiguous, but I do not see how it could be otherwise and still get *near to* an analysis of such a phenomenon.

Now, as I have pointed out in these concluding notes, this does raise some serious methodological questions. Foucault reminds us that the epistemologies of the western world have been dominated by a metaphysics that leaves unobjectifiable aspects of phenomena, on the one hand, and a positivism that seeks objectification at the expense of speculation and interpretation, on the other hand (see, for example, *The Order of Things: An Archaeology of the Human Sciences*, 1974).

I have, of course, attempted to outline a methodology (especially in my Introduction to this study) that recognises this problem and attempts an accommodation. If I say, in a characteristic, broad, generalising sweep that this or that is the case, my audience may respond with: "Show us the evidence! Where is the empirical support? Is this falsifiable?" I may, in response, be able to offer up this case study or that. They may respond further, with: "This is not enough; it is partial, inconclusive, and in comparison to the generalisation, is meagre support!" I may then say, "but this seems typical, this seems likely, this is what I believe I know is the situation."

Will this satisfy my respondents? Whether it does or not may, largely, depend on their 'reading' of *me*.

I am reminded of this problem when looking at Gurvitch. He has, for example, attempted to approach problems of the individual and the collective in his writings on the sociology of knowledge:

"...the sociology of knowledge cannot assert itself unless it admits that collective knowledge is in a dialectical relationship with individual knowledge. The history of civilisation bears witness to the fact that collective knowledge exists and that it is based on collective judgements, which recognise the veracity of collective experiences and institutions. The abandonment of the concept of the self-contained consciousness (the closed consciousness turned in on itself), in favour of the open consciousness in a close and constant relation with the world, has made it possible to acknowledge that the interpretation of consciousness and their partial fusion are as real as the individual consciousness. Thus, all consciousness appears to involve a dialectic between the 'Me', the 'Other' and the 'We', and the objections to the possibility of collective knowledge are concentrated on *acts of judgement,* which are related to reflection and the spoken word, and might seem to be individual."

(G. Gurvitch, 'The Social Framework of Knowledge', 1971, p.14. First published in French in 1966)

At the close of my section on 'Youth', I turned my particular attention to the question of sexual relations. I would emphasise here that the period of the early 1960s epitomises, in the terms of popular music, this over-stated concern with the personal/sexual relations of everyday life. It is not only The Beatles' work that is saturated with such concerns, it is a very general phenomenon. This seems to me to underline the central dominance of the individual, as distinct from the peripheral, significance of the collective, at this time, and in this mode. And yet there can be little doubt that the importance of the collective is to be recognised; if not easily seen, in the development of popular music in the late-1950s and early-1960s. Again, we can acknowledge the fact that a relation of personal to public exists as a vital force, a dynamic, of that era.

Time and time again, though, we see a rejection of this in the writings on The Beatles. *In A Cellarful of Noise* written in 1964 Brian Epstein falls foul of the same problem:

> "Them. . .John...Paul...George. . .and Ringo. Collectively, the four most famous names in the world. Extraordinary young men who have dire-ctly altered the lives of hundreds, even thousands of people, who have affected the entire balance of the entertainment industry, who have kicked up so much dust that in all our lifetimes, it will not completely settle."
>
> *(p.91)*

As I have indicated with other writers in this study, Epstein then attempts to close off our access to The Beatles phenomenon:

> "They have defied analysis, though not for a year or two has there been a shortage of analysts prepared to devote an amazing amount of time to delving, scratching and soul-bearing to look for the reason for the inhuman grip of The Beatles."
>
> *(Epstein, p.92)*

In considering the ideas of Epstein and Gurvitch, for example, I have underlined an issue raised in the chapter on 'The Beatles'; namely, that an 'Idealist' analysis will tend to reify cultural relations and processes. I would suggest that studying Popular Culture is full of such pitfalls. I have argued in these concluding notes that an accommodation is necessary for the biographical and the contextual. It is all too easy to go on as if the phenomenon we identify, for example, The Beatles phenomenon, has ceased to be about human beings and social relations. A good many of the 'pop music histories' fall into this mode. They extract the particular performer or performers from their cultural matrix and discuss *them.* They have become free-floating, not dependent, umbilically related to their cultural creation. It is, of course, very difficult to avoid these problems, but as I have argued, it is essential that we try.

There is an interesting, related problem here in any view we may hold of music as a language. Many writers over the years, not the least of which has been Levi-Strauss (*Mythologies, etc.*), have argued that music, as an art form, is not a language in that the conditions of artistic production remain individualistic. They are not collective in the sense that we normally understand of a language.

Artists may aspire the artistic product into a collective language. But it is still not commonly held in cultural terms. One clearly thinks of the work of Brecht in an oppositional sense to this, notably in the way he synthesises the artistic production with the political theory and action, in a Gramscian mode.

I extended my concerns in 'The Beatles' section to survey the issue of myth making. Again, in these concluding notes, I have discussed the role of idol and hero, and attempted to evaluate the concepts in relation to The Beatles phenomenon. It seems evident to me that the process whereby The Beatles reached the prominence they did is tied to the myth-making side of the 'Pop' industry. In the 1962-64 period, more and more observers wrote in awed tones (and euphemistically?) of The Beatles. I have quoted some of them. Some critics wrote them down - or off. However, what is significant is that The Beatles became famous, and infamous, and, therefore, justified the coverage given to them. The attention they received legitimated the recent history of their emergence as 'The Fab Four' - the greatest. It then seemed more than appropriate, even necessary, in terms of the pheno-menon-event, to say more and more about them. Most of the post-1964 'more and more' that was said was, however gratifying, an uncritical (in the widest sense) acceptance of who they were and what they were all about. They *were* The Beatles, they *were* successful, they *were* there!

The efforts of the journalist here, or the music critics there, usually produced and reproduced the notion that The Beatles were worthy of all this time and space, and money, being devoted to them. One would note here Adorno's remarks on the importance of the relation between the relations of production and the forces of production, in the light of my own remarks on the problematic relation between rock and the commercial nexus.

The extent of the cultural capital invested into the description of The Beatles' situation was enormous. What might be very important is who or what was excluded while this process of incorporation was going on? Contemporaneous careers to The Beatles were clearly important up to 1962-3-4, but do they tend to be pushed into the background in comparison to The Beatles after 1962? I think they do. Yet it must be true to say that The Beatles phenomenon encompasses the careers, activities, lives, of countless other, lesser, or unacknowledged musicians, *etc.*

In this study I have alluded to what might be called the nature of capitalist relations and the sense of *accidentalness* of The Beatles' success. I would reaffirm that feeling here, and place the emphasis where I have. By which interrelation of complex cultural factors did The Beatles become so successful? I have attempted to approach this in my study.

I have also considered, at some length, the 'obtrusiveness of art' (to paraphrase Kant): many writers on music, and especially folk, popular or popularised music, have reminded us that the development of musical forms and activities has, in terms of modern industrial society, been dominated by the bourgeoisie. Now this is not surprising. But it is never a simplistic situation. One characteristic feature, as discussed by Weber, has been the attempt in bourgeois society to disembody music. There has, of course, been great, if uneven, resistance to this, in the insistence of the relation between music and dance. But even in the 'left-wingish' musically illustrated/supportive days of the late-1960s, an awful lot of sitting around was done (often accompanied by dope smoking) rather than 'bopping'.

This is germane to my discussion in general, and I would go further to suggest that the intrusion of Rock and Roll has been of particular relevance. A whole era of musical activity, involvement and association has been stimulated by Rock and Roll in the post-War years. I have raised this and set it against the elitist and pessimistic notions extended about mass culture. Kurt Blaukopf recognises this conflict in his essay 'Musical Behaviour in Industrial Societies':

> ". . .has the theory according to which the rise of
> the media inevitably leads to an overall decrease
> of musical activities been invalidated by the

resuscitation of musical activities in industrial countries? Are environmental changes brought about by technology responsible for the emergence of new types of musical activities undertaken by large sections of the young generation in many industrial countries?"

(Essay to be found in 'Cultures', UNESCO Journal. Vol I, No.I. 1973, p.213)

Without over-stressing the point, is this also shades of 'Soundscape' or 'The Sound of the City'?

These comments by Blaukopf underline the notion of 'spontaneous musical activities'. This is underlined, perhaps, by such repeated facts that, for example, The Beatles *et al* could not, at the outset at least, read or write music. Then again, a great deal of money was later spent on equipment. (Remember, for example, George Harrison's comment to Epstein on the signing of the Parlaphone contract in 1962: "Order some new guitars!"

It would seem appropriate to echo Adorno in suggesting that the new technologies of music - for example, the phonograph record - cannot be seen to have reduced the amount of musical activity, but on the contrary to have popularised a whole, vast area of music and invite active participation. Skiffle and Rock and Roll are candidates here. But I was recently reminded that this aspect of direct musical influence in people's lives may not only be seen in post-War terms. Dennis Potter's TV production, *Pennies from Heaven*, might be typical?

But again, this is not to suggest that these musical activities came 'out of nowhere' - even if it seems like they did.

I have emphasised in this study, and in these concluding notes, my concern about social development, social change and my optimism despite the problems associated with what Blaukopf has called an epoch of 'historical acceleration'.

I would see here some related remarks by Métraux and Margaret Mead:

"A world of music is in the making in which the great wealth of the musical languages evolved throughout history converge to create an artistic form which conveys the variety of feelings, concepts and aspirations of man in contemporary society."

(G. S. Métraux, in Cultures, UNESCO Journal on Music and Society, 1973)

"... It will be the child - and not the parent and the grandparent - that represents what is to come."

(M. Mead, from 'Culture and Commitment. A Study of the Generation Gap', 1970)

Some may feel that these truisms are naïve, or do not need re-stating. But I must admit that I do. After all else, the existence of a phenomenon such as The Beatles gives me hope and encouragement. So:

'Why don't we do it in the road?'

Epilogue

"Mary; Mary! What are you doing?"

"Nothing! I was just watching the train go by."

"Well, come in, and shut the door."

"Okay, Mum."

Mary came in from the mean and smoke black-ened yard. She put the bucketful of coal down beside the fire.

"I don't know why you stay here, Mum. Why don't you get yourself a nice council flat or something?"

"I'm happy enough here. I know you don't think it's as nice as where you and Robin are."

"It's not that, Mum. It's just that it's so run down here now. And don't you get lonely? You said last time I came that Mrs Mar-sden had gone."

"Well I suppose I could move. Could have years

The train rattled on, exposing as it did the nakedness of the houses, seemingly caught unawares.

Here, he, the observer, was passing through, 'touching', the scene spread out before him, coming to his eye; adding to his consciousness. He speculated about the awe-inspiring task of comm-unication, with all this before him, all this assembled and ordered humanity. There was with him still an ambivalent feeling toward communication. Why should he seek out this further experience? Why speculate, why comm-unicate, however tenuous? It surely did not matter, he could not do it all, be fully satisfied? Really meaningful communic-ation is in the eye of the beholder. It is difficult for the loner. He was capable of outgoing argument and discussion; he was well versed in the art of making words count in a verbal contest. But this is, of course, another thing altogether. This skill had come through years of presenting a public persona. He thought that many people might say that they knew him. What they knew in fact was the public expression of him. In short, they knew what they were allowed to. That was how he perceived the situation of how others perceived him. His isol-ation, his enclave, was decidedly of his calling this day. And yet, he knew above all else that he was a social product. He would argue that his knowledge and consciousness was culturally determ-

ago. When your Dad was alive he was all for moving. He said that it was all changed in this neighbourhood, with his work gone and most of his friends moved on. But we were happy enough here as a family. You seemed happy most of the time."

"Yes, I was. I wasn't running it down like that. But even since I moved out it has got worse. Hardly anyone lives here now!"

"That's because them at the Council don't give a damn about the place. They could have kept the place up if they had wanted. But all the money was put into places like yours and the Council sent us round letters saying we ought to move out and let them knock it all down. But it used to be grand 'round here. I remember after the War, when your Dad came home; all the people then. It was hard, mind you."

The old woman moved forward on her seat and poked at the grade-three coal fire burning in the

ined. His reality was socially constructed; he could neither fully escape from, nor fully claim to be his own man. On numerous occasions he found that the past and the present ram each other, like aspects of a life bound on a course to somewhere else. This was not *déjà vu*, a clinical process, but undoubtedly a social process.

Music and literature had the greatest role to play in this respect. He reflected that his continuous and extensive involvement in Rock and Roll was a constant source, almost a fund really, of experience and experiment. The experiences; many happy, enjoyable and stimulating, some gruesome; were to paraphrase Mr Micawber, always turning up!

He did certainly feel that one of the delights of being part of a culture, of being human, is having the advanced facility to remember and reflect upon the past. The older one gets, the more there is to fall back on. He had often heard himself say this, usually while trying, in his half vain, half modest, manner, to relate aspects of culture, social phenomenon, to persons younger than himself or to those less versed in the mysteries of the academy. He would most invariably go on to add, as a necessary caveat, that that did not mean the more mature had the right *per se* to use their own past as a blunt weapon with which to beat the young. No, he was certain that while a recognition of our pasts, individual and collective, is

time-burnt grate. The light from the fire illuminated her face and the cosy old room around her in the way that it had done for years; for generations. Mary looked at this face, and remembered those times of which her mother now spoke. They seemed long ago and far away now, and yet at this moment, here, she realised that they were not that remote. Experience was etched in her mother's face just as it was written over this room, this neighbourhood.

"It was hard, mind you. Making ends meet. Bringing you children up. But we had some fun."

"It's a pity most of your friends have left."

"Yes, but at least you're not too far away, and Jack and Alice come often enough.

It's funny, you know, I was looking out some old papers for Jack the other day. You know he's doing this thing on the 1960s. Anyway, I sat all afternoon looking through the

certainly important in relating our situation to the present and the future, we could not, as individuals, escape from the consequences of it. It was no good being in your thirties, and having experienced the span of the post-War years, and trying to behave as a twenty-year-old.

He was sure that age carries a responsibility with it in the sense that history related to others may help them to discover more about the nature of human society in their terms. As youth recedes from us we have a tendency to lose sight of it; perhaps deliberately? Perhaps because we have so much to remember, reflect upon, interpret? He reminded himself that often he had been 'picked up' on his use of the word 'recede', when discussing the person in history. He had defended his contention that recede was right in the sense that our past did seem to move away from our present position, as distinct from our development (or prograss as many would call it) taking us away into the future. The future is clearly as 'imp-ortant' as the past, but the former is just less tangible. After all, he reflected, our pasts, personal and collective, are not an immobilised panorama, something to put in the album or hang on the wall! The use we make of histories, the very concept of relating the past, does surely suggest an active relationship with such phenomenon? We may, for example, decide to 'take hold' of the past and make some use of it. However, as he well knew, this was not an inevitable

papers. I found this story of those Beatles lads, and their great mansions they bought down south. I was thinking that for all their money and that, their families were missing out with them not being at home, like."

"Has Jack come for the papers yet?"

"No, I expect he will come over on the weekend."

The room grew darker and rain flecked the window. Time and tide.

"Do you want me to make you some tea before I go to collect the children?"

"No, it's alright, Mary, you get off now."

"What are you laughing at?"

"Oh, I was just thinking about your Dad and me. What we used to be like when we were your age. In the summer we would get you all to bed and go and sit out the front on the kitchen chairs. And he was always fooling about, trying to kiss me - and that

process of reasoning. It had to be worked at. He had always thought that it was particularly dishonest to pretend to the young that the reasoning activity amongst social scientists was not beset with problems. It was not, after all, just a question of philosophising about how many angels could dance on the head of a pin; it was essentially about what is to be done! The political philosophy of possessive individualism, the rationale behind capitalism, was a conceptual framework that had celebrated the presence of *the* individual at the centre of all things. He knew this. Our own impressions of people and our feelings about their impressions of us are important. We not only perceive ourselves, or at least what we think we see in the 'mirror' and beyond, we also see ourselves as we think others do, may or should see us. Our attitude to how others see us is related to our view of the relationships we enter into, voluntarily or otherwise.

The longer we live, the more people we know, he thought. Another truism. But how well do we handle that accumulation of experiences?

This he had often asked of his relationships. The way that he, and so many of his associates, handled their personal and public life was not as systematic as they would hope people might see their academic pursuits. He was always being 'drawn away' from the recognised academy, to go out 'there' and bloody well do something. Did he

I can remember it as if it were yesterday. Do you know what he was always saying?"

"No?"

"He used to look up and down, and say, 'No one will be watching us, why don't we do it in the road?"

care whether others took a dim view of this? "Now that is another question," he thought to himself!

"Jack, Jack! What are you thinking about?"

"Oh, lovers and friends."

BIBLIOGRAPHY

ADLER, B.: *Beatles Love Letters*, 1964

ALDRIDGE, A.: *Beatles Illustrated Lyrics* (2 Vols), 1969 & 1971.

'The Beatles Sinister Song Book': *The Observer* (article), Nov. 1967.

ANDERSON, P.: 'Components of the National Culture', *New Left Review* 50, 1968.

ANDRESKI, S.L.: *Social Sciences as Sorcery.* 1972.

ARON, R.: *Progress and Disillusion*, 1968.

BELZ, C. *The Story of Rock*, 1969

BEYNON, H.*Working for Ford,* 1973.

BARBU, Z. in 'Approaches to Popular Culture', CWE Bigsby, 1976

BLAUKOPF, K.: 'Musical Behaviour in Industrial Societies in Cultures', UNESCO Journal, Vol 1, No.1, 1973.

BOGDANOR, V. AND SKIDELSKY, R.: *The Age of Affluence.* 1971

BOOKER, C.: *The Neophiliacs*, 1969.

BOR, W.: *The Making of Cities,* 1972.

BRAUN, M.: *Love Me Do; The Beatles Progress*, 1964

BROOK, E. AND FINN, D.: 'Working Class Images of Society and Community Studies', essay in Working Papers in Cultural Studies, No. 10, 1977.

BURKE, J.: *A Hard Days Night*, 1964

Story of Pop: series and Beatles Special (Ed. by Pascall, J.), 1973.

CARR, R. and TYLER, T. *The Beatles: An Illustrated Record.*

Community Development Project Collective (CDP)
    The Costs of Industrial Change, 1977
    Gilding the Ghetto, 1977

CDP Vauxhall, Liverpool publication, Oxford University Team. 1976

COHEN, P. and ROBINS, D. *Knuckle Sandwich*, 1978

COHEN, S. *Revolt into Style or Style into Revolt*, *Times Higher Education Supplement*, 30-4-76.

COHEN, S. and TAYLOR, L.: *Escape Attempts*, 1976

COHN, N. *Pop from the Beginning*, 1969

COHN, N. AND PEELLAERT, G.: *Rock Dreams*, 1974

CONNOLLY, R.: *That'll Be The Day (book version of the screenplay)*, 1973

DAVIES, H.: *The Beatles*, 1968 (revised ed. 1978)

DILELLO, R.: *The Longest Cocktail Party*, 1973

DEAN, J. (Ed): *The Beatles Book* (monthly fanzine), 1963-69

EISEN, J. *The Age of Rock* (two volumes) 1969 and 1970

ELLIS, R. *The Big Beat Scene*, 1961

EPSTEIN, B.: *A Cellarful of Noise*, 1964
    The Boys Who Made the Mersey Beat, 1963

EVANS, M.: 'The Cunard Yanks' (in *The Story of Pop*), 1973

FLETCHER, C.: 'Beat Gangs on Merseyside' (in *Youth in New Society*, Ed. by Raison, T.), 1966

FOUCAULT, M.: *The Order of Things*, 1974
                The Archaeology of Knowledge, 1972

FRITH, S.: *The Sociology of Rock.* 1978.

FYVEL, T. R.: T*he Insecure Offenders: Rebellious Youth in the Welfare State*, 1961

GALBRAITH, J. K.: *The Affluent Society,* 1958

GILLETT, C. *The Sound of the City*, 1971

GOLDMANN, L.: *The Hidden God*, 1964
    The Human Sciences and Philosophy, 1969

GRIFFEN, A.: *On the Scene at the Cavern*, 1964.

GUNN, T.: *The Sense of Movement*, 1957

GURVITCH, G.: *The Social Frameworks of Knowledge*, 1971

HALL, S. and JEFFERSON, T. (Eds.): *Resistance through Rituals*, 1975

HALL, S. and WHANNEL, P.: *The Popular Arts*, 1964

HARRY, B.: *Merseybeat: The Beginnings of The Beatles*, 1977

HEILPERN, J.: Brian Epstein (article on), *The Observe,* 1-9-68

HOGGART, R.: *The Uses of Literacy*, 1960

HOUSE, J.: *The Beatles Quiz Book*, 1964

INCE, D. E.: A Report on a Project with Unattached Young People in an Area of High Social Need in Liverpool, 1971

JAHN, M.: *Rock from Elvis Presley to The Rolling Stones*, 1975

JOHNSON, P.: 'The Menace of Beatlism', *New Statesman*, 28-2-64

KONIG, R.: *The Restless Image*, 1973

LAWTON, R. and CUNNINGHAM, C. Merseyside: Social and Economic Studies, 1970

LEFEBVRE, H.: *Everyday Life in the Modern World*, 1968

LENNON, C.: *A Twist of Lennon*, 1978

LOWENTHAL, L.: *Literature and the Image of Man*, 1957
Literature, Popular Culture and Society, 1968

LUKACS, G.: *The Ontology of Social Being: On Marx*, 1978

LUKAS, R. C.: *From Metternick to The Beatles*, 1973

LYND, R.: *Knowledge for What?*, 1938

MCCABE, P. and SCHONFIELD, R.: *Apple to the Core: The Unmaking of The Beatles*, 1973

MCGOUGH, R. (with Patten, B. and Henri, A.): *The Mersey Sound*, 1967

MCQUAIL, D.: *Towards a Sociology of Mass Communications*, 1969

MANNING, P. and Truzzi, M.: *Youth and Sociology*, 1972

MARCUS, G.: *Mystery Train*, 1977

MARX, K.: *Capital*, 1867, Penguin edition, 1979

MAY and PHILLIPS: *British Beat*, 1974

MAYS, J. B. *The Young Pretenders*, 1965

MAZAROS, I.: *The Necessity for Social Control*, 1971

MEAD, M.: *Culture and Commitment: A Study of the Generation,* Gap, 1970.

MELLERS, W.L: *Twilight of the Gods*, 1976

MELLY, G.: *Revolt into Style*, 1970

METRAUX, G. S. in 'Cultures' *op. cit.*

MILLER, J. (Ed.): *The Rolling Stone Illustrated History of Rock and Roll*, 1976

Daily Mirror: 'The Beatles in America', 1965

MUCHNICK, D.: *Urban Renewal in Liverpool*, 1970

MUNGHAM, G. & PEARSON G.: *Working Class Youth Culture*, 1976.

MURDOCK, G. and MCCRON, R.: 'Youth and Class: The Career of a Confusion' in Mungham and Pearson, 1976

MUSGROVE, F.: *Youth and the Social Order*, 1964

NEVILLE, R.: *Playpower*, 1970

Newsom Report, 1963

NUTTALL, J.: *Bomb Culture*, 1968

PARKIN, F.: *Class, Inequality and Political Order*, 1971

PATRICK, J.: *A Glasgow Gang Observed*, 1973

PEYSER, J.: 'The Beatles and The Beatless' in Eisen, 1969

Rolling Stone Interviews (Two Vols), 1974

ROSENBERG, H.: *The Tradition of the New*, 1970
ROSZAK, T.: *The Making of the Counter Culture*, 1969
SHEPHERD, B.: *The True Story of The Beatles*, 1964
SHEPHERD, J. *et al.*: *Who's Music: A Sociology of Musical Languages*, 1977
SHONFIELD, A.: *British Economic Policy since the War*, 1958
SILLITOE, A.: *Saturday Night and Sunday Morning*, 1958
    The Loneliness of the Long-Distance Runner, 1959
    Key to The Door, 1961
SMITH, W.: *Scientific Survey of Merseyside*, 1953
SWINGWOOD, A.: *The Myth of Mass Culture*, 1977
WHITCOMB, I.: *After the Ball,* 1972
WILLIAMS, A. and MARSHALL, W.: *The Man Who Gave The Beatles Away*, 1975
WILLIAMS, R. *Base and Superstructure in Marxist Cultural Theory* (in *New Left Review* 82. Dec.1973)
WILLIS, P.: *Learning to Labour* , 1978

Printed in the United Kingdom
by Lightning Source UK Ltd.
113230UKS00001B/6